Shakespeare's Rhetorical Figures

Shakespeare's Rhetorical Figures:
An Outline

by Gideon Rappaport

One Mind Good Press
San Diego, California

One Mind Good Press
San Diego, CA

[ISBN: 979-8-218-27871-7]

Contents

Preface

The word *figure* comes from the Latin *figura*, a translation of the Greek word *schema*. As used in the study of grammar and rhetoric from ancient to modern times, it refers to an intentional deviation from simple, normal, common speech and writing. Any effort by one person to entertain, to instruct, or to persuade another through the use of language, particularly in poetry, will necessarily involve the use of figures — modifications of the normal forms of words, phrases, and sentences — to achieve whatever may be the aim of the speech or writing. "Rhetorical figures" are also called "figures of speech" and have been variously classified as "schemes" and "tropes."

Here are a few examples of the kinds of modifications to which the phrase "rhetorical figure" refers:

Let's say that I have not understood something you have said. I might reply "What?" This is common speech for "I don't understand what you said." But it could also mean "I didn't hear what you said." Both of those longer phrases are themselves common speech, and either would be clear enough. But suppose that instead of making any of these replies I say one of the following:

a. "What are you trying to say?"; or
b. "I don't get it"; or
c. "I'm not sure that I've taken your point"; or
d. "Please explain your explanation"; or
e. "What can you mean, my dear, what can you possibly mean?"

With each of these replies I have more effectively conveyed not only a literal meaning but also a particular tone and a telling attitude, altering the effect that my words will now have on you. And I have used the following rhetorical figures to do so:

a. apoplanesis (making my lack of understanding a function of your failed effort to be clear);
b. metaphor ("get it");
c. meiosis plus metaphor ("I'm not sure" and "taken your point");
d. polyptoton plus parechesis with consonance ("explain/explanation"[1] and repetition of *p*, *pl*, *ex*, and *n* sounds); and
e. symploce plus diacope ("What can you/what can you" and "can you mean/can you possibly mean").

By the use of these figures the statement that I did not understand what you said is enhanced, sharpened, intensified, even made comical or dramatic, conveying a great deal more of both information and emotion.

---

1 Borrowed from Byron (*Don Juan*, Dedication 2.8).

The unsurpassed literary art of Shakespeare grew out of his visionary genius developed in accordance with the worldview and tastes of the time. But it was rooted in the poet's internalization of over two hundred inherited figures of speech that he had learned in school, including the nine in the examples above. As I have written in *Appreciating Shakespeare*,

> By the time [Shakespeare] began writing, he had mastered them all. Then he devoted his working life to engaging them in the service of a poetic language more vivid, fluid, and imaginative than they had ever served before.
>
> We are not to think of Shakespeare's obviously rhetorical patterning of language, verbal artifice, and wordplay as merely decoration. It is the very medium of thought and feeling…. As Shakespeare matured, his use of figures of speech became more and more subtle, rhetoric and meaning more absorbed into one another. But from the Renaissance viewpoint, even in the highly figured speech of earlier plays—like *A Midsummer Night's Dream, Richard II,* and *Romeo and Juliet*—the use of formal rhetorical devices does not obscure the speaker's passion but rather expresses it.[2]

The three sections of *Shakespeare's Rhetorical Figures: An Outline* are intended to aid students, teachers, actors, directors, audiences, and readers in understanding and appreciating that art. The book has four goals:

1. To increase the understanding of Shakespeare's meanings;
2. To increase appreciation for Shakespeare's artistry in getting those meanings across to his audience and to us;
3. To see in examples how Shakespeare uses each rhetorical figure in practice; and
4. To provide a quick and easy way to know the nature and pronounce the name of any particular rhetorical figure.

This book is a companion to the important scholarly work of Sister Miriam Joseph (1898-1982). In none of the Shakespeare courses that I took in high school, college, or graduate school was I counseled to read Sister Miriam Joseph's book *Shakespeare's Use of the Arts of Language*. I knew it existed; I had looked things up in it and even quoted it. But reading it straight through was a revelation. I already knew that Shakespeare was the greatest artist of language the world has known. Sister Joseph's study brought into sharp clarity what that art was. This book presents her arrangement of the figures and her examples in both outline and dictionary form.

The first section, the **Overview**, offers in a general outline the structure of the theory of the arts of language as it developed to serve the Trivium, the first three of the seven liberal arts, namely grammar, logic, and rhetoric. Based on that structure Sister Joseph arranged the over two hundred figures of speech used by Shakespeare under four headings: "Grammar" and the three modes of rhetorical speech identified by Aristotle, namely "*Logos,*" "*Pathos,*" and "*Ethos.*" To produce her arrangement, Sister Joseph examined all the schools of language in

---

2 Gideon Rappaport, *Appreciating Shakespeare* (San Diego: One Mind Good Press, 2022), page 43.

he long tradition beginning with Aristotle and developed by the grammarians, logicians, and rhetoricians of Rome, the Middle Ages, and the Renaissance, discovering in the process that despite their particular differences all the various schools exhibit the same essential theory of language composition.

Based on Sister Joseph's arrangement, the second and longest section, the **Outline of Shakespeare's Rhetorical Figures with Examples**, presents in outline form all of the rhetorical figures included in her study with examples of Shakespeare's use of each. Added to the examples of Sister Joseph are some of my own and some from other sources.[3]

The third section, the **Glossary of Figures with Pronunciations**, lists alphabetically all of the traditional rhetorical figures used by Shakespeare as identified by Sister Joseph, including some of the multiple names by which many were known. It also lists in italics the terms for the categories of figures. The entry for each rhetorical figure includes a brief definition and a simplified pronunciation guide and is cross-referenced to the examples in the Outline. The Glossary thus serves as both a dictionary of terms and an index to Shakespearean examples.

In introducing *Shakespeare's Use of the Arts of Language*, Sister Joseph writes that

> The extraordinary power, vitality, and richness of Shakespeare's language are due in part to his genius, in part to the fact that the unsettled linguistic forms of his age promoted to an unusual degree the spirit of free creativeness, and in part to the theory of composition then prevailing. It is this last which accounts for those characteristics of Shakespeare's language which differentiate it most from the language of today, not so much in the words themselves as in their collocation. The difference in habits of thought and in methods of developing a thought results in a corresponding difference in expression principally because the Renaissance theory of composition, derived from an ancient tradition, was permeated with formal logic and rhetoric, while ours is not. (SMJ 3)

Her reorganization of the figures under the headings "Grammar," "*Logos*," "*Pathos*," and "*Ethos*," Sister Joseph writes,

> makes the numerous figures more significant by ordering them in groups fulfilling four fundamental functions, somewhat as the periodic table makes the chemical elements more significant by ordering them in families having similar properties. By thus correlating the figures with the whole body of theory in logic and in the parts of rhetoric other than elocution[,] this reorganization emphasizes the completeness of the pattern and the

---

3 Books consulted include Harold F. Brooks, Introduction to the Arden Edition of *A Midsummer Night's Dream* (New York: Methuen, 1979), pages xlv–liii; Ward Farnsworth, *Farnsworth's Classical English Rhetoric* (Boston: David R. Godine, 2011); Richard A. Lanham, *A Handlist of Rhetorical Terms* (Berkeley: University of California Press, 1969); Kate Emery Pogue, *Shakespeare's Figures of Speech: A Reader's Guide* (Bloomington, Indiana: iUniverse, 2009); *Merriam-Webster's Collegiate Dictionary*, Eleventh Edition (2003); and *Webster's New International Dictionary*, Second Edition, Unabridged (1946).

Online sources include "Elizabethan Rhetorical Figures," Virginia Commonwealth University, http://www.people.vcu.edu/~bgriffin/399/Elizabethan%20Rhetorical%20Figures.html; "Figure of Speech," Wikipedia, https://en.wikipedia.org/wiki/Figure_of_speech; "Glossary of Rhetorical Terms," University of Kentucky, https://mcl.as.uky.edu/glossary-rhetorical-terms; and *Silva Rhetoricae* of Brigham Young University, http://rhetoric.byu.edu/.

interdependence of its parts, for every part gains meaning from its relation to the other parts and to the whole. (SMJ 36–37)

…This reclassification of the figures makes no claim to apodictic exactitude. Their classification, by whatever method, has always proved baffling, for one figure may fit into any one of a number of classes, and some figures may not fit precisely into any one…[Yet] in addition to making the figures more intelligible and significant, the reorganization here presented accentuates the basic agreement of the Renaissance rhetoricians and logicians among themselves and with the ancient tradition. (SMJ 39)

Sister Joseph's goal was "To awaken attention to features which characterized the art of composition and of imaginative apprehension in Shakespeare's day" by describing "the intricate pattern of the arts of language taken for granted by Shakespeare and his contemporary audience" (SMJ 48). Because that pattern provides access to a crucial dimension of meaning in Shakespeare's works, Sister Joseph's manifold illuminations merit study.

The aim of this work is not to substitute for Sister Joseph's indispensable book but to make easily accessible, in both outline and dictionary form, her arrangement of the rhetorical figures and their logical interrelations that Shakespeare had at his disposal. It is intended as a reference work to help deepen the appreciation of Shakespeare's accomplishment in bringing the traditional arts of language to the highest conceivable pitch of mastery.

Acknowledgements:

I am grateful to Tom Feltham for copyediting, Chuck Eng for book design, Yochanan Shaked for the cover art, and John Ladd for proofreading. Special thanks go to Mark Wadia for technical and moral support.

List of Abbreviations

Abbreviations of Shakespeare's Works

A&C	*Antony and Cleopatra*		More	*Sir Thomas More*
Ado	*Much Ado about Nothing*		MSND	*A Midsummer Night's Dream*
AWEW	*All's Well That Ends Well*		MV	*The Merchant of Venice*
AYLI	*As You Like It*		MWW	*The Merry Wives of Windsor*
CE	*A Comedy of Errors*		Oth	*Othello*
Cor	*Coriolanus*		Per	*Pericles*
Cym	*Cymbeline*		P&T	*"The Phoenix and the Turtle"*
E3	*Edward III*		Q1	*Quarto 1*
F1	*First Folio*		R&J	*Romeo and Juliet*
1H4	*Henry IV, Part I*		R2	*Richard II*
2H4	*Henry IV, Part II*		R3	*Richard III*
H5	*Henry V*		RL	*The Rape of Lucrece*
1H6	*Henry VI, Part I*		Shrew	*The Taming of the Shrew*
2H6	*Henry VI, Part II*		Son	*Sonnet*
3H6	*Henry VI, Part III*		T&C	*Troilus and Cressida*
H8	*Henry VIII*		Temp	*The Tempest*
Ham	*Hamlet*		Timon	*Timon of Athens*
JC	*Julius Caesar*		Titus	*Titus Andronicus*
KJ	*King John*		TN	*Twelfth Night*
LC	*"A Lover's Complaint"*		TNK	*The Two Noble Kinsmen*
Lear	*King Lear*		TGV	*The Two Gentlemen of Verona*
LLL	*Love's Labor's Lost*		V&A	*Venus and Adonis*
Mac	*Macbeth*		WT	*The Winter's Tale*
MM	*Measure for Measure*			

Other Abbreviations

Abbott   E. A. Abbott, *A Shakespearian Grammar* (London: Macmillan, 1874)

MWCD   *Merriam-Webster's Collegiate Dictionary*, Eleventh Edition

ff.   and the following pages

RAL   Richard A. Lanham, *A Handlist of Rhetorical Terms* (Berkeley, California: University of California Press, 1969)

SMJ   Sister Miriam Joseph, *Shakespeare's Use of the Arts of Language* (Philadelphia, Pennsylvania: Paul Dry Books, 2005)

Tilley   Morris Palmer Tilley, *A Dictionary of the Proverbs in England in the Sixteenth and Seventeenth Centuries* (Ann Arbor: University of Michigan Press, 1950), https://babel.hathitrust.org/cgi/pt?id=mdp.39015016495585&view=1up&seq=9

Triv   Sister Miriam Joseph, *The Trivium: The Liberal Arts of Logic, Grammar, and Rhetoric: Understanding the Nature and Function of Language*, edited by Marguerite McGlinn (Philadelphia, Pennsylvania: Paul Dry Books, 2002)

WNID   *Webster's New International Dictionary*, Unabridged, Second Edition

Overview

This Overview offers a general outline of the theory of the arts of language as arranged by Sister Miriam Joseph in *Shakespeare's Use of the Arts of Language*. **Boldface** numbers refer to the specific rhetorical figures, which are exemplified in the Outline of Shakespeare's Rhetorical Figures with Examples and listed alphabetically in the Glossary of Figures with Pronunciations.

Grammar

    Schemes of Grammar

        Schemes of Words

            Addition (**1–3**)

            Subtraction (**4–7**)

            Lengthening (in English, altering the stress) of Syllables (**8**)

            Shortening (in English, altering the stress) of Syllables (**9**)

            Exchange of Letters (**10**)

            Exchange of Sounds (**11**)

            Modulation of Voice (**12**)

        Schemes of Construction

            Alteration of Word Order (**13–19**)

            Omission (**20–21, 22A, 23–26**)

            Addition of Conjunctions (**27**)

            Variation of Rhythm (**28–30**)

            Transition (**31**)

            Grammatical Exchange (**32–36**)

    Vices of Language (**37–53**)

      Excess Verbiage (**45–49**)

  Figures of Repetition (**54–70**)

Outline of Shakespeare's Rhetorical Figures with Examples

Note: Each figure is assigned a number in **boldface** both in this Outline and in the Glossary. The quotations from Shakespeare's works under each figure are cited in the chronological order of the works as listed in *The Riverside Shakespeare*, Second Edition, and line references are to that edition. Where quotations differ from the *Riverside* text, the source text is indicated. Quotations from Sister Miriam Joseph, *Shakespeare's Use of the Arts of Language*, are indicated by the initials (SMJ) and the relevant page number in that work. For other references see the List of Abbreviations.

Grammar

  Schemes of Grammar

    Schemes of Words

      Addition

1 Prosthesis — "addition of a syllable at the beginning of a word" (SMJ 51)

Enrings the barky fingers of the elm
(MSND IV.i.44)

Nor, by my will, assubjugate his merit
(T&C II.iii.192)

I hold you as a thing enskied, and sainted
(MM I.iv.34)

Enwheel thee round!
(Oth II.i.87)

Beweep this cause again, I'll pluck ye out
(Lear I.iv.302)

2 Epenthesis — adding a syllable in the middle of a word (SMJ 51)

Give Mutius burial with our bretheren
(Titus I.i.348)

> I have but with a cursorary eye
> O'er glanc'd the articles
>> (H5 V.ii.77, Q3; F1 "curselarie," Q1–2 "cursenary")

> Lie blist'ring 'fore the visitating sun
>> (TNK I.i.146)

3 Proparalepsis, also Paragoge—"addition of a syllable at the end of a word"
(SMJ 51)

> put *l* to sore, then sorel jumps from thicket
>> (LLL IV.ii.58)
>>> [sore = a buck in its fourth year; sorel = a buck in its third year]

> And bid her hasten all the house to bed
>> (R&J, III.iii.156)

> Unto our climatures and countrymen
>> (Ham I.i.125)

Subtraction-Elision

4 Aphaeresis—subtracting a syllable from the beginning of a word (SMJ 52)

> Why, sir, what 'cerns it you if I wear pearl and gold?
>> (Shrew V.i.75)

> she looks as pale as any clout in the versal world
>> (R&J II.iv.205–206)

> I have scap'd by miracle
>> (1H4 II.iv.165–66)

> 'Gainst Fortune's state would treason have pronounc'd
>> (Ham II.ii.511)

> use every man after his desert, and who shall scape whipping
>> (Ham II.ii.529–30)

> The King hath cause to plain
>> (Lear III.i.39)

> Point against point, rebellious arm 'gainst arm
>> (Mac I.ii.56)

Now spurs the lated traveller apace
    (Mac III.iii.6)

Then shall we hear their 'larum, and they ours
    (Cor I.iv.9)

5 Syncope—subtracting a letter or syllable from the middle of a word (SMJ 52)

And whe'r he run, or fly, they know not whether
    (V&A 304)

For I ne'er saw true beauty till this night
    (R&J I.v.53)

pray heartly pardon me
    (MWW III.iii.227)

O'ermaster't as you may
    (Ham I.v.140)

You shall do marvell's wisely, good Reynaldo
    (Ham II.i.3)

That were I ta'en here, it would scarce be answer'd
    (TN III.iii.28)

Hence broker, lackey, ignomy and shame
Pursue thy life and live aye with thy name
    (T&C V.x.33, F1)

Weary sev'nights, nine times nine
    (Mac I.iii.22)

Let's make us med'cines of our great revenge
    (Mac IV.iii.214)

And gape at wid'st to glut him
    (Temp I.i.60)

6 Synaloepha, also spelled Synalepha—elision of one of two vowels or of a single
    vowel (SMJ 52)

Had made his course t'illume that part of heaven
    (Ham I.i.37)

T'invite the Troyan lords after the combat
    (T&C III.iii.236)

> Win us with honest trifles, to betray 's
> In deepest consequence.
> (Mac I.iii.125–26)

> There's one did laugh in 's sleep
> (Mac II.ii.20)

> Take't, 'tis yours. What is't?
> (Cor I.ix.81)

> Believe't not lightly—though I go alone
> (Cor IV.i.29)

> Timon: They're welcome all, let 'em have kind admittance.
>   Music, make their welcome!
> First Lord: You see, my lord, how ample y' are belov'd
> (Timon I.ii.128–30)

> Though you would seek t'unsphere the stars with oaths
> (WT I.ii.48)

7 Apocope—subtraction of the last syllable of a word "as bet for better" (SMJ 53)

> With Clifford and the haught Northumberland
> (3H6 II.i.169)

> I have rememb'red me, thou s' hear our counsel
> (R&J I.iii.9)

> And when I ope my lips let no dog bark!
> (MV I.i.94)

> Season your admiration for a while
> With an attent ear
> (Ham I.ii.192–93)

>   to make inquire
> Of his behavior
> (Ham II.i.4–5)

> As seld I have the chance
> (T&C IV.v.150)

>   whose low sounds
> Reverb no hollowness
> (Lear I.i.153–54)

Which are t' intrinse t' unloose
   (Lear II.ii.75)

8 Diastole, also Eciasis — lengthening (in English altering the stress) of a syllable
   (SMJ 53)

Why thy can**ón**ized bones, hearsèd in death
   (Ham I.iv.47, but cf., Abbott §491)

That thou, dead corse, again in **cóm**plete steel
   (Ham I.iv.52, but cf., Abbott §492)

The pangs of **dés**pis'd love, the law's delay
   (Ham III.i.71; F1 "**dís**priz'd")

And power, unto itself most **cóm**men**dá**ble
   (Cor IV.vii.51, cf., Abbott §490)

9 Systole — shortening (in English altering the stress) of a syllable (SMJ 53)

Why thy **can**ónized bones, hearsèd in death
   (Ham I.iv.47, but cf., Abbott §491)

That thou, dead corse, again in cóm**plete** steel
   (Ham I.iv.52, but cf., Abbott §492)

The pangs of dés**pis'd** love, the law's delay
   (Ham III.i.71; F1 "díspriz'd")

And power, unto itself most cóm**men**dáble
   (Cor IV.vii.51, cf., Abbott §490)

10 Metathesis — transposition or exchange of letters in a word, as Peacham's *brust*
   for *burst* (SMJ 53)

Must be to him that makes the camp a cestron [for *cistern*]
   (TNK V.i.46)

11 Antisthecon — exchange of one sound for another in a word, "as *wrang* for
   wrong, usually for the sake of rhyme" (SMJ 53)

Troilus: But to the sport abroad — are you bound thither?
Aeneas: In all swift haste.
Troilus: Come, go we then togither.
   (T&C I.i.115–16, Q1 2nd state and F1)

Which better than the first, O dear heaven, bless!
Or, ere they meet, in me, O nature, cesse!
   (AWEW V.iii.71–72)

12 Tasis—"not precisely a figure…a sweet and pleasant modulation or
tunableness of the voice in pronunciation" (SMJ 53–54), apparently referred
to in the following:

The tune of Imogen!
   (Cym V.v.238)

Schemes of Construction

Alteration of Word Order

13 Hyperbaton—the general term for the alteration of normal word order, including
figures **14–19** below (SMJ 54)

14 Anastrophe—unusual word order (SMJ 54)

Now is the winter of our discontent
Made glorious summer by this son of York;
And all the clouds that low'r'd upon our house
In the deep bosom of the ocean buried.
   (R3 I.i.1–4)

Bullingbrook: I thought you had been willing to resign.
King Richard: My crown I am, but still my griefs are mine.
   (R2 IV.i.190–91)

Did ever dragon keep so fair a cave?
   (R&J III.ii.74)

Of something nearly that concerns yourselves
   (MSND I.i.126)

Does it not, think thee, stand me now upon—
   (Ham V.ii.63, but cf., Abbott §204)

    Yet I'll not shed her blood,
Nor scar that whiter skin of hers than snow.
   (Oth V.ii.3–4)

For Banquo's issue have I fil'd my mind,
For them the gracious Duncan have I murther'd
    (Mac III.i.64–65)

May soon return to this our suffering country
Under a hand accurs'd!
    (Mac III.vi.48–49)

Whither indeed, before thy here-approach
    (Mac IV.iii.133)

                Jove's lightnings, the precursors
O' th' dreadful thunderclaps, more momentary
And sight-outrunning were not.
    (Temp I.ii.201–203)

                I'll resolve you
(Which to you shall seem probable) of every
These happen'd accidents
    (Temp V.i.248–50)

15 Tmesis—putting a word or words between the parts of a compound word
    (SMJ 55)

                how heinous e'er it be,
To win thy after-love I pardon thee
    (R2 V.iii.34–35)

This is not Romeo, he's some other where.
    (R&J I.i.198)

Writes me that man, how dearly ever parted
    (T&C III.iii.96)

16 Hysteron Proteron—putting first that which occurs later (SMJ 55)

When yellow leaves, or none, or few do hang
Upon those boughs which shake against the cold
    (Son 73.2–3)

Th' *Antoniad*, the Egyptian admiral,
With all their sixty, fly and turn the rudder
    (A&C III.x.2–3)

17 Hypallage—exchange or application of words (A) in a perverted, absurd, or awkward way or (B) in a transferred epithet (SMJ 55–56)

A: Awkward or absurd application of words (with profound implication in the last example)

The eye of man hath not heard, the ear of man hath not seen, man's hand is not able to taste, his tongue to conceive, nor his heart to report, what my dream was.
    (MSND IV.i.211–14, cf., 1 Corinthians 2:9)

I see a voice! Now will I to the chink,
To spy and I can hear my Thisby's face.
    (MSND V.i.192–93)

Will it please you to see the epilogue, or to hear a Bergomask dance between two of our company?
    (MSND V.i.352–54)

All his successors (gone before him) hath done't; and all his ancestors (that come after him) may.
    (MWW I.i.14–16)

To be a well-favor'd man is the gift of fortune, but to write and read comes by nature.
    (Ado III.iii.14–16)

Elbow: Prove it before these varlets here, thou honorable man, prove it.
Escalus: Do you hear how he misplaces?
    (MM II.i.86–88)

For to a vision so apparent rumor
Cannot be mute
    (WT I.ii.270–71)

Every man shift for all the rest, and let no man take care for himself
    (Temp V.i.256–57)

B: Transferred epithet

Doing annoyance to the treacherous feet,
Which with usurping steps do trample thee
    (R2 III.ii.16–17)

And never brandish more revengeful steel
    (R2 IV.i.50)

With rainy marching in the painful field
    (H5 IV.iii.111)

This was the most unkindest cut of all
    (JC III.ii.183)

Alas, what ignorant sin have I committed?
    (Oth IV.ii.70)

And by the happy hollow of a tree
Escap'd the hunt
    (Lear II.iii.2–3)

He rais'd the house with loud and coward cries.
    (Lear II.iv.43)

Or have we eaten on the insane root
That takes the reason prisoner?
    (Mac I.iii.84–85)

           this bird
Hath made his pendent bed and procreant cradle
    (Mac I.vi.7–8)

With Tarquin's ravishing strides, towards his design
Moves like a ghost
    (Mac II.i.55–56)

         Our Italy
Shines o'er with civil swords
    (A&C I.iii.44–45)

Forgive my fearful sails!
    (A&C III.xi.55)

18 Parenthesis—"interrupts a sentence by interposing words" (SMJ 295), "a word, phrase, or sentence inserted as an aside in a sentence complete in itself" (RAL)

         yea, my gravity,
Wherein (let no man hear me) I take pride,
Could I, with boot, change for an idle plume
    (MM II.iv.9–11, cf., 2 Corinthians 11:21, 23)

If you'll bestow a small (of what you have little)
Patience awhile, you'll hear the belly's answer.
    (Cor I.i.125–26)

> Upon a time—unhappy was the clock
> That strook the hour!—it was in Rome—accurs'd
> The mansion where!—'twas at a feast—O would
> Our viands had been poison'd, or at least
> Those which I heav'd to head!—the good Posthumus
> (What should I say? He was too good to be
> Where ill men were, and was the best of all
> Amongst the rar'st of good ones), sitting sadly,
> Hearing us praise our loves of Italy…
>   (Cym V.v.153–61)

>   Ha' not you seen, Camillo
> (But that's past doubt; you have, or your eye-glass
> Is thicker than a cuckold's horn), or heard
> (For to a vision so apparent rumor
> Cannot be mute), or thought (for cogitation
> Resides not in that man that does not think)
> My wife is slippery?
>   (WT I.ii.267–73)

>   Then was this island
> (Save for the son that she did litter here,
> A freckled whelp, hag-born) not honor'd with
> A human shape.
>   (Temp I.ii.281–84)

>   I'll resolve you
> (Which to you shall seem probable) of every
> These happen'd accidents
>   (Temp V.i.248–50)

19 Epergesis, also Appositio—"interrupts by interposing a word in apposition as an added interpretation" (SMJ 295), i.e., use of appositives or appositive phrases, sometimes including Metaphors **138** (SMJ 57)

> Her father and myself, lawful espials,
>   (Ham III.i.31, F1)

> Antiquity forgot, custom not known,
> The ratifiers and props of every word,
>   (Ham IV.v.105–106)

Behold, these are the tribunes of the people,
The tongues o' th' common mouth.
    (Cor III.i.21–22)

                    the thunder,
That deep and dreadful organ pipe,
    (Temp III.iii.97–98)

                    He,
A most unbounded tyrant,
    (TNK I.ii.62–63)

Omission

20 Eclipsis, or Ellipsis—"omission of a word easily understood" (SMJ 58)

We'll calm the Duke of Norfolk, you your son
    (R2 I.i.159)

As fire drives out fire, so pity pity—
    (JC III.i.171)

…and my father died within's two hours
    (Ham III.ii.127)

And he to England shall along with you
    (Ham III.iii.4)

For what, alas, can these my single arms?
    (T&C II.ii.135)

Desire them home
    (T&C IV.v.157)

He that conceals him, death
    (Lear II.i.63)

Duncan: Dismay'd not this
    Our captains, Macbeth and Banquo?
Sergeant: Yes,
    As sparrows eagles; or the hare the lion.
    (Mac I.ii.33–35)

Haply you shall not see me more, or if,
A mangled shadow.
    (A&C IV.ii.26–27)

21 Zeugma—using one verb to govern a number of clauses with which it is grammatically congruent (SMJ 58); in Prozeugma (or Protozeugma) the common verb or adjective is expressed in the first clause, in Mesozeugma in a middle clause, in Hypozeugma in the final clause—cf., **22A** Syllepsis (A)

How Tarquin wronged me, I Collatine
  (RL 819)

But passion lends them power, time means, to meet
  (R&J II.Prol.13)

As you on him, Demetrius dote on you!
  (MSND I.i.225)

Our blood to us, this to our blood is born
  (AWEW I.iii.131)

            wishing clocks more swift?
Hours, minutes? noon, midnight?
  (WT I.ii.289–90)

22A Syllepsis (A)—using one verb to govern a number of clauses with at least one of whose subjects it lacks grammatical congruence (SMJ 58), cf., **21** Zeugma; for **22B** Syllepsis (B) (using "a word having simultaneously two different meanings, although it is not repeated") see under *Logos*: Topics of Invention: Artificial Arguments: Division (A): Notation and Conjugates: Ambiguity

Nor God, nor I, delights in perjur'd men.
  (LLL V.ii.346)

Love loving not itself, none other can
  (R2 V.iii.88)

                like seely beggars
Who sitting in the stocks refuge their shame,
That many have and others must sit there
  (R2 V.v.25–27)

She has deceiv'd her father, and may thee
  (Oth I.iii.293)

            The poop was beaten gold,
Purple the sails
  (A&C II.ii.192–93)

I have no more to reckon, he to spend.
    (Timon III.iv.56)

My pray'rs to heaven for you, my loyalty,
Which ever has and ever shall be growing
    (H8 III.ii.177–78)

23 Hypozeuxis — (A) giving every clause in a series its own subject and verb; (B)
    iteration (Puttenham, per SMJ 58)

A: Each clause having its own subject and verb

Madam, the guests are come, supper serv'd up, you call'd, my young lady
ask'd for, the nurse curs'd in the pantry, and every thing in extremity.
    (R&J I.iii.100–102)

B: Iteration

What? I love, I sue, I seek a wife
    (LLL III.i.189, Q1, F1)

Blessed are clouds, to do as such clouds do!
    (LLL V.ii.204)

24 Diazeugma — using one subject with many verbs (SMJ 59)

          he bites his lip, and starts,
Stops on a sudden, looks upon the ground,
Then lays his finger on his temple; straight
Springs out into fast gait, then stops again,
Strikes his breast hard
    (H8 III.ii.113–18)

25 Brachylogia — "omission of conjunctions between words" (SMJ 59)

Paris: Beguil'd, divorced, wronged, spited, slain! …
Capulet: Despis'd, distressed, hated, martyr'd, kill'd!
    (R&J IV.v.55, 59)

With bracelets of thy hair, rings, gawds, conceits,
Knacks, trifles, nosegays, sweetmeats
    (MSND I.i.33–34)

> O Fates, come, come,
> Cut thread and thrum,
> Quail, crush, conclude, and quell!
> (MSND V.i.285–87)

> Are all thy conquests, glories, triumphs, spoils,
> Shrunk to this little measure?
> (JC III.i.149–50)

> The courtier's, soldier's, scholar's, eye, tongue, sword
> (Ham III.i.151)

> Hoo, hearts, tongues, figures, scribes, bards, poets, cannot
> Think, speak, cast, write, sing, number, hoo!
> His love to Antony.
> (A&C III.ii.16–18)

26 Asyndeton—"omitting conjunctions between clauses" (SJM 59)

> Call up her father.
> Rouse him, make after him, poison his delight,
> Proclaim him in the streets; incense her kinsmen
> (Oth I.i.67–69)

> Is whispering nothing?
> Is leaning cheek to cheek? is meeting noses?
> Kissing with inside lip? stopping the career
> Of laughter with a sigh…horsing foot on foot?
> Skulking in corners? wishing clocks more swift?
> (WT I.ii.284–89)

> All hail, great master, grave sir, hail! I come
> To answer thy best pleasure; be't to fly,
> To swim, to dive into the fire, to ride
> On the curl'd clouds
> (Temp I.ii.189–92)

Addition of Conjunctions

27 Polysyndeton—using a conjunction between every two phrases or clauses (SMJ 59)

> Your love says, like an honest gentleman,
> An' a courteous, and a kind, and a handsome,
> And, I warrant, a virtuous
>   (R&J II.v.55–57)

> an ass-head and a coxcomb and a knave
>   (TN V.i.206–207)

> 'Tis as I should entreat you wear your gloves,
> Or feed on nourishing dishes, or keep you warm,
> Or sue to you to do a peculiar profit
> To your own person
>   (Oth III.iii.77–80)

> If there be cords, or knives,
> Poison, or fire, or suffocating streams,
> I'll not endure it.
>   (Oth III.iii.388–90)

>   So we'll live,
> And pray, and sing, and tell old tales, and laugh
> At gilded butterflies, and hear poor rogues
> Talk of court news; and we'll talk with them too
>   (Lear V.iii.11–14)

Variation of Rhythm

28 Isocolon, also Parison—using "phrases or clauses…of equal length and usually of corresponding structure" (SMJ 59)

> Gloucester: Fairer than tongue can name thee, let me have
>   Some patient leisure to excuse myself.
> Lady Anne: Fouler than heart can think thee, thou canst make
>   No excuse current but to hang thyself.
>   (R3 I.ii.81–84)

Your reasons at dinner have been sharp and sententious:
pleasant without scurrility, witty without affection,
audacious without impudency, learned without opinion,
and strange without heresy.
  (LLL V.i.2–6)

This royal throne of kings, this sceptered isle,
This earth of majesty, this seat of Mars [etc.]
  (R2 II.i.40–51)

My care is loss of care, by old care done,
Your care is gain of care, by new care won;
  (R2 IV.i.194–98)

Juliet: I shall forget, to have thee still stand there…
Romeo: And I'll still stay, to have thee still forget
  (R&J II.ii.172–74)

Our instruments to melancholy bells,
Our wedding cheer to a sad burial feast [etc.]
  (R&J IV.v.86–89)

By his best arrow with the golden head,
By the simplicity of Venus' doves,
By that which knitteth souls and prospers loves
  (MSND I.i.170–72)

And therefore is wing'd Cupid painted blind…
And therefore is Love said to be a child
  (MSND I.i.235, 238)

And for her sake do I rear up her boy;
And for her sake I will not part with him.
  (MSND II.i.136–37)

Demetrius: …in the wood
Helena: …in the temple, in the town…
  (MSND II.i.237–38)

You both are rivals, and love Hermia;
And now both rivals to mock Helena
  (MSND III.ii.155–56)

As Caesar lov'd me, I weep for him; as he was fortunate, I
rejoice at it; as he was valiant, I honor him; but, as he was
ambitious, I slew him. There is tears for his love; joy for his
fortune; honor for his valor; and death for his ambition.
   (JC III.ii.24–29)

Queen: Hamlet, thou hast thy father much offended.
Hamlet: Mother, you have my father much offended.
Queen: Come, come, you answer with an idle tongue.
Hamlet: Go, go, you question with a wicked tongue.
   (Ham III.iv.9–12)

29 Homoioteleuton—the use of like endings of words (in English not distinguished from Homoioptoton, the use of like case endings), as -ly in the
example (SMJ 60)

How churlishly I chid Lucetta hence,
When willingly I would have had her here!
How angerly I taught my brow to frown
   (TGV I.ii.60–62)

30 Hirmus (also spelled Heirmos, Hyrmos, Irmus)—use of a periodic or
suspended sentence (SMJ 60)

       Tell my friends,
Tell Athens, in the sequence of degree,
From high to low throughout, that whoso please
To stop affliction, let him take his haste,
Come hither, ere my tree hath felt the axe,
And hang himself.
   (Timon V.i.207–212)

Transition

31 Metabasis—"telling what has been said and what is to follow" (SMJ 60)

       This is most brave,
That I, the son of a dear father murthered,
Prompted to my revenge by heaven and hell,
Must like a whore unpack my heart with words,
And fall a-cursing like a very drab,
A stallion. Fie upon't, foh!

> About, my brains! Hum—I have heard
> That guilty creatures sitting at a play
> Have by the very cunning of the scene
> Been struck so to the soul, that presently
> They have proclaim'd their malefactions:
> For murther, though it have no tongue, will speak
> With most miraculous organ. I'll have these players
> Play something like the murder of my father
> Before mine uncle. I'll observe his looks,
> I'll tent him to the quick. If 'a do blench,
> I know my course.
> (Ham II.ii.582–98)

Grammatical Exchange

32 Enallage—"the deliberate use of one case, person, gender, number, tense, or mood for another" (SMJ 61), cf., **37** Solecismus

Shifts in person or case of the pronoun:

And hang more praise upon deceased I
(Son 72.7)

Is she as tall as me?
(A&C III.iii.11)

So saucy with the hand of she here—what's her name
(A&C III.xiii.98)

With female fairies will his tomb be haunted,
And worms will not come to thee [for *him*]
(Cym IV.ii.217–18)

Singular verb with plural subject:

But see where Somerset and Clarence comes!
(3H6 IV.ii.3)

is there not wars? is there not employment?
(2H4 I.ii.72–73)

Whiles I threat, he lives:
Words to the heat of deeds too cold breath gives.
(Mac II.i.60–61)

Never was waves nor wind more violent
    (Per IV.i.59)

Plural verb with singular subject:

The posture of your blows are yet unknown
    (JC V.i.33)

                more than the scope
Of these delated articles allow
    (Ham I.ii.37–38)

Equality of two domestic powers
Breed scrupulous faction
    (A&C I.iii.47–48)

33 Hendiadys — use of two nouns joined by "and" in place of a noun with its
    modifier (sometimes two coordinate adjectives joined by "and" in place of
    two cumulative adjectives) (SMJ 61)

To have the due and forfeit of my bond
    (MV IV.i.37)

ponderous and marble jaws
    (Ham I.iv.50)

youth and observation
    (Ham I.v.101)

book and volume of my brain
    (Ham I.v.103)

abstract and brief chronicles of the time
    (Ham II.ii.524–25)

full of sound and fury
    (Mac V.v.27)

The heaviness and the guilt within my bosom
Takes off my manhood.
    (Cym V.ii.1–2)

34 "Hendiadys in Reverse" — modifying a noun with a figurative adjective ("Here
    Shakespeare's creative art…outruns the precepts of the figurists, who…did
    not describe a turn of words like this.") (SMJ 62)

> at once pluck out
> The multitudinous tongue
>   (Cor III.i.155–56)

35 Graecismus—use of a Greek idiom (usually by the confusion of two English constructions) (SMJ 62)

> That York is most unmeet of any man
>   (2H6 I.iii.164)

> I do not like the Tower, of any place [combining *more than any place* and *of all places*]
>   (R3 III.i.68)

> This is the greatest error of all the rest
>   (MSND V.i.246)

> Of all men else I have avoided thee
>   (Mac V.viii.4)

36 Anthimeria—"substitution of one part of speech for another" (SMJ 62)

> For goodness, growing to a plurisy,
> Dies in his own too much.
>   (Ham IV.vii.117–18)

> And many such-like as's of great charge
>   (Ham V.ii.43)

> To ransack Troy, within whose strong immures
>   (T&C Prol. 8)

> Kingdom'd Achilles in commotion rages
>   (T&C II.iii.175)

> I true? How now? what wicked deem is this?
>   (T&C IV.iv.59)

> All cruels else subscribe
>   (Lear III.vii.65)

> report
> That I am sudden sick. Quick, and return.
>   (A&C I.iii.4–5)

What you shall know mean time
Of stirs abroad
    (A&C I.iv.81–82)

                        shap'd out a man
Whom this beneath world doth embrace and hug
    (Timon I.i.43–44)

his complexion is perfect gallows
    (Temp I.i.29–30)

Come pat betwixt too early and too late
    (H8 II.iii.84)

                It more imports me
Than all the actions that I have foregone,
Or futurely can cope
    (TNK I.i.172–74)

Using pronouns, adjectives, and nouns as verbs:

If thou thou'st him some thrice, it shall not be amiss
    (TN III.ii.45–46)

Shall dizzy with more clamor Neptune's ear
    (T&C V.ii.174)

Lord Angelo dukes it well
    (MM III.ii.94)

If it [the wind] hath ruffian'd so upon the sea
    (Oth II.i.7)

when the thunder would not peace at my bidding
    (Lear IV.vi.102–103)

And that which most with you should safe my going
    (A&C I.iii.55)

            a hand that kings
Have lipp'd
    (A&C ii.v.29–30)

I'll unhair thy head
    (A&C II.v.64)

>   since Julius Caesar,
> Who at Philippi the good Brutus ghosted
>   (A&C II.vi.12–13)

Had our great palace the capacity
To camp this host
    (A&C IV.viii.32–33)

Wouldst thou be window'd in great Rome
    (A&C IV.xiv.72)

had I come coffin'd home
    (Cor II.i.176)

>   fall down, and knee
> The way into his mercy
>   (Cor V.i.5–6)

a Jack guardant cannot office me from my son Coriolanus
    (Cor V.ii.62–63)

>   My affairs
> Are servanted to others
>   (Cor V.ii.82–83)

Lov'd me above the measure of a father,
Nay, godded me indeed
    (Cor V.iii.10–11)

>   my true lip
> Hath virgin'd it e'er since
>   (Cor V.iii.47–48)

>   and nature prompts them
> In simple and low things to prince it much
>   (Cym III.iii.84–85)

'Tis still a dream, or else such stuff as madmen
Tongue and brain not
    (Cym V.iv.145–46)

But that the good mind of Camillo tardied
My swift command
    (WT III.ii.162–63)

> Bosom up my counsel
> (H8 I.i.112)

> give us the bones
> Of our dead kings, that we may chapel them
> (TNK I.i.49–50)

> they have skiff'd
> Torrents
> (TNK I.iii.37–38)

Vices of Language

37 Solecismus—the ignorant misuse of cases, genders, and tenses (and presumably parts of speech) (SMJ 64), cf., **32** Enallage

> Nathaniel: *Laus Deo, bone intelligo.*
> Holofernes: *Bone?*—*bone* for *bene*, Priscian a little scratched, 'twill serve.
>   (LLL V.i.27–29, "*bone…bene*" Theobald conjecture; "*bene…bene*" Q1, F1)

> … she gives you to notify that her husband will be absence from his house between ten and eleven… He's a very jealousy man.
>   (MWW II.ii.83–90)

> And didst thou not…desire me to be no more so familiarity with such poor people…?
>   (2H4 II.i.98–100)

38 Barbarismus—mispronunciation of words, especially by a foreign speaker (SMJ 65)

> Sir Hugh Evans (Welsh): Fery goot. I will make a prief of it in my note-book, and we will afterwards ork upon the cause with as great discreetly as we can.
>   (MWW I.i.144–46)

> Dr. Caius (French): I pray you bear witness that me have stay six or seven, two tree hours for him, and he is no-come.
>   (MWW II.iii.36)

> Fluellen (Welsh): th' athversary…is digt himself four yard under the countermines. By Cheshu, I think 'a will plow up all
>   (H5 III.ii.60–63)

> Macmorris (Irish): By Chrish law, 'tish ill done!…O, 'tish ill done
>   (H5 III.ii.88–93)

Jamy (Scottish): It sall be vary gud, gud feith, gud captens bath, and I sall quit you with gud leve, as I may pick occasion; that sall I, mary.
    (H5 III.ii.102–104)

39 Soraismus, also spelled Soriasmus—ignorant or pedantic mingling of different languages, also called Mingle-mangle (SMJ 65)

Most barbarous intimation! yet a kind of insinuation, as it were *in via*, in way, of explication; *facere*, as it were, replication, or rather *ostentare*, to show, as it were, his inclination…to insert again my *haud credo* for a deer.
    (LLL IV.ii.13–19)

he clepeth a calf, "cauf"; half, "hauf"; neighbor *vocatur* "nebor";…it insinuateth me of insanie: *ne intelligis, domine*?
    (LLL V.i.22–26, "insanie" Theobald conjecture; "infamie" Q1, F1)

I do, *sans question*.
    (LLL V.i.86)

Allons! we will employ thee.
    (LLL V.i.152, "*Allons!*" Rowe; "Alone" Q1, F1)

but we will put it (as they say) to *fortuna della guerra*
    (LLL V.ii.529–31, "*de la guerra*" Theobald conjecture; "delaguar" Q1, F1)

Pray you go and vetch me in my closet *une boîte en verd*, a box, a green-a box
    (MWW I.iv.45–46, "*une boîte en*" Hart conjecture; "vnboyteene" F1)

40 Heterogenium—"answering something utterly irrelevant to what is asked" (SMJ 66)

But sure he is stark mad:
When I desir'd him to come home to dinner,
He ask'd me for a thousand marks in gold:
"'Tis dinner time," quoth I: "My gold!" quoth he.
"Your meat doth burn," quoth I: "My gold!" quoth he.
"Will you come home?" quoth I: "My gold!" quoth he;
"Where is the thousand marks I gave thee, villain?"
"The pig," quoth I, "is burn'd": "My gold!" quoth he.
    (CE II.i.59–66)

Juliet: No, no! But all this did I know before.
         What says he of our marriage? what of that?
Nurse: Lord, how my head aches! What a head have I!

     It beats as it would fall in twenty pieces.
     My back a' t' other side—ah, my back, my back! ...
Juliet: I' faith, I am sorry that thou art not well.
     Sweet, sweet, sweet nurse, tell me, what says my love?
Nurse: Your love says, like an honest gentleman,
     An' a courteous, and a kind, and a handsome,
     And, I warrant, a virtuous—Where is your mother?
   (R&J II.v.46–57)

41 Amphibologia, or Amphibology—"ambiguity of grammatical structure, often
   occasioned by mispunctuation" (SMJ 66)—see also under *Logos*: Logical
   Argumentation: Syllogistic Reasoning: Fallacious Reasoning: Material
   Fallacy: Ambiguity of Language

If we offend, it is with our good will.
That you should think, we come not to offend,
But with good will. To show our simple skill,
That is the true beginning of our end.
Consider then, we come but in despite.
We do not come, as minding to content you,
Our true intent is. All for your delight
We are not here. That you should here repent you,
The actors are at hand; and, by their show,
You shall know all, that you are like to know.
   (MSND V.i.108–117)

[intentional mispunctuation of:
  If we offend, it is with our good will
  That you should think we come not to offend,
  But with good will to show our simple skill:
  That is the true beginning of our end.
  Consider then, we come—but in despite
  We do not come—as minding to content you.
  Our true intent is all for your delight.
  We are not here that you should here repent you.
  The actors are at hand, and, by their show,
  You shall know all that you are like to know.]

Cassio: Dost thou hear, mine honest friend?
Clown: No, I hear not your honest friend; I hear you.
   (Oth III.i.21–22)

42 Tapinosis—"the use of a base word to diminish the dignity of a person or
 thing" (SMJ 67)

O monstrous arrogance! Thou liest, thou thread, thou thimble,
Thou yard, three-quarters, half-yard, quarter, nail!
Thou flea, thou nit, thou winter-cricket thou!
Brav'd in mine own house with a skein of thread?
Away, thou rag, thou quantity, thou remnant
　　(Shrew IV.iii.107–111)

Quis, quis, thou consonant?
　　(LLL V.i.52)

in which cage of rushes I am sure you are not prisoner
　　(AYLI III.ii.370–71)

I see no more in you than in the ordinary
Of nature's sale-work
　　(AYLI III.v.42–43)

Therefore, you clown, abandon—which is in the vulgar
leave—the society—which in the boorish is company—of
this female—which in the common is woman; which
together is, abandon the society of this female, or, clown
thou perishest; or to thy better understanding, diest
　　(AYLI V.i.47–52)

And they have been grand-jurymen since before Noah was a sailor.
　　(TN III.ii.16–17)

to awaken your dormouse valor
　　(TN III.ii.19–20)

you are now sail'd into the north of my lady's opinion, where you will hang
like an icicle on a Dutchman's beard, unless you do redeem it
　　(TN III.ii.26–28)

O thou dissembling cub! what wilt thou be
When time hath sow'd a grizzle on thy case?
　　(TN V.i.164–65)

Achilles! a drayman, a porter, a very camel.
　　(T&C I.ii.249)

43 Cacemphaton, or Aischrologia (also spelled Aschrologia)—(A) foul or scurrilous speech, or (B) "an unpleasing combination of sounds such as results from excessive alliteration" (SMJ 68)

A: Foul speech

Agamemnon, how if he had biles—full, all over, generally?…And those biles did run—say so—did not the general run then? Were not that a botchy core?…Then would come some matter from him… The plague of Greece upon thee, thou mongrel beef-witted lord!
    (T&C II.i.2–13)

There's Ulysses and old Nestor, whose wit was mouldy ere your grandsires had nails on their toes, yoke you like draught-oxen
    (T&C II.i.104–106)

the vengeance on the whole camp! or rather, the Neapolitan bone-ache! for that methinks is the curse depending on those that war for a placket.
    (T&C II.iii.17–20)

What music will be in him when Hector has knock'd out his brains, I know not; but I am sure none, unless the fiddler Apollo get his sinews to make catlings on.
    (T&C III.iii.301–304)

Yes, your beggar of fifty; and his use was to put a ducat in her clack-dish. The Duke had crochets in him. He would be drunk too
    (MM III.ii.125–28)

He's now past it, yet…he would mouth with a beggar, though she smelt brown bread and garlic.
    (MM III.ii.182–84)

B: Unpleasing combination of sounds, cacophony

The preyful Princess pierc'd and prick'd a pretty pleasing pricket
    (LLL IV.ii.56)

Lady Mac.: I heard the owl scream and the crickets cry.
                Did not you speak?
Macbeth: When?
Lady Mac.:   Now.
Macbeth: As I descended?
Lady Mac.: Ay.

Macbeth: Hark! Who lies i' th' second chamber?
Lady Mac.: Donalbain.
Macbeth: This is a sorry sight.
Lady Mac.: A foolish thought, to say a sorry sight.
   (Mac II.ii.15–19)

44 Cacosyntheton—awkward or misleading placement of words, "as when an adjective improperly follows a noun or when there is any other unpleasing order of words" (SMJ 68)

A soul feminine saluteth us
   (LLL IV.ii.81)

I combat challenge of this latten bilbo
   (MWW I.i.162)

My name is Pistol call'd
   (H5 IV.i.62)

I am the poor duke's constable, and my name is Elbow
   (MM II.i.47–48)

Prove it before these varlets here, thou honorable man, prove it. [transposition of *honorable men* and *varlet*—see also **52** Acyrologia]
   (MM II.i.86–87)

Excess Verbiage—"employing many words to say little or to repeat the same thing inanely, dilutedly, tediously, garrulously" (SMJ 68)

45 Tautologia, also Tautology—"vain repetition of the same idea" in different words (SMJ 68)

I know the more one sickens the worse at ease he is…that
the property of rain is to wet and fire to burn…that a great
cause of the night is lack of the sun
   (AYLI III.ii.23–28)

Polonius: What do you read, my lord?
Hamlet: Words, words, words.
   (Ham II.ii.191–92)

an act hath three branches—it is to act, to do, to perform
   (Ham V.i.11–12)

If the man go to this water and drown himself, it is…he goes
 (Ham V.i.16–17)

he that is not guilty of his own death shortens not his own life
 (Ham V.i.19–20)

Lepidus: What manner o' thing is your crocodile?
Antony: It is shap'd sir, like itself, and it is as broad as it has breadth. It is
          just so high as it is, and moves with its own organs. It lives by that
          which nourisheth it, and the elements once out of it, it transmigrates.
Lepidus: What color is it of?
Antony: Of it own color too.
Lepidus: 'Tis a strange serpent.
Antony: 'Tis so, and the tears of it are wet.
    (A&C II.vii.41–49)

46 Perissologia, also Macrologia—"the addition of a superfluous clause which
   adds nothing to the meaning" (SMJ 69)

I do despise a liar as I do despise one that is false, or as I despise one that is
not true.
    (MWW I.i.68–70)

47 Parelcon—"the addition of a superfluous word, as of *that* [and also *and*] in
   the following" (SMJ 69)

Till that the weary very means do ebb?
    (AYLI II.vii.73)

when that I was and a little tine boy
    (TN V.i.389)

He that has and a little tine wit—
    (Lear III.ii.74)

48 Pleonasmus—"the needless telling of what is already understood" (SMJ 69)

I saw the wound, I saw it with mine eyes—
    (R&J III.ii.52)

Falstaff: Pistol!
Pistol: He hears with ears.
Evans: The tevil and his tam! What phrase is this? "He hears with ear"?
           Why, it is affectations.
    (MWW I.i.147–50)

I can hear it with mine own ears
    (2H4 II.ii.65–66)

his biting is immortal; those that do die of it do seldom or never recover.
    (A&C V.ii.246–48)

49 Homiologia—"tedious and inane repetition" (SMJ 69)

An old lord of the Council rated me the other day in the street about you, sir,
but I mark'd him not, and yet he talk'd very wisely, but I regarded him not,
and yet he talk'd wisely, and in the street too.
    (1H4 I.ii.83–87)

He hath wrong'd me, indeed he hath, at a word he hath. Believe me, Robert
Shallow, esquire, saith he is wrong'd.
    (MWW I.i.105–107)

Where's the roll? where's the roll? where's the roll? Let me see, let me see,
let me see. So, so, so, so, so, so, so; yea, marry, sir. Ralph Mouldy! Let them
appear as I call; let them do so, let them do so. Let me see, where is Mouldy?
    (2H4 III.ii.96–100)

when I lay at Clement's Inn—I was then Sir Dagonet in Arthur's
show—there was a little quiver fellow, and 'a would manage you his piece
thus, and 'a would about and about, and come you in and come you in.
"Rah, tah, tah," would 'a say, "bounce" would 'a say, and away again would
'a go, and again would 'a come. I shall ne'er see such a fellow.
    (2H4 III.ii.279–86)

I will not excuse you, you shall not be excus'd, excuses shall not be admit-
ted, there is no excuse shall serve, you shall not be excus'd
    (2H4 V.i.4–6)

Or, clown, thou perishest; or to thy better understanding, diest; or (to wit) I
kill thee, make thee away, translate thy life into death
    (AYLI V.i.51–53)

That he's mad, 'tis true, 'tis true 'tis pity,
And pity 'tis 'tis true—a foolish figure [of speech]
    (Ham II.ii.97–98)

As I say…(as I say)…(as I said)…(as I said)…(as I said) and (as I say)…for,
as you know…(if you be rememb'red)…(if you be rememb'red)…as I told
you…I hope here be truths…(as I say)…I hope here be truths.
    (MM II.i.97–133)

50 Periergia—"overlabor to seem fine and eloquent, especially in a slight matter" (SMJ 70), related to Declamatio (de-cla-MA-ti-o), "elaborately ornamental or rehearsed speech" (RAL29), and Circumlocution, talking all around the subject, neither included in SMJ

after his undressed, unpolished, uneducated, unpruned, untrained, or rather unlettered, or ratherest unconfirmed fashion
  (LLL IV.ii.16–18)

Anointed, I implore so much expense of thy royal sweet breath as will utter a brace of words
  (LLL V.ii.522–23)

My duty to you both, on equal love.
Great Kings of France and England: that I have labor'd
With all my wits, my pains, and strong endeavors
To bring your most imperial Majesties
Unto this bar and royal interview,
Your mightiness on both parts best can witness [etc.]
  (H5 V.ii.23–67)

Full thirty times hath Phoebus' cart gone round
Neptune's salt wash and Tellus' orbed ground,
And thirty dozen moons with borrowed sheen
About the world have times twelve thirties been,
Since love our hearts and Hymen did our hands
Unite commutual in most sacred bands.
  (Ham III.ii.155–60)

Most radiant, exquisite, and unmatchable beauty—
  (TN I.v.170–71)

51 Bomphiologia—"bombastic speech" (SMJ 70), speech exhibiting braggadocio

I am a rogue if I were not at half-sword with a dozen of them two hours together. I have scap'd by miracle. I am eight times thrust through the doublet, four through the hose, my buckler cut through and through, my sword hack'd like a hand-saw—*ecce signum!* I never dealt better since I was a man…if I fought not with fifty of them, I am a bunch of radish. If there were not two or three and fifty upon poor old Jack, then am I no two-legg'd creature.
  (1H4 II.iv.164–188)

> At my nativity
> The front of heaven was full of fiery shapes
> Of burning cressets, and at my birth
> The frame and huge foundation of the earth
> Shak'd like a coward.
>   (IH4 III.i.13–17)

Whoreson dog! I give him satisfaction! Would he had been one of my rank!…I am not vex'd more at any thing in th' earth; a pox on't! I had rather not be so noble as I am. They dare not fight with me because of the Queen my mother. Every Jack slave hath his bellyful of fighting, and I must go up and down like a cock that nobody can match.
>   (Cym II.i.14–22)

> Thou injurious thief,
> Hear but my name, and tremble…
>   To thy further fear,
> Nay, to thy mere confusion, thou shalt know
> I am son to th' Queen…
>   Art not afeard? …
>   Die the death!
> When I have slain thee with my proper hand,
> I'll follow those that even now fled hence,
> And on the gates of Lud's-Town set your heads.
> Yield, rustic mountaineer.
>   (Cym IV.ii.86–100)

52 Cacozelia — (A) "Affected diction, especially the coining of fine words out of Latin" (SMJ 72); (B) "ignorant misapplication of words…malapropism" (SMJ 75), including mistaking a word in one language for a word in another

A: Affected diction

Armado: There is remuneration, for the best ward of mine honor is rewarding my dependents…
Costard: Now will I look to his remuneration. Remuneration! O, that's the Latin word for three farthings: three farthings—remuneration… Remuneration: why, it is a fairer name than French crown! I will never buy and sell out of this word.
>   (LLL III.i.131–42)

Armado: Sir, it is the King's most sweet pleasure and affection to congratulate the Princess at her pavilion in the posteriors of this day, which the rude multitude call the afternoon.

Holofernes: The posterior of the day, most generous sir, is liable, congruent, and measurable for the afternoon. The word is well cull'd, chose, sweet, and apt…

    (LLL V.i.87–93)

O, he's the courageous captain of compliments… Ah, the immortal *passado*, the *punto reverso*, the *hay!*… The pox of such antic, lisping, affecting phantasimes ["fantasticoes" Q1], these new tuners of accent!

    (R&J II.iv.19–29)

Therefore, you clown, abandon—which is in the vulgar leave—the society— which in the boorish is company—of this female—which in the common is woman; which together is, abandon the society of this female

    (AYLI V.i.47–51)

Osric: Sir, here is newly come to court Laertes, believe me, an absolute gentleman, full of most excellent differences, of very soft society, and great showing; indeed, to speak sellingly [Q2 *uncorrected*; "feelingly" Q2 *corrected*] of him, he is the card or calendar of gentry; for you shall find in him the continent of what part a gentleman would see.

Hamlet: Sir, his definement suffers no perdition in you, though I know to divide him inventorially would dozy th' arithmetic of memory, and yet but yaw neither in respect of his quick sail; but in the verity of extolment, I take him to be a soul of great article, and his infusion of such dearth and rareness as, to make true diction of him, his semblable is his mirror, and who else would trace him, his umbrage, nothing more.

Osric: Your lordship speaks most infallibly of him.

Hamlet: The concernancy, sir? Why do we wrap the gentleman in our more rawer breath?

    (Ham V.ii.106–123)

Osric: The King, sir, hath wager'd with him six Barbary horses, against the which he has impawn'd, as I take it, six French rapiers and poniards, with their assigns… Three of the carriages, in faith, are very dear to fancy…and of very liberal conceit.

Hamlet: What call you the carriages?…Why is this all impawn'd, as you call it?

    (Ham V.ii.147–64)

Viola (as Cesario): Most excellent accomplish'd lady, the heavens rain odors on you!…My matter hath no voice, lady, but to your own most pregnant and vouchsafed ear.

Sir Andrew: [*aside*] "Odors," "pregnant," and "vouchsafed"; I'll get 'em all three all ready.

(TN III.i.84–91)

Combinations of **52** Cacozelia, **51** Bomphiologia, **44** Cacosyntheton, and classical allusions, the third burlesquing Marlowe's *Tamburlaine* (SMJ 73 substantially):

Ha, thou mountain-foreigner! Sir John, and master mine,
I combat challenge of this latten bilbo.
Word of denial in thy *labras* here!
Word of denial! Froth and scum, thou liest!
(MWW I.i.161–64)

Pistol: I will retort the sum in equipage.
Falstaff: I will not lend thee a penny.
Pistol: Why then the world's mine oyster,
           Which I with sword will open.
(MWW II.ii.1–4)

These be good humors indeed! Shall packhorses,
And hollow pamper'd jades of Asia,
Which cannot go but thirty mile a day,
Compare with Caesars and with Cannibals
And Troiant Greeks? Nay, rather damn them with
King Cerberus, and let the welkin roar.
Shall we fall foul for toys?
(2H4 II.iv.163–69)

What? Shall we have incision? shall we imbrue?
Then death rock me asleep, abridge my doleful days!
Why then let grievous, ghastly, gaping wounds
Untwind the Sisters Three! Come, Atropos, I say!
(2H4 II.iv.196–99)

Combination of **51** Bomphiologia, **39** Soraismus, and **44** Cacosyntheton:

Nym: Will you shog off? I would have you solus.
Pistol: "Solus," egregious dog? O viper vile!
          The "solus" in thy most mervailous face,
          The "solus" in thy teeth, and in thy throat…
          I do retort the "solus" in thy bowels,
          For I can take, and Pistol's cock is up,
          And flashing fire will follow
      (H5 II.i.45–53)

B: Malapropism

Speed: …But, Launce, how say'st thou that my master is become a notable
              lover?…
Launce: A notable lubber —as thou reportest him to be.
      (TGV II.v.41–46)

Speed: …what news with your mastership?
Launce: With my master's ship [Theobald conjecture; "Mastership" F1]? why,
              it is at sea.
      (TGV III.i.280–82)

Holofernes: Th' allusion holds in the exchange.
Dull: 'Tis true indeed, the collusion holds in the exchange.
Holofernes: …I say, th' allusion holds in the exchange.
Dull: And I say, the pollution holds in the exchange…
      (LLL IV.ii.41–47)

saying thus, or to the same defect [for *effect*]
      (MSND III.i.38–39)

one must come in with a bush of thorns and a lantern, and say he comes to
disfigure [for *figure* or *prefigure*], or to present, the person of Moonshine
      (MSND III.i.59–61)

the flowers of odious [for *odorous*] savors sweet
      (MSND III.i.82)

I have an exposition [for *disposition*] of sleep come upon me
      (MSND IV.i.39)

My young master doth expect your reproach [for *approach*]
      (MV II.v.19–20)

the gentleman had drunk himself out of his five sentences [for *senses*]
    (MWW I.i.174–75)

I will marry her, sir, at your request; but if there be no great love in the
beginning, yet heaven may decrease [for *increase*] it upon better acquaintance…
But if you say, "Marry her," I will marry her; that I am freely dissolv'd [for
resolved], and dissolutely [for *resolutely*].
    (MWW I.i.245–52)

But, indeed, she is given too much to allicholy [for *melancholy*] and musing
    (MWW I.iv.153–54)

I will be thy adversary [for *advocate*] toward Anne Page
    (MWW II.iii.94–95)

William:	… *Singulariter, nominativo, hic, haec, hoc* …
Evans:	What is your genitive case plural, William? …
William:	*Genitivo, horum, harum, horum.*
Mistress Quickly:	Vengeance of Jinny's case! Fie on her! never name her, child, if she be a whore… You do ill to teach the child such words. He teaches him to "hic" and to "hac," which they'll do fast enough of themselves, and to call "horum,"—fie upon you!

    (MWW IV.i.41–68)

he's an infinitive [for *infinite*] thing upon my score… [A]nd he is indited [for
invited] to dinner
    (2H4 II.i.24–28)

you cannot one bear with another's confirmities [for *infirmities*]
    (2H4 II.iv.57–58)

you shall comprehend [for *apprehend*] all vagrom [for *vagrant*] men
    (Ado III.iii.25)

We have here recover'd [for *discovered*] the most dangerous piece of lechery [for
treachery] that ever was known in the commonwealth
    (Ado III.iii.167–68)

I would have some confidence [for *conference*] with you that decerns [for
concerns] you nearly
    (Ado III.v.2–3)

Comparisons are odorous [for *odious*]
    (Ado III.v.16)

Our watch, sir, have indeed comprehended [for *apprehended*] two aspicious [for *suspicious*] persons
    (Ado III.v.45–46)

only get the learned writer to set down our excommunication [for *examination* or *communication*], and meet me at the jail
    (Ado III.v.63–64)

Is our whole dissembly [for *assembly*] appear'd?
    (Ado IV.ii.1)

Dost thou not suspect [for *respect*] my place? Dost thou not suspect my years?…No, thou villain, thou art full of piety [for *impiety*]
    (Ado IV.ii.74–79)

By this time our sexton hath reform'd [for *informed*] Signior Leonato of the matter; and, masters, do not forget to specify [for *testify*]…
    (Ado V.i.253–55)

French Soldier: *O Seigneur Dieu!*
Pistol: O Signieur Dew should be a gentleman…
           O Signieur Dew, thou diest on point of fox,
           Except, O signieur, thou do give to me
           Egregious ransom.
    (H5 IV.iv.6 11)

Out, hyperbolical fiend! [the rhetorical term for *exaggerated* used here to mean *vehement*]
    (TN IV.ii.25)

he's the very devil incardinate [for *incarnate*]
    (TN V.i.181–82)

My wife, sir, whom I detest [for *protest* or *attest*] before heaven and your honor
    (MM II.i.69–70)

Marry, sir, by my wife, who, if she had been a woman cardinally [for *carnally*] given
    (MM II.i.79–80)

53 Acyrologia, or Acyron—"use of a word repugnant or contrary to what is meant" (SMJ 77)

Yea, or else it were a pity, but they should suffer salvation [for *damnation*], body and soul.
(Ado III.iii.2–3)

if they should have any allegiance [for *treachery*] in them
(Ado III.iii.5–6)

First, who think you the most desartless [for *deserving*] man to be constable?
(Ado III.iii.9–10)

You are thought here to be the most senseless [for *sensible*] and fit man for the constable of the watch
(Ado III.iii.22–23)

let us obey [for *command*] you to go with us
(Ado III.iii.175–76)

Marry, sir, I would have some confidence [for *conference*] with you that decerns [for *concerns*] you nearly.
(Ado III.v.2–3)

O villain! thou wilt be condemn'd into everlasting redemption [for *perdition* or *damnation*] for this.
(Ado IV.ii.56–57)

No, thou villain, thou art full of piety [for *impiety*], as shall be prov'd upon thee by good witness.
(Ado IV.ii.78–79)

I humbly give you leave [for *beg your leave*] to depart, and if a merry meeting may be wish'd, God prohibit [*provide* or some other antonym for *prohibit*] it!
(Ado V.i.325–26)

I…do bring in here before your good honor two notorious benefactors [for *malefactors*]
(MM II.i.48–50)

precise villains they are, that I am sure of, and void of all profanation [for *profession*, *reverence*, or another antonym for *profanation*] in the world that good Christians ought to have.
(MM II.i.54–56)

Prove it before these varlets here, thou honorable man, prove it. [transposing *honorable men* and *varlet* — see also **44** Cacosyntheton]
(MM II.i.86–87)

Figures of Repetition

54 Alliteration, also Paroemion or Paromoeion — repetition of initial sounds of words (SMJ 78–79)

A hell-hound that doth hunt us all to death
(R3 IV.iv.48)

It were a shame to let this land by lease
(R2 II.i.110)

And for the day confin'd to fast in fires,
Till the foul crimes…
(Ham I.v.11–12)

With witchcraft of his wits… / O wicked wit
(Ham I.v.43–44)

For a more blusterous birth had never babe
(Per III.i.28)

55 Assonance — repetition of internal vowel sounds (not in SMJ)

He's here in double trust:
First, as I am his kinsman and his subject
(Mac I.vii.12–13)

Full fadom five thy father lies,
Of his bones are coral made:
Those are pearls that were his eyes
(Temp I.ii.397–99)

56 Consonance — repetition of internal consonant sounds (not in SMJ)

Teaching stern murder how to butcher thee
(R2 I.ii.32)

57 Parechesis — repetition of the same sound in words close together, in effect combining **54** Alliteration, **55** Assonance, and **56** Consonance in various ways (RAL 71–72, not in SMJ)

… and he it was that might rightly say, *Veni, vidi, vici*;
which to annothanize in the vulgar—O base and obscure
vulgar!—*videlicet*
    (LLL IV.i 67–69)

For never was a story of more woe
    (R&J V.iii.309)

    … and you shall put
This night's great business into my dispatch,
Which shall to all our nights and days to come
Give solely sovereign sway and masterdom.
    (Mac I.v.67–70)

58 Rhyme—(A) Masculine Rhyme: rhyming on the final stressed syllable;
(B) Feminine Rhyme, rhyming on the final stressed and following unstressed
syllable; (C) Triple Rhyme: rhyming on three final syllables, usually with one
stressed syllable followed by two unstressed syllables; (D) Internal Rhyme:
rhyming with at least one word in the middle of a verse line (not in SMJ)

(A) Masculine Rhyme:

Shall I compare thee to a summer's day? …
Rough winds do shake the darling buds of May
    (Son 18.1,3)

Our dates are brief, and therefore we admire…
And rather make them born to our desire
    (Son 123.5,7)

When every case in law is right;
No squire in debt, nor no poor knight
    (Lear III.ii.87–88)

(B) Feminine Rhyme:

I should in thought control your times of pleasure…
Being your vassal bound to stay your leisure
    (Son 58.2,4)

Thyself thou gav'st, thy own worth then not knowing…
So thy great gift, upon misprision growing
    (Son 87.9,11)

When nobles are their tailors' tutors;
No heretics burn'd, but wenches' suitors
    (Lear III.ii.83–84)

(C) Triple Rhyme:

Thanks, i' faith, for silence is only commendable
In a neat's tongue dried and a maid not vendible.
    (MV I.i.111–12)

(D) Internal Rhyme:

Then will two at once woo one
    (MSND III.ii.118)

When the hurly-burly's done
    (Mac I.i.3)

Thrice to thine, and thrice to mine
    (Mac I.iii.35)

Double, double, toil and trouble
    (Mac IV.i.10)

59 Anaphora — "beginning a series of clauses with the same word" (SMJ 79)

How many makes the hour full complete,
How many hours brings about the day,
How many days will finish up the year,
How many years a mortal man may live
    (3H6 II.v.26–29)

Was ever woman in this humor woo'd?
Was ever woman in this humor won?
    (R3 I.ii.227–28)

For happy wife, a most distressed widow;
For joyful mother, one that wails the name;
For one being sued to, one that humbly sues [etc.]
    (R3 IV.iv.98–104)

This royal throne of kings, this sceptered isle,
This earth of majesty, this seat of Mars,
This other Eden, demi-paradise,
This fortress built by Nature for herself…
This happy breed of me, this little world,
This precious stone set in the silver sea [etc.]
    (R2 II.i.40–51)

With mine own tears I wash away my balm,
With mine own hands I give away my crown,
With mine own tongue deny my sacred state,
With mine own breath release all duteous oaths
    (R2 IV.i.207–10)

I conjure thee by Rosaline's bright eyes,
By her high forehead and her scarlet lip,
By her fine foot, straight leg, and quivering thigh
    (R&J II.i.17–19)

Our instruments to melancholy bells,
Our wedding cheer to a sad burial feast;
Our solemn hymns to sullen dirges change;
Our bridal flowers serve for a buried corse
    (R&J IV.v.86–89)

I swear to thee, by Cupid's strongest bow,
By his best arrow with the golden head,
By the simplicity of Venus' doves,
By that which knitteth souls and prospers loves…
By all the vows that ever men have broke
    (MSND I.i.169–75)

And for her sake do I rear up her boy;
And for her sake I will not part with him.
    (MSND II.i.136–37)

                    Show men dutiful?
Why, so didst thou. Seem they grave and learned?
Why, so didst thou. Come they of noble family?
Why, so didst thou. Seem they religious?
Why, so didst thou.
    (H5 II.ii.127–31)

O now, for ever

Farewell the tranquil mind! farewell content!
Farewell the plumed troops and the big wars
That makes ambition virtue!
    (Oth III.iii.347–50)

Are you not Pericles? Like him you spake,
Like him you are!
    (Per V.iii.32–33)

60 Epistrophe, also Antistrophe—ending a series of clauses with the same word
    (SMJ 79–80)

Bullingbrook: Mistake not, uncle, further than you should.
York: Take not, good cousin, further than you should.
    (R2 III.iii.15–16)

Stirr'd up by God, thus boldly for his king.
My Lord of Herford here, whom you call king,
Is a foul traitor to proud Herford's king
    (R2 IV.i.133–35)

Lady Cap.: Verona's summer hath not such a flower.
Nurse: Nay, he's a flower, in faith, a very flower.
    (R&J I.iii.77–78)

Lady Cap.:   And then I hope thou wilt be satisfied.
Juliet: Indeed I never shall be satisfied
    (R&J III.v.92–93)

This man hath bewitch'd the bosom of my child…
And interchang'd love-tokens with my child
    (MSND I.i.27, 29)

Hermia: His folly, Helena, is no fault of mine.
Helena: None but your beauty; would that fault were mine!
    (MSND I.i.200–201)

I love thee not; therefore pursue me not.
    (MSND II.i.188)

Thou toldst me they were stol'n unto this wood;
And here am I, and wode within this wood
    (MSND II.i.191–92)

That if it would but apprehend some joy,
It comprehends some bringer of that joy
      (MSND V.i.19–20)

I will buy with you, sell with you, talk with you, walk
with you, and so following; but I will not eat with you,
drink with you, nor pray with you.
      (MV I.iii.35–38)

I'll have my bond, speak not against my bond,
I have sworn an oath that I will have my bond.
      (MV III.iii.4–5)

If thou has any sound or use of voice,
Speak to me.
If there be any good thing to be done
That may to thee do ease, and grace to me,
Speak to me.
      (Ham I.i.128–32)

A fine woman! a fair woman! a sweet woman!
      (Oth IV.i.178–79)

              Why I should fear I know not,
Since guiltiness I know not; but yet I feel I fear.
      (Oth V.ii.38–39)

61 Symploce—beginning and ending a series of clauses with the same words, a
      combination of **59** Anaphora and **60** Epistrophe (SMJ 79)

Son: How will my mother for a father's death
                Take on with me, and ne'er be satisfied!
Father: How will my wife for slaughter of my son
                Shed seas of tears, and ne'er be satisfied!
King Henry: How will the country for these woeful chances
                Misthink the King, and not be satisfied!
      (3H6 II.v.103–108)

Queen Marg: I had an Edward, till a Richard kill'd him;
                I had a Harry, till a Richard kill'd him;
                Thou hadst an Edward, till a Richard kill'd him;
                Thou hadst a Richard, till a Richard kill'd him.

Duchess: I had a Richard too, and thou didst kill him;
                      I had a Rutland too, thou holp'st to kill him.
Queen Marg: Thou hadst a Clarence too, and Richard kill'd him.
     (R3 IV.iv.40–46)

Where be the bending peers that flattered thee?
Where be the thronging troops that followed thee?
     (R3 IV.iv.95–96)

If lusty love should go in quest of beauty,
Where should he find it fairer than in Blanch?
If zealous love should go in search of virtue,
Where should he find it purer than in Blanch?
If love ambitious sought a match of birth,
Whose veins bound richer blood than Lady Blanch?
     (KJ II.i.426–31)

O, what men dare do! What men may do! What men daily
do, not knowing what they do!
     (Ado IV.i.19–20)

That Angelo's forsworn, is it not strange?
That Angelo's a murtherer, is't not strange?
That Angelo is an adulterous thief,
An hypocrite, a virgin-violator,
Is it not strange? and strange?
     (MM V.i.38–42)

62 Epanalepsis—"repetition at the end of a clause or sentence of the word with
     which it begins" (SMJ 80); see also **63** Antimetabole

Blood hath bought blood, and blows have answer'd blows;
Strength match'd with strength, and power confronted power
     (KJ II.i.329–30)

Old Gaunt indeed, and gaunt in being old.
     (R2 II.i.74)

Bound to himself! What doth he with a bond
That he is bound to?
     (R2 V.ii.67–68)

Open the door, or I will break it open.
     (R2 V.iii.45)

This love feel I, that feel no love in this.
  (R&J I.i.182)

What though he love your Hermia? Lord, what though?
  (MSND II.ii.109)

Weigh oath with oath, and you will nothing weigh.
  (MSND III.ii.131)

Cassius from bondage will deliver Cassius.
  (JC I.iii.90)

hear me for my cause, and be silent, that you may hear.
Believe me for mine honor, and have respect to mine
honor, that you may believe.
  (JC III.ii.13–16)

Remember March, the ides of March remember
  (JC IV.iii.18)

        Purpose so barr'd, it follows
Nothing is done to purpose.
  (Cor III.i.148–49)

63 Antimetabole, also Chiasmus—repeating the words of a phrase in reverse
    order to produce a contrasting sense, the A-B-B-A or mirror image structure
    of a phrase or clause in sound or in meaning; technically, antimetabole is
    the "repetition of the same words in transposed order" and Chiasmus is
    the inversion of the syntactical order of words in parallel phrases or clauses
    (WNID), but the two are "virtual synonyms" (RAL10) (SMJ 81); see also **62**
    Epanalepsis

Stanley: Richmond is on the seas.
Richard: There let him sink, and be the seas on him!
  (R3 IV.iv.462–63)

Old Gaunt indeed, and gaunt in being old.
  (R2 II.i.74)

Ay, no, no ay
  (R2 IV.i.201)

This love feel I, that feel no love in this.
  (R&J I.i.182)

My husband lives that Tybalt would have slain,
And Tybalt's dead that would have slain my husband.
    (R&J III.ii.105–106)

Friar Lawrence: Not body's death, but body's banishment.
Romeo: Ha, banishment? Be merciful, say "death"
    (R&J III.iii.11–12)

Blubb'ring and weeping, weeping and blubb'ring
    (R&J III.iii.87)

Romeo: For nothing can be ill if she be well.
Balthasar: Then she is well and nothing can be ill
    (R&J V.i.16–17)

Hermia: I would my father look'd but with my eyes.
Theseus: Rather your eyes must with his judgment look.
    (MSND I.i.56–57)

Some true love turn'd, and not a false turn'd true
    (MSND III.ii.91)

You of your wife, and me of my consent,
Of my consent that she should be your wife
    (MSND IV.i.158–59)

Chief Justice: You have misled the youthful prince.
Falstaff: The young prince hath misled me.
    (2H4 I.ii.144–45)

till all graces be in one woman, one woman shall not come in my grace
    (Ado II.iii.28–30)

who…if he be not fellow with the best king, thou shalt find the best king of
good fellows
    (H5 V.ii.241–43)

                Your gentleness shall force,
More than your force move us to gentleness.
    (AYLI II.vii.102–103)

The fool doth think he is wise, but the wise man knows himself to be a fool.
    (AYLI V.i.31–32)

Suit the action to the word, the word to the action
    (Ham III.ii.17–18)

For 'tis a question left us yet to prove,
Whether love lead fortune, or else fortune love
    (Ham III.ii.202–203)

                    but heaven hath pleas'd it so
To punish me with this, and this with me
    (Ham III.iv.173–74)

So thou mayst say the king lies by a beggar, if a beggar dwells near him; or the
church stands by thy tabor, if thy tabor stand by the church.
    (TN III.i.8–10)

Some rise by sin, and some by virtue fall
    (MM II.i.38)

the goodness that is cheap in beauty makes beauty brief in goodness
    (MM III.i.181–82)

Elbow: … Bless you, good father friar.
Duke: And you, good brother father.
    (MM III.ii.11–12)

Fair is foul, and foul is fair
    (Mac I.i.11)

Plainly as heaven sees earth and earth sees heaven
    (WT I.ii.315)

Antimetabole with **66** Polyptoton (SMJ 84):

Deposing thee before thou wert possess'd,
Which art possess'd now to depose thyself
    (R2 II.i.107–108)

I wasted time, and now doth time waste me
    (R2 V.v.49)

Mercutio: … Follow me this jest now, till thou hast worn out thy pump, that
              when the single sole of it is worn, the jest may remain, after the
              wearing, soly singular.
Romeo: O single-sol'd jest, soly singular for the singleness!
    (R&J II.iv.61–66)

When he is best, he is a little worse than a man, and when he is worst, he is
little better than a beast.
   (MV I.ii.88–89)

Grief joys, joy grieves, on slender accident
   (Ham III.ii.199)

Timon: What dost thou think 'tis worth?
Apemantus: Not worth my thinking.
   (Timon I.i.213–14)

64 Anadiplosis—"repetition of the last word of one clause or sentence at the
beginning of the next" (SMJ 82); see also Climax **65**

Come, I have learn'd that fearful commenting
Is leaden servitor to dull delay;
Delay leads impotent and snail-pac'd beggary.
   (R3 IV.iii.51–53)

Northumberland: he doth attend
          To speak with you, may it please you to come down.
King Richard: Down, down I come, like glist'ring Phaeton
   (R2 III.iii.176–78)

Bullingbrook: As my true service shall deserve your love.
King Richard: Well you deserve; they well deserve to have
           That know the strong'st and surest way to get.
   (R2 III.iii.199–201)

Aumerle: it is no more
     Than my poor life must answer.
Duchess: Thy life answer?
   (R2 V.ii.82–83)

Paris: Poor soul, thy face is much abus'd with tears.
Juliet: The tears have got small victory by that
   (R&J IV.i.29–30)

Helena: Yet Hermia still loves you; then be content.
Lysander: Content with Hermia? No I do repent…
   (MSND II.ii.110–11)

Iago: Indeed!
Othello: Indeed? ay, indeed…
                Is he not honest?
Iago: Honest, my lord?
Othello: Honest, ay, honest…
                What dost thou think?
Iago: Think, my lord?
   (Oth III.iii.101–105)

Cornwall: There shall he sit till noon.
Regan: Till noon? Till night, my lord, and all night too.
   (Lear II.ii.134–35)

Messenger: Madam,
                She was a widow—
Cleopatra: Widow? Charmian, hark…
                Bear'st thou her face in mind? Is't long or round?
Messenger: Round, even to faultiness.
   (A&C III.iii.26–30)

Husband win, win brother
   (A&C III.iv.18)

Anadiplosis with Antimetabole **63**:

Friar Lawrence: Not body's death, but body's banishment.
Romeo: Ha, banishment? Be merciful, say "death"
   (R&J III.iii.11–12)

You of your wife, and me of my consent,
Of my consent that she should be your wife
   (MSND IV.i.158–59)

65 Climax, also Gradation—Anadiplosis **64** carried through three or more clauses
      (SMJ 83); see also under *Logos*: Logical Argumentation: Syllogistic Reasoning:
      Simple Syllogism: Sorites

wherein cunning, but in craft? wherein crafty, but in
villainy? wherein villainous, but in all things?
   (1H4 II.iv.457–58)

Benedick: Only foul words—and thereupon I will kiss thee.
Beatrice: Foul words is but foul wind, and foul wind is but foul
                breath, and foul breath is noisome; therefore I will
                depart unkiss'd.
      (Ado V.ii.50–54)

For your brother and my sister no sooner met but they
look'd; no sooner look'd but they lov'd; no sooner lov'd
but they sigh'd; no sooner sigh'd but they ask'd one
another the reason; no sooner knew the reason but they
sought the remedy
      (AYLI V.ii.32–37)

And let the kettle to the trumpet speak,
The trumpet to the cannoneer without,
The cannons to the heavens, the heaven to earth
      (Ham V.ii.275–77)

66 Polyptoton—repetition of conjugates, words having the same derivation but
      different terminations (SMJ 83, 162); see also under *Logos*: Topics of Invention:
      Artificial Arguments: Division (A): Notation and Conjugates

But day doth daily draw my sorrows longer,
And night doth nightly make grief's length seem stronger.
      (Son 28.13–14; SMJ accepts emendation of "length" to "strength")

And Death once dead, there's no more dying then.
      (Son 146.14)

Unheedful vows may heedfully be broken
      (TGV II.vi.11)

As ending anthem of my endless dolor
      (TGV III.i.242)

Which harm within itself so heinous is
As it makes harmful all that speak of it.
      (KJ III.i.40–41)

With eager feeding food doth choke the feeder
      (R2 II.i.37)

and that word "grace"
In an ungracious mouth is but profane
    (R2 II.iii.88–89)

A king, woe's slave, shall kingly woe obey.
    (R2 III.ii.210)

York: For taking so the head, your whole head's length.
Bullingbrook: Mistake not, uncle, further than you should.
York: Take not, good cousin, further than you should
    (R2 III.iii.14–16)

Worst in this royal presence may I speak,
Yet best beseeming me to speak the truth.
    (R2 IV.i.115–16)

Romeo: O, wilt thou leave me so unsatisfied?
Juliet: What satisfaction canst thou have to-night?
    (R&J II.ii.125–26)

Some say the lark makes sweet division;
This doth not so, for she divideth us.
    (R&J III.v.29–30)

Flower as she was, deflowered by him
    (R&J IV.v.37)

Hermia: The more I hate, the more he follows me.
Helena: The more I love, the more he hateth me.
    (MSND I.i.198–99)

I followed fast, but faster he did fly
    (MSND III.ii.416)

If it were so, it was a grievous fault,
And grievously hath Caesar answer'd it.
    (JC III.ii.79–80)

    Or rather say, the cause of this defect,
For this effect defective comes by cause:
Thus it remains, and the remainder thus.
    (Ham II.ii.102–104)

it out-Herods Herod
    (Ham III.ii.13–14)

The Greeks are strong, and skillful to their strength,
Fierce to their skill, and to their fierceness valiant
    (T&C I.i.7–8)

       This woman's answer sorts,
For womanish it is to be from thence.
    (T&C I.i.106–107)

       Spirits are not finely touch'd
But to fine issues
    (MM I.i.35–36)

The tempter or the tempted, who sins most, ha?
Not she; nor doth she tempt
    (MM II.ii.163–64)

       I am a man
More sinn'd against than sinning.
    (Lear III.ii.59–60)

And so his knell is knoll'd.
    (Mac V.ix.16)

The loyalty well held to fools does make
Our faith mere folly
    (A&C III.xiii.42–43)

       hardness ever
Of hardiness is mother
    (Cym III.vi.21–22)

   society is no comfort
To one not sociable
    (Cym IV.ii.12–13)

Polyptoton with **63** Antimetabole:

Mercutio: Follow me this jest now, till thou hast worn out thy pump, that when
         the single sole of it is worn, the jest may remain, after the wearing,
         soly singular.
Romeo: O single-sol'd jest, soly singular for the singleness!
    (R&J II.iv.61–66)

67 Diaphora — "repetition of a common name so as to perform two logical
functions: to designate an individual and to signify the qualities connoted
by the common name" (SMJ 84)

My lord is not my lord
   (Oth III.iv.124)

         Is man so hateful to thee,
That art thyself a man?
   (Timon IV.iii.52–53)

68 Ploce, sometimes also Epanodos, Traductio, and Antistrophe — (A) repetition
of a proper name to designate a person and to signify his qualities (Peacham
and Day, SMJ 84); or (B) the "speedy iteration of one word with some little
intermission" (Puttenham, SMJ 85), especially "Emphatic repetition of a word
with pregnant reference to its special significance" (WNID)—cf., **69** Diacope

A: Repetition of proper name

1 Petitioner: … My Lord Protector will come this way by and by…
2 Petitioner: Marry, the Lord protect him… Come back, fool. This is the Duke of
               Suffolk and not my Lord Protector…
1 Petitioner: I pray, my lord, pardon me, I took ye for my Lord Protector.
Queen [*reading*]: "To my Lord Protector"?…
               And as for you, that love to be protected
               Under the wings of our Protector's grace…
   (2H6 I.iii.1–38)

Was't Hamlet wrong'd Laertes? Never Hamlet!
If Hamlet from himself be ta'en away,
And when he's not himself does wrong Laertes,
Then Hamlet does it not, Hamlet denies it
   (Ham V.ii.233–36)

B: Emphatic repetition with a small intermission

[See the repetition of *iron, look, eyes, see, tears*, etc. in *King John*]
   (KJ IV.i)

Grace me no grace, nor uncle me no uncle
   (R2 II.iii.87)

Shall kin with kin and kind with kind confound
   (R2 IV.i.141)

Ay, hand from hand, my love, and heart from heart
   (R2 V.i.82)

Doth grace for grace and love for love allow
   (R&J II.iii.86)

Who, all as hot, turns deadly point to point
   (R&J III.i.160)

confounding oath on oath
   (MSND III.ii.93)

When truth kills truth
   (MSND III.ii.129)

Weigh oath with oath, and you will nothing weigh
   (MSND III.ii.131)

Some there be that shadows kiss,
Such have but a shadow's bliss.
   (MV II.ix.66–67)

Harry to Harry shall, hot horse to horse
   (1H4 IV.i.122–23)

O, I have lost my reputation! I have lost the immortal part of myself,
and what remains is bestial. My reputation, Iago, my reputation!
   (Oth II.iii.262–65)

Ay, you did wish that I would make her turn.
Sir, she can turn, and turn; and yet go on
And turn again; and she can weep, sir, weep;
And she's obedient, as you say, obedient;
Very obedient.
   (Oth IV.i.252–56)

Othello: Thy husband knew it all.
Emilia: My husband?
Othello: Thy husband.
Emilia: That she was false to wedlock? …
                              My husband?
Othello: Ay, 'twas he that told me on her first…
Emilia: My husband?
Othello: What needs this iterance, woman? I say, thy husband.
   (Oth V.ii.139–50)

> O, let me not be mad, not mad, sweet heaven!
> Keep me in temper, I would not be mad!
>   (Lear I.v.46–47)

>   Give my thy hand,
> Thou hast been rightly honest—so hast thou—
> And thou—and thou—and thou. You have serv'd me well
>   (A&C IV.ii.10–12)

> Here come moe voices.—
> Your voices? For your voices I have fought;
> Watch'd for your voices; for your voices bear
> Of wounds two dozen odd; battles thrice six
> I have seen, and heard of; for your voices have
> Done many things, some less, some more. Your voices?
> Indeed I would be consul.
>   (Cor II.iii.125–31)

> Menenius: Hear me speak!
>   As I do know the consul's worthiness,
>   So can I name his faults.
> Sicinius: Consul? what consul?
> Menenius: The consul Coriolanus.
> Brutus: He consul!
> All Plebeians: No, no, no, no, no.
>   (Cor III.i.275–79)

> Coriolanus: The word is "mildly." Pray you let us go.
>   Let them accuse me by invention; I
>   Will answer in mine honor.
> Menenius: Ay, but mildly.
> Coriolanus: Well, mildly be it then. Mildly!
>   (Cor III.ii.142–45)

>   does not the stone rebuke me
> For being more stone than it?
>   (WT V.iii.37–38)

> What shall I do? say what? what shall I do?
>   (Temp I.ii.300)

Anne Bullen? No; I'll no Anne Bullens for him,
There's more in't than fair visage. Bullen?
No, we'll no Bullens.
　　(H8 III.ii.87–89)

69 Diacope — repetition of a word or short phrase with one or more other words
between them, usually exclamatory (SMJ 87), cf., **68** Ploce (B)

A horse, a horse! my kingdom for a horse!
　　(R3 V.iv.7, 13)

O Romeo, Romeo, wherefore art thou Romeo?
　　(R&J II.ii.33)

To be, or not to be…
　　(Ham III.i.55)

　　　　　　To die, to sleep —
No more, and by a sleep…
　　　　　　To die, to sleep —
To sleep, perchance to dream…
　　(Ham III.i.59–64)

Even now, now, very now…
　　(Oth I.i.88)

Light, I say, light!
　　(Oth I.i.144)

She swore, in faith, 'twas strange, 'twas passing strange;
'Twas pitiful, 'twas wondrous pitiful.
　　(Oth I.iii.160–61)

Work on,
My medicine, work!
　　(Oth IV.i.44–45, Q1)

But yet the pity of it, Iago! O Iago, the pity of it, Iago!
　　(Oth IV.i.195–96)

Put out the light, and then put out the light
　　(Oth V.ii.7)

To-morrow, and to-morrow, and to-morrow
　　(Mac V.v.19)

Help, Charmian, help, Iras, help
  (A&C IV.xv.12)

I am dying, Egypt, dying.
  (A&C IV.xv.41)

But kiss, one kiss!
  (Cym II.ii.17)

A pretty one, a very pretty one.
  (WT III.iii.71)

Diacope with **70** Epizeuxis (see below, page 64):

70 Epizeuxis—repetition of a word or short phrase with no other words between
  them (SMJ 87)

"No, no!" quoth she, "sweet Death, I did but jest…"
  (V&A 997)

To thee, to thee, my heav'd-up hands appeal…
  (RL 638)

Arm, arm, my name!
  (R2 III.ii.86)

A little little grave
  (R2 III.iii.154)

O Romeo, Romeo
  (R&J II.ii.33)

O blessed, blessed night!
  (R&J II.ii.139)

O Tybalt, Tybalt, the best friend I had!
  (R&J III.ii.61)

It did, it did, alas the day
  (R&J III.ii.72)

Is't not enough, is't not enough, young man
  (MSND II.ii.125)

Enough, enough, my lord; you have enough.
I beg the law, the law, upon his head.
  (MSND IV.i.154–55)

Blow, blow, thou winter wind
    (AYLI II.vii.174)

Reputation, reputation, reputation!
    (Oth II.iii.262)

By heaven, I do not, I do not, gentlemen.
    (Oth V.ii.232)

O Desdemona, Desdemona, dead, O, o, o.
    (Oth V.ii.281 Q1)

Howl, howl, howl, howl, O you are men of stones.
    (Lear V.iii.258 Q1)

        Thou'lt come no more,
Never, never, never, never, never.
    (Lear V.iii.308–309)

O horror, horror, horror!
    (Mac II.iii.64)

Fly, good Fleance, fly, fly, fly!
    (Mac III.iii.17)

Out, out, brief candle!
    (Mac V.v.23)

But why, why, why?…Well, is it, is it?
    (A&C III.vii.2–4)

2 Lord: Fare thee well, fare thee well.
Apemantus: Thou art a fool to bid me farewell twice.
2 Lord: Why, Apemantus?
Apemantus: Shouldst have kept one to thyself, for I mean to give thee none
    (Timon I.i.262–66)

Swift, swift, you dragons of the night
    (Cym II.ii.48)

One, two, three: time, time!
    (Cym II.ii.51)

O no, no, no, 'tis true.
    (Cym II.iv.106)

There is no tongue that moves, none, none i' th' world,
So soon as yours could win me.
    (WT I.ii.20–21)

O, I hope some god,
Some god hath put his mercy in your manhood
    (TNK I.i.71–72)

70 Epizeuxis and **69** Diacope together:

And my large kingdom for a little grave,
A little little grave, an obscure grave
    (R2 III.iii.153–54)

O Tybalt, Tybalt, the best friend I had!
O courteous Tybalt
    (R&J III.ii.61–62)

It did, it did, alas the day, it did!
    (R&J III.ii.72)

O Cressid! O false Cressid! false, false, false!
    (T&C V.ii.178)

Fly, good Fleance, fly, fly, fly!
    (Mac III.iii.17)

        O Antony,
Antony, Antony! Help, Charmian, help, Iras, help;
Help, friends below…
    (A&C IV.xv.11–13)

Logos
Topics of Invention

Topics of Invention—*Invention* is the general term for coming up with or figuring out what to say about the subject of a composition, how to develop or amplify the idea, from the Latin *invenire* (to come upon or discover, as distinct from the modern sense of original fabrication, which may or may not be involved in the process), the method being to draw the subject of a composition through a variety of established *Topics* or *Places* (from the Greek *topos*, place, via the Latin name of Aristotle's work *Topica*) (SMJ 9092).

Examples of Shakespeare's use of the term *invention* for this process:

> How can my Muse want subject to invent
> While thou dost breathe…
> For who's so dumb that cannot write to thee,
> When thou thyself dost give invention light?
> (Son 38.1–2, 7–8)

> If there be nothing new, but that which is
> Hath been before, how are our brains beguil'd,
> Which laboring for invention bear amiss
> The second burthen of a former child!
> (Son 59.1–4)

> O, what excuse can my invention make?
> (RL 225)

> Much like a press of people at a door,
> Throng her inventions, which shall go before.
> (RL 1301–1302)

> Here are only numbers ratified, but for the elegancy, facility, and golden cadence of poesy, *caret* [= it is lacking]. Ovidius Naso was the man. And why indeed "Naso," but for smelling out the odoriferous flowers of fancy, the jerks [= strokes] of invention?
> (LLL IV.ii.121–25)

> if your love
> Can labor aught in sad invention,
> Hang her an epitaph upon her tomb
>   (Ado V.i.282–84)

>   and in his brain,
>   … he hath strange places [i.e., of invention] cramm'd
> With observation, the which he vents
> In mangled forms.
>   (AYLI II.vii.38–42)

>   Women's gentle brain
> Could not drop forth such giant-rude invention
>   (AYLI IV.iii.33–34)

> Go, write it in a martial hand, be curst and brief. It is no matter
> how witty, so it be eloquent and full of invention.
>   (TN III.ii.42–44)

> I am about it, but indeed my invention
> Comes from my pate as birdlime does from frieze,
> It plucks out brains and all. But my Muse labors,
> And thus she is deliver'd:
>   (Oth II.i.125–28)

Inartificial Arguments—Testimony of Others

71 Testimony of Supernatural Powers—testimony of scripture, of "oracles, soothsayers, augurs, prodigies, dreams, apparitions, ghosts, witches, prophecies,"
whether "for good or evil" (SMJ 92), and of curses, premonitions, trial by
combat, and circumstantial evidence, which are located "On the borderline
between the supernatural and the human forms of testimony" (SMJ 96–97)

> Spirit: The duke yet lives that Henry shall depose;
>   But him out-live, and die a violent death…
>   By water shall he die, and take his end…
>   Let him shun castles.
>   Safer shall he be upon the sandy plains
>   Than where castles mounted stand.
> (2H6 I.iv.30–37)

Though not by war, by surfeit die your king…
Edward thy son…
Die in his youth…
Thyself a queen…
Outlive thy glory…
Rivers and Dorset…Lord Hastings…
                              God, I pray him
That none of you may live his natural age,
But by some unlook'd accident cut off!
    (R3 I.iii.196–213)

O, I have pass'd a miserable night,
So full of fearful dreams…
I, trembling, wak'd, and for a season after
Could not believe but that I was in hell,
Such terrible impression made my dream.
    (R3 I.iv.2–63)

Stanley did dream the boar did rase our helms,
And I did scorn it and disdain to fly.
Three times to-day my foot-cloth horse did stumble,
And started when he look'd upon the Tower,
As loath to bear me to the slaughter-house.
    (R3 III.iv.82–86)

I do remember me, Henry the Sixt
Did prophesy that Richmond should be king,
When Richmond was a little peevish boy
    (R3 IV.ii.95–97)

Thus Margaret's curse falls heavy on my neck.
"When he," quoth she, "shall split thy heart with sorrow,
Remember Margaret was a prophetess."
    (R3 V.i.25–27)

By the apostle Paul, shadows to-night
Have strook more terror to the soul of Richard
Than can the substance of ten thousand soldiers
Armed in proof and led by shallow Richmond.
    (R3 V.iii.216–219)

Receive thy lance, and God defend the right!
    (R2 I.iii.101)

O God, I have an ill-divining soul!
Methinks I see thee now, thou art so low,
As one dead in the bottom of a tomb.
    (R&J III.v.54–56)

In sooth, I know not why I am so sad…
    (MV I.i.1)

Beware the ides of March.
    (JC I.ii.18)

When beggars die there are no comets seen;
The heavens themselves blaze forth the death of princes.
    (JC II.ii.30–31)

Woe to the hand that shed this costly blood!
Over thy wounds now do I prophesy…
A curse shall light upon the limbs of men;
Domestic fury and fierce civil strife
Shall cumber all the parts of Italy…
And Caesar's spirit, ranging for revenge,
With Ate by his side come hot from hell,
Shall in these confines with a monarch's voice
Cry "Havoc!" and let slip the dogs of war
    (JC III.i.258–73)

                Caesar, thou art reveng'd,
Even with the sword that kill'd thee.
    (JC V.iii.45–46)

The ghost of Caesar hath appear'd to me
Two several times by night; at Sardis once,
And this last night, here in Philippi fields.
I know my hour is come.
    (JC V.v.17–20)

This bodes some strange eruption to our state…
In the most high and palmy state of Rome,
A little ere the mightiest Julius fell,
The graves stood tenantless and the sheeted dead
Did squeak and gibber in the Roman streets.
As stars with trains of fire, and dews of blood,
Disasters in the sun; and the moist star…
Was sick almost to doomsday with eclipse.
And even the like precurse of fear'd events,
As harbingers preceding still the fates
And prologue to the omen coming on,
Have heaven and earth together demonstrated
Unto our climatures and countrymen.
    (Ham I.i.69, 113–25)

Thou wouldst not think how ill all's here about my heart…
It is but foolery, but it is such a kind of gain-giving as would perhaps trouble a
woman.
    (Ham V.ii.212–16)

Trifles light as air

Are to the jealious confirmations strong
As proofs of holy writ
    (Oth III.iii.322–24)

These late eclipses in the sun and moon portend no good to us… Love cools,
friendship falls off, brothers divide: in cities, mutinies; in countries, discord; in
palaces, treason; and the bond crack'd 'twixt son and father. This villain of mine
comes under the prediction… 'Tis strange.
    (Lear I.ii.103–117)

But 'tis strange;

And oftentimes, to win us to our harm,
The instruments of darkness tell us truths,
Win us with honest trifles, to betray 's
In deepest consequence.
    (Mac I.iii.122–26)

Ross: Thou seest the heavens, as troubled with man's act,
           Threatens his bloody stage. By th' clock 'tis day,
           And yet dark night strangles the travelling lamp.
           Is't night's predominance, or the day's shame,
           That darkness does the face of earth entomb,
           When living light should kiss it?
Old Man: 'Tis unnatural
           Even like the deed that's done. On Tuesday last,
           A falcon, tow'ring in her pride of place,
           Was by a mousing owl hawk'd at, and kill'd.
Ross: And Duncan's horses (a thing most strange and certain)
           Beauteous and swift, the minions of their race,
           Turn'd wild in nature, broke their stalls, flung out,
           Contending 'gainst obedience, as they would make
           War with mankind.
Old Man: 'Tis said, they eat each other.
Ross: They did so — to th'amazement of mine eyes
           That look'd upon't.
  (Mac II.iv.5–20)

Soothsayer: If thou dost play with him at any game,
             Thou art sure to lose; and of that natural luck,
             He beats thee 'gainst the odds. Thy lustre thickens
             When he shines by. I say again, thy spirit
             Is all afraid to govern thee near him;
             But he away, 'tis noble.
  (A&C II.iii.26–31)

                         The auguries
Say they know not, they cannot tell, look grimly,
And dare not speak their knowledge.
  (A&C IV.xii.4–6)

My temple stands in Ephesus, hie thee thither,
And do upon mine altar sacrifice.
There, when my maiden priests are met together
Before the people all,
Reveal how thou at sea didst lose thy wife.
To mourn thy crosses, with thy daughter's, call
And give them repetition to the life.

Or perform my bidding, or thou livest in woe;
Do't, and happy, by my silver bow!
Awake, and tell thy dream.
    (Per V.i.240–49)

When as a lion's whelp shall, to himself unknown, without seeking find, and be
embrac'd by a piece of tender air; and when from a stately cedar shall be lopp'd
branches, which, being dead many years, shall after revive, be jointed to the
old stock, and freshly grow; then shall Posthumus end his miseries, Britain be
fortunate and flourish in peace and plenty.
    (Cym V.iv.138–44)

Yet, for a greater confirmation
(For in an act of this importance 'twere
Most piteous to be wild), I have dispatch'd in post
To sacred Delphos, to Apollo's temple,
Cleomenes and Dion, whom you know
Of stuff'd sufficiency. Now, from the oracle
They will bring all, whose spiritual counsel had,
Shall stop or spur me.
    (WT II.i.180–87)

Cleomenes: But of all, the burst
                And ear-deaf'ning voice o' th' oracle,
                Kin to Jove's thunder, so surprised my sense,
                That I was nothing…
Dion: When the oracle
                (Thus by Apollo's great divine seal'd up)
                Shall the contents discover, something rare
                Even then will rush to knowledge.
    (WT III.i.8–21)

I do refer me to the oracle:
Apollo be my judge!
    (WT III.ii.115–16)

Hermione is chaste, Polixenes blameless, Camillo a true subject, Leontes a jeal-
ous tyrant, his innocent babe truly begotten, and the King shall live without an
heir, if that which is lost be not found.
    (WT III.ii.132–36)

> Dreams are toys;
> Yet for once, yea, superstitiously,
> I will be squar'd by this.
> (WT III.iii.39–41)

if ever truth were pregnant by circumstance…there is such unity in the proofs.
The mantle of Queen Hermione's; her jewel about the neck of it; the letters of
Antigonus found with it, which they know to be his character
(WT V.ii.30–35)

I do believe it
Against an oracle.
(Temp IV.i.11–12)

Testimony of Men

72 Apodixis—argument based on the experience of many (SMJ 97)

Beseech you, sir, be merry; you have cause
(So have we all) of joy; for our escape
Is much beyond our loss. Our hint of woe
Is common: every day some sailor's wife,
The masters of some merchant, and the merchant
Have just our theme of woe; but for the miracle
(I mean our preservation), few in millions
Can speak like us. Then wisely, good sir, weigh
Our sorrow with our comfort.
(Temp II.i.1–9)

73 Martyria—argument based on one's own experience (SMJ 97)

Before my God, I might not this believe
Without the sensible and true avouch
Of mine own eyes.
(Ham I.i.56–58)

These are kind creatures. Gods, what lies I have heard!
Our courtiers say all's savage but at court.
Experience, O, thou disprov'st report!
(Cym IV.ii.32–34)

74 Proverb, also Adage (or Paroemia), Maxim, Apothegm, Sententia or Sentence, Aphorismus (A) or Aphorism, Gnome—the first two "represent the testimony of many men," the last five "the wisdom of one" (SMJ 98), "yet since the people sometimes seize upon and popularize the wise sayings of one man, a sharp line cannot be drawn between these two types of generalization" (SMJ 98); "The most difficult thing for the modern reader to remember is that the proverb…has been for most of formal rhetoric's history a means of *proof* rather than a substantiating ornament" (RAL 84); for **202** Aphorismus (B) see under *Logos*: Logical Argumentation: Syllogistic Reasoning: Disputation.

All places that the eye of heaven visits
Are to a wise man ports and happy havens.
   (R2 I.iii.275–76)

Where words are scarce, they are seldom spent in vain,
For they breathe truth that breathe their words in pain.
   (R2 II.i.7–8)

For nought so vile that on the earth doth live
But to the earth some special good doth give;
Nor aught so good but, strain'd from that fair use,
Revolts from true birth, stumbling on abuse.
   (R&J II.iii.17–20)

they stumble that run fast.
   (R&J II.iii.94)

The course of true love never did run smooth
   (MSND I.i.134)

Nerissa: … they are as sick that surfeit with too much as they that starve with nothing. It is no mean happiness therefore to be seated in the mean: superfluity comes sooner by white hairs, but competency lives longer.
Portia: Good sentences, and well pronounc'd.
Nerissa: They would be better if well follow'd.
   (MV I.ii.5–11)

Fast bind, fast find—
A proverb never stale in thrifty mind.
   (MV II.v.54–55)

… the devil shall have his bargain, for he was never yet a breaker of proverbs. He will give the devil his due.
   (1H4 I.ii.117–19)

Friendship is constant in all other things
Save in the office and affairs of love;
Therefore all hearts in love use their own tongues.
Let every eye negotiate for itself,
And trust no agent
    (Ado II.i.175–79; cf., "When love puts in, friendship is gone," Tilley, L549)

Truly by your office you may, but I think they that touch pitch will be defil'd.
    (Ado III.iii.56–57; cf., Ecclesiasticus 13:1 and Tilley, P358)

Orleans: "Ill will never said well."
Constable: I will cap that proverb with "There is flattery in friendship."
Orleans: And I will take up that with "Give the devil his due."
Constable: Well plac'd. There stands your friend for the devil; have at the very
           eye of that proverb with "A pox of the devil."
Orleans: You are better at proverbs, by how much "A fool's bolt is soon
           shot."
    (H5 III.vii.113–22; Tilley, I41, F41, D273, F515)

Fashion it thus: that what he is, augmented,
Would run to these and these extremities;
And therefore think him as a serpent's egg,
Which, hatch'd, would as his kind grow mischievous,
And kill him in the shell.
    (JC II.i.30–34)

Beauty provoketh thieves sooner than gold.
    (AYLI I.iii.110)

Truly, and to cast away honesty upon a foul slut were to put good meat into an
unclean dish.
    (AYLI III.iii.35–37; cf., Tilley, M834)

                      Foul deeds will rise,
Though all the earth o'erwhelm them, to men's eyes.
    (Ham I.ii.256–57; cf., Tilley, M1315)

But virtue, as it never will be moved,
Though lewdness court it in a shape of heaven,
So lust, though to a radiant angel link'd,
Will sate itself in a celestial bed
And prey on garbage.
    (Ham I.v.53–57)

Take these again, for to the noble mind
Rich gifts wax poor when givers prove unkind.
   (Ham III.i.99–100; cf., "A gift is valued by the mind of the giver," Tilley, G97)

What to ourselves in passion we propose,
The passion ending, doth the purpose lose.
   (Ham III.ii.194–95)

For use almost can change the stamp of nature
   (Ham III.iv.168; cf., Tilley, C551, C932)

So full of artless jealousy is guilt,
It spills itself in fearing to be spilt.
   (Ham IV.v.19–20; cf., Tilley, C606, F117, W333)

When sorrows come, they come not single spies,
But in battalions
   (Ham IV.v.78–79; cf., Tilley, M1012)

There's a divinity that shapes our ends,
Rough-hew them how we will
   (V.ii.10–11)

Lady, *"Cucullus non facit monachum"*: that's as much to say as I wear not motley
in my brain.
   (TN I.v.55–57; cf., Tilley, H586)

That she belov'd knows nought that knows not this:
Men prize the thing ungain'd more than it is.
That she was never yet that ever knew
Love got so sweet as when desire did sue.
Therefore this maxim out of love I teach:
Achievement is command; ungain'd, beseech;…
   (T&C I.ii.288–93)

Isabel: We cannot weigh our brother with ourself.
      Great men may jest with saints; 'tis wit in them,
      But in the less foul profanation…
      That in the captain's but a choleric word,
      Which in the soldier is flat blasphemy…
Angelo: Why do you put these sayings upon me?
   (MM II.ii.126–33)

"Cucullus non facit monachum": honest in nothing but in his clothes.
    (MM V.i.262–63; cf., Tilley, H586)

Who steals my purse steals trash…
But he that filches from me my good name
Robs me of that which not enriches him,
And makes me poor indeed.
    (Oth III.iii.157–61)

        Wouldst thou have that
Which thou esteem'st the ornament of life,
And live a coward in thine own esteem,
Letting "I dare not" wait upon "I would,"
Like the poor cat i' th' adage?
    (Mac I.vii.41–45; cf., Tilley, C144)

They said they were an-hungry; sigh'd forth proverbs—
That hunger broke stone walls, that dogs must eat,
That meat was made for mouths, that the gods sent not
Corn for the rich men only. With these shreds
They vented their complainings
    (Cor I.i.205–209; cf., Tilley, H811, M828 [quoting this passage])

75 Diatyposis—"commending profitable rules and precepts to another" (SMJ 101),
    sometimes ironically as in the examples from *Timon of Athens*

        for, brother, men
Can counsel and speak comfort to that grief
Which they themselves not feel, but tasting it,
Their counsel turns to passion, which before
Would give preceptial med'cine to rage,
Fetter strong madness in a silken thread,
Charm ache with air, and agony with words.
No, no, 'tis all men's office to speak patience
To those that wring under the load of sorrow,
But no man's virtue nor sufficiency
To be so moral when he shall endure
The like himself.
    (Ado V.i.20–31)

And these few precepts in thy memory
Look thou character. Give thy thoughts no tongue,
Nor any unproportion'd thought his act… [etc.]
This above all: to thine own self be true,
And it must follow, as the night the day,
Thou canst not then be false to any man.
   (Ham I.iii.58–80)

                Love all, trust a few,
Do wrong to none. Be able for thine enemy
Rather in power than use, and keep thy friend
Under thy own life's key. Be check'd for silence,
But never tax'd for speech.
   (AWEW I.i.64–68)

You great benefactors, sprinkle our society with thankfulness. For your own
gifts, make yourselves prais'd; but reserve still to give, lest your deities be
despis'd. Lend to each man enough, that one need not lend to another; for were
your godheads to borrow of men, men would forsake the gods. Make the meat
be belov'd more than the man that gives it. Let no assembly of twenty be without a score of villains.
   (Timon III.vi.70–77)

               Go, live rich and happy,
But thus condition'd: thou shalt build from men;
Hate all, curse all, show charity to none,
But let the famish'd flesh slide from the bone
Ere thou relieve the beggar. Give to dogs
What thou deniest to men.
   (Timon IV.iii.525–30)

Every man shift for all the rest, and let no man take care for himself; for all is
but fortune.
   (Tempest V.i.256–57)

76 Apomnemonysis — quoting "for authority the testimony of approved authors"
   (SMJ 104)

Holofernes: … I beseech your society.
Nathaniel: And thank you too; for society, saith the text, is the happiness of life.
Holofernes: And certes the text most infallibly concludes it.
   (LLL IV.ii.159–64; no source yet identified)

> Yet their own authors faithfully affirm
> That the land Salique is in Germany…
> 　　　Besides, their writers say…
> For in the book of Numbers is it writ,
> When the man dies, let the inheritance
> Descend unto the daughter.
> 　(H5 I.ii.43–45, 64–68, 98–100; cf., Numbers 27:8)

> For what says Quinapalus? "Better a witty fool than a foolish wit."
> 　(TN I.v.35–36)

77 Epicrisis—adding the speaker's own opinion to a cited authority, agreeing,
　disagreeing, or making exceptions (SMJ 103)

> You know that I held Epicurus strong,
> And his opinion; now I change my mind,
> And partly credit things that do presage.
> 　(JC V.i.76–78)

78 Chria—"a very short exposition of a deed or word, with the name of the author
　[or authority] recited" (SMJ 103)

> Armado:　…Comfort me, boy: what great men have been in love?
> Moth:　　Hercules, master.
> Armado:　Most sweet Hercules! More authority, dear boy, name more; and,
> 　　　　　sweet my child, let them be men of good repute and carriage.
> Moth:　　Samson, master; he was a man of good carriage, great carriage, for he
> 　　　　　carried the town gates on his back like a porter; and he was in love
> 　(LLL I.ii.64–72)

> There was never any thing so sudden but the fight of two rams, and Caesar's
> thrasonical brag of "I came, saw, and overcame."
> 　(AYLI V.ii.30–32)

> 　　　A kind of conquest
> Caesar made here, but made not here his brag
> of "Came, and saw, and overcame." With shame
> (The first that ever touch'd him) he was carried
> From off our coast, twice beaten
> 　(Cym III.i.22–26)

79 Orcos — "an oath affirming that one speaks the truth" (SMJ 103)

> If I in act, consent, or sin of thought
> Be guilty of the stealing that sweet breath
> Which was embounded in this beauteous clay,
> Let hell want pains enough to torture me.
>   (KJ IV.iii.135–38)

> Cesario, by the roses of the spring,
> By maidhood, honor, truth, and every thing,
> I love thee so, that maugre all thy pride,
> Nor wit nor reason can my passion hide.
>   (TN III.i.149–52)

> So come my soul to bliss, as I speak true;
> So speaking as I think, alas, I die.
>   (Oth V.ii.250–51)

80 Euche — a vow to keep a promise (SMJ 104)

> When ever Buckingham doth turn his hate
> Upon your Grace, but with all duteous love
> Doth cherish you and yours, God punish me
> With hate in those where I expect most love!
> When I have most need to employ a friend,
> And most assured that he is a friend,
> Deep, hollow, treacherous, and full of guile
> Be he unto me! This do I beg of God,
> When I am cold in love to you or yours.
>   (R3 II.i.32–40)

> This is the day which, in King Edward's time,
> I wish'd might fall on me when I was found
> False to his children and his wive's allies;
> This is the day wherein I wish'd to fall
> By the false faith of him whom most I trusted…
> That high All-Seer, which I dallied with,
> Hath turn'd my feigned prayer on my head,
> And given in earnest what I begg'd in jest.
>   (R3 V.i.13–22)

I…swear here, by the honor of my blood,
My father's purposes have been mistook…
My lord, these griefs shall be with speed redress'd,
Upon my soul, they shall…
I promis'd you redress of these same grievances
Whereof you did complain, which, by mine honor,
I will perform with a most Christian care.
   (2H4 IV.ii.54–60, 113–15)

Hamlet: Give me one poor request.
Horatio: What is't, my lord, we will.
Hamlet: Never make known what you have seen tonight.
Both: My lord, we will not.
Hamlet: Nay, but swear't.
Horatio: In faith,
    My lord, not I.
Marcellus: Nor I, my lord, in faith.
Hamlet: Upon my sword.
Marcellus: We have sworn, my lord, already.
Hamlet: Indeed, upon my sword, indeed.
Ghost: Swear…   [*They swear.*]
   (Ham I.v.142–81)

'Tis not the many oaths that makes the truth,
But the plain single vow that is vow'd true.
What is not holy, that we swear not by,
But take the High'st to witness. Then pray you tell me,
If I should swear by Jove's great attributes
I lov'd you dearly, would you believe my oaths
When I did love you ill? This has no holding,
To swear by Him whom I protest to love
That I will work against Him; therefore your oaths
Are words and poor conditions, but unseal'd—
   (AWEW IV.ii.21–30)

Othello: Now by yond marble heaven,
    In the due reverence of a sacred vow
    I here engage my words.
Iago: Do not rise yet.
    Witness, you ever-burning lights above,
    You elements that clip us round about,

> Witness that here Iago doth give up
> The execution of his wit, hands, heart,
> To wrong'd Othello's service!
>   (Oth III.iii.460–67)

Why should I think you can be mine, and true
(Though you in swearing shake the throned gods),
Who have been false to Fulvia? Riotous madness,
To be entangled with those mouth-made vows,
Which break themselves in swearing!
   (A&C I.iii.27–31)

81 Eustathia—a pledge of constancy (SMJ 105)

Let them pull all about mine ears, present me
Death on the wheel, or at wild horses' heels,
Or pile ten hills on the Tarpeian rock,
That the precipitation might down stretch
Below the beam of sight, yet will I still
Be thus to them.
   (Cor III.ii.1–6)

From my succession wipe me, father…
Not for Bohemia, nor the pomp that may
Be thereat gleaned, for all the sun sees, or
The close earth wombs, or the profound seas hides
In unknown fadoms, will I break my oath
To this my fair belov'd.
   (WT IV.iv.480–92)

82 Asphalia—the offer of surety for another (SMJ 105)

Antonio: Content, in faith, I'll seal to such a bond…
Bassanio: You shall not seal to such a bond for me,
              I'll rather dwell in my necessity.
Antonio: Why, fear not, man. I will not forfeit it.
   (MV I.iii.152–56)

Antonio: I dare be bound again,
            My soul upon the forfeit, that your lord
            Will never more break faith advisedly.
Portia: Then you shall be his surety.
   (MV V.i.251–54)

> Sir, have pity,
> I'll be his surety.
>   (Tempest I.ii.475–76)

83 Euphemismus—prognostication of good (SMJ 106)

This dream is all amiss interpreted,
It was a vision fair and fortunate.
Your statue spouting blood in many pipes,
In which so many smiling Romans bath'd,
Signifies that from you great Rome shall suck
Reviving blood, and that great men shall press
For tinctures, stains, relics, and cognizance.
This by Calphurnia's dream is signified.
   (JC II.ii.83–90)

Last night the very gods show'd me a vision…
I saw Jove's bird, the Roman eagle, wing'd
From the spungy south to this part of the west,
There vanish'd in the sunbeams, which portends
(Unless my sins abuse my divination)
Success to th' Roman host.
   (Cym IV.ii.346–52)

> For the Roman eagle,
From south to west on wing soaring aloft,
Lessen'd herself, and in the beams o' th' sun
So vanish'd; which foreshow'd our princely eagle,
Th' imperial Caesar, should again unite
His favor with the radiant Cymbeline,
Which shines here in the west.
   (Cym V.v.470–76)

There's nothing ill can dwell in such a temple.
If the ill spirit have so fair a house,
Good things will strive to dwell with't.
   (Temp I.ii.458–60)

84 Paraenesis — warning of impending evil (SMJ 106)

> O Buckingham, take heed of yonder dog!
> Look when he fawns he bites; and when he bites,
> His venom tooth will rankle to the death.
> Have not to do with him, beware of him…
>   (R3 I.iii.288–91)

> Shalt see thy other daughter will use thee kindly, for though she's as like this as
> a crab's like an apple, yet… She will taste as like this as a crab does to a crab.
>   (Lear I.v.14–19)

> Winter's not gone yet, if the wild geese fly that way…thou shalt have as many
> dolors for thy daughters as thou canst tell in a year.
>   (Lear II.iv.46–55)

85 Ominatio — prognostication of evil (SMJ 106)

> And if you crown him, let me prophesy,
> The blood of English shall manure the ground,
> And future ages groan for this foul act.
> Peace shall go sleep with Turks and infidels,
> And in this seat of peace tumultuous wars
> Shall kin with kin and kind with kind confound.
> Disorder, horror, fear, and mutiny
> Shall here inhabit, and this land be call'd
> The field of Golgotha and dead men's skulls.
> O, if you raise this house against this house,
> It will the woefullest division prove
> That ever fell upon this cursed earth.
>   (R2 IV.i.136–47)

> Calphurnia here, my wife, stays me at home:
> She dreamt to-night she saw my statuë,
> Which, like a fountain with an hundred spouts,
> Did run pure blood; and many lusty Romans
> Came smiling and did bathe their hands in it.
> And these does she apply for warnings and portents
> And evils imminent, and on her knee
> Hath begg'd that I will stay at home to-day.
>   (JC II.ii.75–82)

This bodes some strange eruption to our state.
(Ham I.i.69)

Come Hector, come, go back.
Thy wife hath dreamt, thy mother hath had visions,
Cassandra doth foresee, and I myself
Am like a prophet suddenly enrapt
To tell thee that this day is ominous:
Therefore come back.
(T&C V.iii.62–67)

I have great comfort from this fellow. Methinks he hath no drowning mark upon him, his complexion is perfect gallows. Stand fast, good Fate, to his hanging… If he be not born to be hang'd, our case is miserable.
(Temp I.i.28–33)

Artificial Arguments—"derived from a subject by the art of topical investigation"
(SMJ 108)

Definition

86 Definitio, or Definition—as defined by the logicians, the explanation of "the nature or essence of a subject in terms of its genus and difference" (SMJ 108), that is, the kind of thing it is and that which distinguishes it from others of its kind, in particular, its properties

Define, define, well-educated infant.
(LLL I.ii.94)

In our last conflict four of his five wits went halting off, and now is the whole man govern'd with one; so that if he have wit enough to keep himself warm, let him bear it for a difference between himself and his horse, for it is all the wealth that he hath left to be known a reasonable creature.
(Ado I.i.65–71)

poor Ophelia
Divided from herself and her fair judgment,
Without the which we are pictures, or mere beasts
(Ham IV.v.84–86)

Essence vs. Property

A base foul stone, made precious by the foil
Of England's chair, where he is falsely set
     (R3 V.iii.250–51)

Sweet love, I see, changing his property,
Turns to the sourest and most deadly hate.
     (R2 III.ii.135–36)

the property of rain is to wet and fire to burn.
     (AYLI III.ii.26–27)

So they loved as love in twain
Had the essence but in one,
Two distincts, division none:
Number there in love was slain…
Property was thus appalled,
That the self was not the same;
Single nature's double name
Neither two nor one was called.
     (P&T 25–28, 37–40)

          his voice was propertied
As all the tuned spheres
     (A&C V.ii.83–84)

Substance vs. Shadow

But Henry now shall wear the English crown,
And be true king indeed, thou but the shadow.
     (3H6 IV.iii.49–50)

          grief has so wrought on him,
He takes false shadows for true substances.
     (Titus III.ii.79–80)

Each substance of a grief hath twenty shadows
     (R2 II.ii.14)

Ah me, how sweet is love itself possess'd,
When but love's shadows are so rich in joy!
     (R&J V.i.10–11)

the very substance of the ambitious is merely the shadow of a dream.
    (Ham II.ii.257–59)

'Tis but the shadow of a wife you see,
The name, and not the thing.
    (AWEW V.iii.307–308)

87 Horismus—the rhetoricians' imaginative form of 86 Definitio (the stricter and
    more precise form of the logicians) (SMJ 108)

        love is not love
Which alters when it alteration finds,
Or bends with the remover to remove.
O no, it is an ever-fixed mark…
It is the star to every wand'ring bark…
Love's not Time's fool…
    (Son 116.2–9)

Jacques: He hath been a courtier, he swears.
Touchstone: If any man doubt that, let him put me to my purgation. I have
            trod a measure, I have flatt'red a lady, I have been politic with my
            friend, smooth with mine enemy, I have undone three tailors, I
            have had four quarrels, and like to have fought one.
    (AYLI V.iv.42–47)

Mad call I it, for to define true madness,
What is't but to be nothing else but mad?
    (Ham II.ii.93–94)

        The feast is sold
That is not often vouch'd, while 'tis a-making,
'Tis given with welcome. To feed were best at home;
From thence, the sauce to meat is ceremony,
Meeting were bare without it.
    (Mac III.iv.32–36)

          This double worship,
Where one part does disdain with cause, the other
Insult without all reason; where gentry, title, wisdom,
Cannot conclude but by the yea and no
Of general ignorance…
[defining government in which plebeians have a voice]
    (Cor III.i.142–46)

88 Systrophe—"the heaping together of many definitions of one thing" (SMJ 109)

> Phebe: Good shepherd, tell this youth what 'tis to love.
> Silvius: It is to be all made of sighs and tears…
>> It is to be all made of faith and service…
>> It is to be all made of fantasy.
>> All made of passion, and all made of wishes,
>> All adoration, duty, and observance,
>> All humbleness, all patience, and impatience,
>> All purity, all trial, all observance
> (AYLI V.ii.83–98)

> Sleep that knits up the ravell'd sleave of care,
> The death of each day's life, sore labor's bath,
> Balm of hurt minds, great nature's second course,
> Chief nourisher in life's feast.
>> (Mac II.ii.34–37)

Division (A), or Divisio—an argument based on logical division of a subject into Genus
and Species, Whole and Parts, Subject and Adjuncts, Cause and Effects, Antecedent and Consequents, Contraries and Contradictories, Similarity and Dissimilarity, Comparison (Greater, Equal, and Less), and Notation and Conjugates; for
174 Division (B), see under *Logos*: Logical Argumentation; Syllogistic Reasoning:
Fallacious Reasoning: Material Fallacy: Ambiguity of Language

Genus/Species

89 Diaeresis—"logical division of a genus into its species" (SMJ 111)

> I have neither the scholar's melancholy, which is emulation; nor the musician's,
> which is fantastical; nor the courtier's, which is proud; nor the soldier's, which
> is ambitious; nor the lawyer's, which is politic; nor the lady's, which is nice; nor
> the lover's, which is all these: but it is a melancholy of mine own, compounded
> of many simples, extracted from many objects, and indeed the sundry con-
> templation of my travels, in which my often rumination wraps me in a most
> humorous sadness.
>> (AYLI IV.i.10–20)

>> The king-becoming graces,
> As justice, verity, temp'rance, stableness,
> Bounty, perseverance, mercy, lowliness,
> Devotion, patience, courage, fortitude…
>> (Mac IV.iii.91–94)

there's no motion

That tends to vice in man, but I affirm
It is the woman's part: be it lying, note it,
The woman's; flattering, hers; deceiving, hers;
Lust and rank thoughts, hers, hers; revenges, hers;
Ambitions, covetings, change of prides, disdain,
Nice longing, slanders, mutability,
All faults that name, nay, that hell knows,
Why, hers, in part or all; but rather, all
    (Cym II.v.20–28)

90 Synecdoche—"a trope [that] heightens meaning by substituting genus for
    species, species for genus, part for whole, whole for part" (SMJ 112)

The locks between her chamber and his will
    (RL 302)

Pour down thy weather
    (KJ IV.ii.109)

To dance our ringlets to the whistling wind
    (MSND II.i.86)

He'll make your Paris Louvre shake for it
    (H5 II.iv.132)

    so the whole ear of Denmark
Is by a forged process of my death
Rankly abus'd
    (Ham I.v.36–38)

Two thousand souls and twenty thousand ducats
Will not debate the question of this straw.
    (Ham IV.iv.25–26)

Yet, poor old heart, he holp the heavens to rain.
    (Lear III.vii.62)

Take thy face hence.
    (Mac V.iii.19)

These are the ushers of Martius: before him he carries noise
    (Cor II.i.158–59)

till new-born chins
Be rough and razorable
   (Temp II.i.249–50)

Like to a pair of lions smear'd with prey
   (TNK I.iv.18)

Whole/Parts

91 Merismus, also Partitio or Partition—dividing a whole into its parts (SMJ 112)

Do you set down your name in the scroll of youth, that are written down old
with all the characters of age? Have you not a moist eye, a dry hand, a yellow
cheek, a white beard, a decreasing leg, an increasing belly? Is not your voice
broken, your wind short, your chin double, your wit single, and every part
about you blasted with antiquity? And will you yet call yourself young?
   (2H4 I.ii.178–85)

                     and then I lov'd thee
And show'd thee all the qualities o' th' isle,
The fresh springs, brine-pits, barren place and fertile.
   (Temp I.ii.336–38)

Misuse of **91** Merismus and of **92** Eutrepismus (cf., **45** Tautologia and
      49 Homiologia) (SMJ 114):

Don Pedro: Officers, what offense have these men done?
Dogberry: Marry, sir, they have committed false report; moreover they have
             spoken untruths; secondarily, they are slanders; sixt and lastly,
             they have belied a lady; thirdly, they have verified unjust things;
             and to conclude, they are lying knaves.
Don Pedro: First, I ask thee what they have done; thirdly, I ask thee what's
             their offense; sixt and lastly, why they are committed; and to
             conclude, what you lay to their charge.
Claudio: Rightly reason'd, and in his own division
   (Ado V.i.213–24)

92 Eutrepismus—numbering and ordering parts of a whole (SMJ 113)

> I am enjoin'd by oath to observe three things:
> First, never to unfold to any one
> Which casket 'twas I chose; next, if I fail
> Of the right casket, never in my life
> To woo a maid in way of marriage;
> Lastly,
> If I do fail in fortune of my choice,
> Immediately to leave you, and be gone.
> (MV II.ix.9–16)

Subject/Adjuncts, Cause/Effects, Antecedent/Consequents:

93 Enumeratio—division "of subject into its adjuncts, a cause into its effects, an antecedent into its consequents" (SMJ 114)

> His humor is lofty, his discourse peremptory, his tongue filed, his eye ambitious, his gait majestical, and his general behavior vain, ridiculous, and thrasonical. He is too picked, too spruce, too affected, too odd as it were, too peregrinate
> (LLL V.i.9–14)

> I will name you the degrees. The first, the Retort Courteous, the second, the Quip Modest; the third, the Reply Churlish; the fourth, the Reproof Valiant; the fift, the Countercheck Quarrelsome; the sixt, the Lie with Circumstance; the seventh, the Lie Direct.
> (AYLI V.iv.91–96)

> Osric: ... believe me, an absolute gentleman, full of most excellent differences, of very soft society, and great showing; indeed, to speak sellingly of him, he is the card or calendar of gentry; for you shall find in him the continent of what part a gentleman would see.
> Hamlet: Sir, his definement suffers no perdition in you, though I know to divide him inventorially would dozy th' arithmetic of memory...
> (Ham V.ii.106–14)

> do you know what a man is? Is not birth, beauty, good shape, discourse, manhood, learning, gentleness, virtue, youth, liberality, and suchlike, the spice and salt that season a man?
> (T&C I.ii.252–55)

94 Propositio—"a brief summary of what is to follow" (SMJ 115)

I do make myself believe that you may most uprighteously do a poor wrong'd
lady a merited benefit; redeem your brother from the angry law; do no stain to
your own gracious person; and much please the absent Duke
    (MM III.i.199–203)

95 Restrictio—"excepting part of a statement already made" (SMJ 115) (RAL 86)

    That it should come to this!
But two months dead, nay, not so much, not two.
    (Ham I.ii.137–38)

    I love and honor him,
But must not break my back to heal his finger.
    (Timon II.i.23–24)

    You good gods,
Let what is here contain'd relish of love,
Of my lord's health, of his content—yet not
That we two are asunder; let that grieve him
    (Cym III.ii.29–32)

I am but sorry, not afeard; delay'd,
But nothing alt'red. What I was, I am:
More straining on for plucking back
    (WT IV.iv.463–65)

96 Prolepsis—"a general statement amplified by dividing it into parts" (SMJ 116)

The course of true love never did run smooth;
But either it was different in blood…
Or else misgraffed in respect of years…
Or else it stood upon the choice of friends…
Or if there were a sympathy in choice,
War, death, or sickness did lay siege to it
    (MSND I.i.134–42)

The middle of humanity thou never knewest, but the extremity of both ends.
When thou wast in thy gilt and thy perfume, they mock'd thee for too much
curiosity; in thy rage thou know'st none, but art despis'd for the contrary.
    (Timon IV.iii.300–304)

97 Epanodos — like **96** Prolepsis, but "repeating the terms of the general proposition in the amplification which particularizes it" (SMJ 116)

> Mine eye and heart are at a mortal war,
> How to divide the conquest of thy sight:
> Mine eye my heart thy picture's sight would bar,
> My heart mine eye the freedom of that right... .
> To 'cide this title is impanelled
> A quest of thoughts, all tenants to the heart,
> And by their verdict is determined
> The clear eye's moiety and the dear heart's part—
> > As thus: mine eye's due is thy outward part,
> > And my heart's right thy inward love of heart.
> (Son 46:1–4, 9–14)

98 Synathroesmus — (A) giving details and then gathering them up in recapitulation; (B) Congeries, heaping together words of different meaning, without recapitulation (SMJ 117)

(A): details with recapitulation

> White-beards have arm'd their thin and hairless scalps
> Against thy majesty; boys, with women's voices,
> Strive to speak big, and clap their female joints
> In stiff unwieldy arms against thy crown;
> Thy very beadsmen learn to bend their bows
> Of double-fatal yew against thy state;
> Yea, distaff-women manage rusty bills
> Against thy seat: both young and old rebel,
> And all goes worse than I have power to tell.
> > (R2 III.ii.112–20)

(B): Congeries (here in antithetical pairs)

> Who can be wise, amaz'd, temp'rate, and furious,
> Loyal, and neutral, in a moment? No man.
> > (Mac II.iii.108–109)

99 Epiphonema—"an epigrammatic summary, gather[ing] into a pithy, sententious utterance what has preceded" (SMJ 117)

O, these are barren tasks, too hard to keep,
Not to see ladies, study, fast, not sleep.
   (LLL I.i.47–48)

Husband, I cannot pray that thou mayst win;
Uncle, I needs must pray that thou mayst lose;
Father, I may not wish the fortune thine;
Grandam, I will not wish thy wishes thrive:
Whoever wins, on that side shall I lose;
Assured loss before the match be play'd.
   (KJ III.i.331–36)

               To end a tale of length,
Troy in our weakness stands, not in her strength.
   (T&C I.iii.136–37)

            Will you rhyme upon't,
And vent it for a mock'ry? Here is one:
"Two boys, an old man (twice a boy), a lane,
Preserv'd the Britains, was the Romans' bane."
   (Cym V.iii.55–58)

100 Disjunctive Proposition—expressing "alternatives that divide the possibilities contemplated" (SMJ 118)

Immaculate and spotless is my mind;
That was not forc'd, that never was inclin'd
   To accessary yieldings, but still pure
   Doth in her poison'd closet yet endure.
   (RL 1656–59)

Straight let us seek, or straight we shall be sought
   (KJ V.vii.79)

The land is burning, Percy stands on high,
And either we or they must lower lie.
   (1H4 III.iii.203–204)

I know no personal cause to spurn at him,
But for the general. He would be crown'd
   (JC II.i.11–12)

Our hearts you see not, they are pitiful;
And pity to the general wrong of Rome…
Hath done this deed on Caesar.
　　(JC III.i.169–72)

Antony:　…that you shall give me reasons
　　　　　Why, and wherein, Caesar was dangerous.
Brutus:　O else were this a savage spectacle.
　　(JC III.i.221–23)

Not that I lov'd Caesar less, but that I lov'd Rome more. Had you rather Caesar
were living, and die all slaves, than that Caesar were dead, to live all freemen?
　　(JC III.ii.21–24)

All the conspirators, save only he,
Did that they did in envy of great Caesar;
He, only in a general honest thought
And common good to all, made one of them.
　　(JC V.v.69–72)

Subjects and Adjuncts

Examples of distinction between subject and adjuncts and of their confusion:

Believe me, king of shadows, I mistook.
Did not you tell me I should know the man
By the Athenian garments he had on?
　　(MSND III.ii.347–49) [adjuncts insufficient to identify subject]

Theseus:　And mark the musical confusion
　　　　　Of hounds and echo in conjunction.
Hippolyta:　　　　　… I never heard
　　　　　So musical a discord, such sweet thunder.
　　(MSND IV.i.117–18) [confusion of adjuncts]

The lunatic, the lover, and the poet
Are of imagination all compact…
And as imagination bodies forth
The forms of things unknown, the poet's pen
Turns them to shapes, and gives to aery nothing
A local habitation and a name.
　　(MSND V.i.15–17) [removal and replacement of adjuncts]

If we offend, it is with our good will.
That you should think, we come not to offend,
But with good will. To show our simple skill… [etc.]
　　(MSND V.i.108–117) [misplacement of adjunct (punctuation), cf.,
　　Amphibologia **41**]

His speech was like a tangled chain; nothing impair'd, but all disorder'd.
　　(MSND V.i.125–26) [referring to the previous example]

A son who is the theme of honor's tongue,
Amongst a grove the very straightest plant,
Who is sweet Fortune's minion and her pride,
Whilst I, by looking on the praise of him,
See riot and dishonor stain the brow
Of my young Harry. O that it could be prov'd
That some night-tripping fairy had exchang'd
In cradle-clothes our children where they lay,
And call'd mine Percy, his Plantagenet!
Then would I have his Harry and he mine.
　　(1H4 I.i.81–90)

And then I stole all courtesy from heaven,
And dress'd myself in such humility
That I did pluck allegiance from men's hearts,
Loud shouts and salutations from their mouths,
Even in the presence of the crowned King.
　　(1H4 III.ii.50–54)

Yet your mistrust cannot make me a traitor…
Treason is not inherited, my lord
　　(AYLI I.iii.56–61)

'Twas I; but 'tis not I. I do not shame
To tell you what I was, since my conversion
So sweetly tastes, being the thing I am.
　　(AYLI IV.iii.135–37)

Duke S.:　If there be truth in sight, you are my daughter.
Orlando:　If there be truth in sight, you are my Rosalind.
Phebe:　　If sight and shape be true,
　　　　　Why then my love adieu!
　　(AYLI V.iv.118–21)

What art thou that usurp'st this time of night,
Together with that fair and warlike form
In which the majesty of buried Denmark
Did sometimes march?
    (Ham I.i.46–49)

Much attribute he hath, and much the reason
Why we ascribe it to him; yet all his virtues,
Not virtuously on his own part beheld,
Do in our eyes begin to lose their gloss,
Yea, like fair fruit in an unwholesome dish,
Are like to rot untasted.
    (T&C II.iii.116–21)

This she? no, this is Diomed's Cressida.
If beauty have a soul, this is not she;
If souls guide vows, if vows be sanctimonies,
If sanctimony be the gods' delight,
If there be rule in unity itself,
This was not she… This is, and is not, Cressid!
    (T&C V.ii.137–46)

I will never trust a man again for keeping his sword clean, nor believe he can
have every thing in him by wearing his apparel neatly.
    (AWEW IV.iii.144–46)

The Duke's in us; and we will hear you speak
    (MM V.i.295)

That which you are, my thoughts cannot transpose
    (Mac IV.iii.21)

    Now does he feel his title
Hang loose about him, like a giant's robe
Upon a dwarfish thief.
    (Mac V.ii.20–22)

    Sure this robe of mine
Does change my disposition.
    (WT IV.iv.134–35)

Clown: …You denied to fight with me this other day, because I was no
            gentleman born. See you these clothes? Say you see them not and
            think me still no gentleman born. You were best say these robes are
            not gentlemen born. Give me the lie, do; and try whether I am not
            now a gentleman born.
Autolycus: I know you are now, sir, a gentleman born.
Clown: Ay, and have been so any time these four hours.
   (WT V.ii.128–37)

Four legs and two voices; a most delicate monster!
   (Tempest II.ii.89–90)

101 Peristasis—amplifying "by detailing the circumstances affecting a person or a
   thing" (SMJ 121)

I…betook myself to walk: the time When? about the sixth hour…Now for the
ground Which?…it is ycliped thy park. Then for the place Where? where, I
mean, I did encounter that obscene and most prepost'rous event…It standeth
north-north-east and by east from the west corner of thy curious-knotted
garden. There did I see that low-spirited swain…
   (LLL I.i.232–47)

                   When and where and how
We met, we woo'd, and made exchange of vow,
I'll tell thee as we pass…
   (R&J II.iii.61–63)

                   What beast was't then
That made you break this enterprise to me?
                      … Nor time, nor place,
Did then adhere, and yet you would make both:
They have made themselves, and that their fitness now
Does unmake you.
   (Mac I.vii.47–54)

I cannot delve him to the root: his father
Was call'd Sicilius, who did join his honor
Against the Romans with Cassibelan,
But had his titles by Tenantius, whom
He serv'd with glory and admir'd success:
So gain'd the sur-addition Leonatus:
And had (besides this gentleman in question)

Two other sons, who in the wars o' th' time
Died with their swords in hand; for which their father,
Then old and fond of issue, took such sorrow
That he quit being, and his gentle lady,
Big of this gentleman, our theme, deceas'd
As he was born. The King he takes the babe
To his protection, calls him Posthumus Leonatus,
Breeds him and makes him of his bedchamber,
Puts to him all the learnings that his time
Could make him the receiver of, which he took,
As we do air, fast as 'twas minist'red,
And in 's spring became a harvest; liv'd in court
(Which rare it is to do) most prais'd, most lov'd,
A sample to the youngest, to th' more mature
A glass that feated them, and to the graver
A child that guided dotards. To his mistress
(For whom he now is banish'd), her own price
Proclaims how she esteem'd him; and his virtue
By her election may be truly read,
What kind of man he is.
    (Cym I.i.28–54)

When shall I hear all through? This fierce abridgment
Hath to it circumstantial branches, which
Distinction should be rich in. Where? how liv'd you?
And when came you to serve our Roman captive?
How parted with your brothers? How first met them?
Why fled you from the court? and whither? These
And your three motives to the battle, with
I know not how much more, should be demanded,
And all the other by-dependances,
From chance to chance; but nor the time nor place
Will serve our long interrogatories.
    (Cym V.v.382–92)

102 Encomium—"high praise and commendation of a person or thing by extolling the inherent qualities or adjuncts" (SMJ 123)

This was the noblest Roman of them all…
His life was gentle, and the elements
So mix'd in him that Nature might stand up
And say to all the world, "This was a man!"
   (JC V.v.68–75)

What a piece of work is a man, how noble in reason, how infinite in faculties, in form and moving, how express and admirable, in action how like an angel, in apprehension, how like a god! the beauty of the world; the paragon of animals
   (Ham II.ii.303–307 F1)

See what a grace was seated on this brow:
Hyperion's curls, the front of Jove himself,
An eye like Mars, to threaten and command,
A station like the herald Mercury
New lighted on a heaven-kissing hill,
A combination and a form indeed,
Where every god did seem to set his seal
To give the world assurance of a man.
   (Ham III.iv.55–62)

Whose beauty did astonish the survey
Of richest eyes, whose words all ears took captive,
Whose dear perfection hearts that scorn'd to serve
Humbly call'd mistress
   (AWEW V.iii.16–19)

103 Taxis—"distribut[ing] to every subject its proper adjunct" (SMJ 123)

As the ox hath his bow, sir, the horse his curb, and the falcon her bells, so man hath his desires; and as pigeons bill, so wedlock would be nibbling.
   (AYLI III.iii.79–82)

                   we may again
Give to our tables meat, sleep to our nights;
Free from our feasts and banquets bloody knives
Do faithful homage and receive free honors;
All which we pine for now.
   (Mac III.vi.33–37)

> Reverend sirs,
> For you there's rosemary and rue; these keep
> Seeming and savor all the winter long…
> …Here's flow'rs for you:
> Hot lavender, mints, savory, marjorum,
> The marigold, that goes to bed wi' th' sun.
> And with him rises weeping. These are flow'rs
> Of middle summer, and I think they are given
> To men of middle age…
> … Now, my fair'st friend,
> I would I had some flow'rs o' th' spring that might
> Become your time of day—and yours, and yours,
> That wear upon your virgin branches yet
> Your maidenheads growing. O Proserpina
> For the flow'rs now, that, frighted, thou let'st fall
> From Dis's wagon! daffadils…
> …violets
> …pale primeroses
> …bold oxlips, and
> The crown imperial; lilies of all kinds
> (The flow'r-de-luce being one). O, these I lack
> To make you garlands of, and my sweet friend,
> To strew him o'er and o'er!
> (WT IV.iv.73–129)

Taxis in madness:

There's rosemary, that's for remembrance; pray you, love, remember. And there is pansies, that's for thoughts…There's fennel for you, and columbines. There's rue for you, and here's some for me…You may wear your rue with a difference. There's a daisy. I would give you some violets, but they wither'd all when my father died.
  (Ham IV.v.175–85)

104 Epitheton—attributing a quality to a person or thing by addition of a modifying adjective (SMJ 124) (RAL 45)

Armado: …my tender juvenal…
Moth: Why tender juvenal? Why tender juvenal?
Armado: I spoke it tender juvenal as a congruent epitheton appertaining to
               thy young days, which we may nominate tender.
      (LLL I.ii.8–15)

banish plump Jack, and banish all the world
      (1H4 II.iv.479–80)

Hamlet: His beard was grisl'd, no?
Horatio: It was, as I have seen it in his life,
               A sable silver'd.
      (Ham I.ii.239–41)

For brave Macbeth (well he deserves that name)
      (Mac I.ii.16)

Why, that's my dainty Ariel!
      (Temp V.i.95)

My tricksy spirit!
      (Temp V.i.226)

Compound epithets:

A pair of star-cross'd lovers
      (R&J Prol. 6)

thou mongrel beef-witted lord
      (T&C II.i.12–13)

          now from head to foot
I am marble-constant
      (A&C V.ii.239–40)

               Had I been thief-stol'n,
As my two brothers, happy!
      (Cym I.vi.5–6)

               Their discipline
(Now wing-led with their courages)
      (Cym II.iv.23–24)

… the Thunderer, whose bolt, you know,
Sky-planted
   (Cym V.iv.95–96)

          Jove's lightning, the precursors
O' th' dreadful thunder-claps, more momentary
And sight-outrunning were not
   (Temp I.ii.201–203)

         I met her Deity
Cutting the clouds towards Paphos; and her son
Dove-drawn with her.
   (Temp IV.i.92–94)

        There stand,
For you are spell-stopp'd.
   (Temp V.i.60–61)

Other examples:

carry-tale, dissentious jealousy (V&A 657)
marrow-eating sickness (V&A 741)
cold-pale weakness (V&A 892)
pity-pleading eyes (RL 561)
world-without-end hour (Son 57.5)
world-without-end bargain (LLL V.ii.789)
woe-wearied tongue (R3 IV.iv.18)
wonder-wounded hearers (Ham V.i.257)
to-and-fro-conflicting wind and rain (Lear III.i.11)
cub-drawn bear (Lear III.i.12)
belly-pinched wolf (Lear III.i.13)
heart-strook injuries (Lear III.i.17)
oak-cleaving thunderbolts (Lear III.ii.5)
all-shaking thunder (Lear III.ii.6)
flower-soft hands (A&C II.ii.210)

105 Antonomasia—(A) substituting "a descriptive phrase for a proper name"
   (SMJ 125); (B) substituting "a proper name for a quality associated with it"
   (SMJ 125)

(A): Substituting a descriptive phrase for a proper name

that same wicked bastard of Venus that was begot of thought, conceiv'd of
spleen, and born of madness, that blind rascally boy that abuses every one's
eyes because his own are out
    (AYLI IV.i.211–14)

This royal throne of kings, this sceptred isle,
This earth of majesty, this seat of Mars,
This other Eden, demi-paradise [etc.]
    (R2 II.i.40–58)

(B): Substituting a proper name for a quality associated with it

This England never did, nor never shall,
Lie at the proud foot of a conqueror,
But when it first did help to wound itself.
    (KJ V.vii.112–14)

This blessed plot, this earth, this realm, this England
    (R2 II.i.50)

Three Judases, each one thrice worse than Judas!
    (R2 III.ii.132)

                            yet you Pilates
Have here deliver'd me to my sour cross,
And water cannot wash away your sin.
    (R2 IV.i.240–42)

                      This is that very Mab
That plats the manes of horses in the night
    (R&J I.iv.88–89)

I am no great Nebuchadnezzar, sir, I have not much skill in grass.
    (AWEW IV.v.20–21)

You would be another Penelope
    (Cor I.iii.82)

106 Periphrasis — "use of a descriptive phrase for a common name, often to give
    an air of solemnity or elevation or to avoid a harsh word" (SMJ 125)

> when that fell arrest
> Without all bail shall carry me away
>   (Son 74.1–2)

I'll put a girdle round about the earth
In forty minutes.
    (MSND II.i.175–76)

I cannot tell what the dickens his name is
    (MWW III.ii.19–20)

You have conspir'd against our royal person,
Join'd with an enemy proclaim'd, and from his coffers
Receiv'd the golden earnest of our death
    (H5 II.ii.167–69)

When we have shuffled off this mortal coil
    (Ham III.i.66)

makes him stand to, and not stand to
    (Mac II.iii.34)

Most sacrilegious murther hath broke ope
The Lord's anointed temple, and stole thence
The life o' th' building!
    (Mac II.iii.67–69)

She made great Caesar lay his sword to bed;
He ploughed her, and she cropp'd.
    (A&C II.ii.227–28)

    for our crowned heads we have no roof,
Save this which is the lion's, and the bear's,
And vault to every thing!
    (TNK I.i.52–54)

107A Metonymy (A)—"the substitution of subject for adjunct, or adjunct for subject" (SMJ 126); for **107B** Metonymy (B) (substitution of cause for effect or effect for cause) see under *Logos*: Topics of Invention: Artificial Arguments: Division (A): Cause and Effect, Antecedent and Consequent

Mine eye and heart are at a mortal war
    (Son 46.1)

"O sir," says answer, "at your best command,
At your employment, at your service, sir."
"No, sir," says question, "I, sweet sir, at yours";
And so ere answer knows what question would…
     (KJ I.i.197–200)

Bell, book, and candle shall not drive me back
     (KJ III.iii.12)

Are you contented to resign the crown?
     (R2 IV.i.200)

Their cheeks are paper.
     (H5 II.ii.74)

Friends, Romans, Countrymen, lend me your ears!
     (JC III.ii.73)

as doublet and hose ought to show itself courageous to petticoat
     (AYLI II.iv.6–7)

          O most wicked speed: to post
With such dexterity to incestious sheets
     (Ham I.ii.156–57)

The serpent that did sting thy father's life
Now wears his crown.
     (Ham I.v.39–40)

Conferring them on younger strengths
     (Lear I.i.40)

               and giddy censure
Will then cry out
     (Cor I.i.268–69)

108 Hypotyposis, or Enargia — "the generic name given to figures of lively
     description or counterfeit representation," of which "the Elizabethans
     recognized many species, each with its own name signifying that it was a
     description of persons, manners, gestures, speech, events, places, or times,
     either real or imaginary" (SMJ 126), which follow below (**109–118**)

109 Prosopographia—"lively description of a person" (SMJ 126) (implied in the first example and illustrated in the second)

I have drawn her picture with my voice.
    (Per IV.ii.95)

My dearest wife was like this maid, and such a one
My daughter might have been. My queen's square brows,
Her stature to an inch, as wand-like straight,
As silver-voic'd, her eye as jewel-like
And cas'd as richly, in pace another Juno;
Who starves the ears she feeds, and makes them hungry,
The more she gives them speech.
    (Per V.i.107–113)

110 Prosopopoeia—"attribution of human qualities to dumb or inanimate creatures" (SMJ 126)

Arthur: There is no malice in this burning coal;
          The breath of heaven hath blown his spirit out,
          And strew'd repentant ashes on his head.
Hubert: But with my breath I can revive it, boy.
Arthur: And if you do, you will but make it blush
          And glow with shame of your proceedings, Hubert…
          All things that you should sue to do me wrong
          Deny their office; only you do lack
          That mercy which fierce fire and iron extends,
          Creatures of note for mercy-lacking uses.
    (KJ IV.i.108–20)

The iron tongue of midnight hath told twelve.
    (MSND V.i.363)

Nor heaven peep through the blanket of the dark
To cry, "Hold, hold!"
    (Mac I.v.53–54)

               The next time I do fight,
I'll make death love me; for I will contend
Even with his pestilent scythe.
    (A&C III.xiii.191–93)

Methinks I hear
Antony call; I see him rouse himself
To praise my noble act. I hear him mock
The luck of Caesar
   (A&C V.ii.283–86)

111 Characterismus—"description of the body or mind" (SMJ 127)

Ay, that's a colt indeed, for he doth nothing but talk of his horse, and he makes it a great appropriation to his own good parts that he can shoe him himself. I am much afeard my lady his mother play'd false with a smith… He doth nothing but frown, as who should say, "And you will not have me, choose." He hears merry tales and smiles not. I fear he will prove the weeping philosopher when he grows old, being so full of unmannerly sadness in his youth… [H]e hath a horse better than the Neapolitan's, a better bad habit of frowning than the Count Palentine; he is every man in no man. If a throstle sing, he falls straight a-cap'ring. He will fence with his own shadow. If I should marry him, I should marry twenty husbands… I say nothing to him, for he understands not me, nor I him. He hath neither Latin, French, nor Italian… He is a proper man's picture, but alas, who can converse with a dumb show? How oddly he is suited! I think he bought his doublet in Italy, his round hose in France, his bonnet in Germany, and his behavior every where… [H]e hath neighborly charity in him, for he borrow'd a box of the ear of the Englishman, and swore he would pay him again when he was able. I think the Frenchman became his surety and seal'd under for another… Very vildly in the morning, when he is sober, and most vildly in the afternoon, when he is drunk. When he is best, he is little worse than a man, and when he is worst, he is little better than a beast… [S]et a deep glass of Rhenish wine on the contrary casket, for if the devil be within, and that temptation without, I know he will choose it… [A] sponge.
   (MV I.ii.40–99)

His nature is too noble for the world;
He would not flatter Neptune for his trident,
Or Jove for 's power to thunder. His heart's his mouth;
What his breast forges, that his tongue must vent,
And, being angry, does forget that ever
He heard the name of death.
   (Cor III.i.254–59)

112 Ethopoeia—"description of natural propensities, manners and affections" (SMJ 127)

> For all the rest,
> They'll take suggestion as a cat laps milk;
> They'll tell the clock to any business that
> We say befits the hour.
> (Temp II.i.288–90)

113 Mimesis—"imitation of gesture, pronunciation, utterance" (SMJ 127)

And here she stands, touch her whoever dare,
I'll bring mine action on the proudest he
That stops my way in Padua. Grumio,
Draw forth thy weapon, we are beset with thieves;
Rescue thy mistress if thou be a man.
Fear not, sweet wench, they shall not touch thee, Kate!
I'll buckler thee against a million.
(Shrew III.ii.233–39)

Sir, his definement suffers no perdition in you, though I know to divide him inventorially would dozy th' arithmetic of memory, and yet but yaw neither in respect of his quick sail; but in the verity of extolment, I take him to be a soul of great article, and his infusion of such dearth and rareness as, to make true diction of him, his semblable is his mirror, and who else would trace him, his umbrage, nothing more.
(Ham V.ii.112–120)

Cries, "Excellent! 'Tis Agamemnon right!
Now play me Nestor, hem, and stroke thy beard,
As he being dress'd to some oration…
'Tis Nestor right. Now play him me, Patroclus,
Arming to answer in a night alarm…
(T&C I.iii.164–71)

Hum?…Ha?…Hum?…Agamemnon?…Ha?…God buy you, with all my heart… If to-morrow be a fair day, by aleven of the clock it will go one way or other. Howsoever, he shall pay for me ere he has me…Fare ye well, with all my heart.
(T&C III.iii.281–99)

114 Dialogismus—"the framing of speech suitable to the person speaking"
(SMJ 128)

> Now your traveller,
> He and his toothpick at my worship's mess,
> And when my knightly stomach is suffic'd,
> Why then I suck my teeth, and catechize
> My picked man of countries. "My dear sir,"
> Thus, leaning on mine elbow, I begin,
> "I shall beseech you"—that is question now;
> And then comes answer like an Absey book:
> "O sir," says answer, "at your best command,
> At your employment, at your service, sir."
> "No, sir," says question, "I, sweet sir, at yours";
> And so ere answer knows what question would,
> Saving in dialogue of compliment,
> And talking of the Alps and Apennines,
> The Pyrenean and the river Po,
> It draws toward supper in conclusion so.
> But this is worshipful society,
> And fits the mounting spirit like myself
>   (KJ I.i.189–206)

Or of a courtier, which could say, "Good morrow, sweet lord! How dost
thou, sweet lord?"
    (Ham V.i.82–83)

> Dear daughter, I confess that I am old;
> Age is unnecessary. On my knees I beg
> That you'll vouchsafe me raiment, bed, and food.
>   (Lear II.iv.154–56)

115 Pragmatographia—"the vivid description of an action or event" (SMJ 128)

> Mechanic slaves
> With greasy aprons, rules, and hammers shall
> Uplift us to the view. In their thick breaths,
> Rank of gross diet, shall we be enclouded,
> And forc'd to drink their vapor…Saucy lictors
> Will catch at us like strumpets, and scald rhymers
> Ballad 's out a' tune. The quick comedians

Extemporally will stage us, and present
Our Alexandrian revels: Antony
Shall be brought drunken forth, and I shall see
Some squeaking Cleopatra boy my greatness
I' th' posture of a whore.
     (A&C V.ii.209–21)

                    His sword, death's stamp,
Where it did mark, it took; from face to foot
He was a thing of blood, whose every motion
Was tim'd with dying cries. Alone he ent'red
The mortal gate of th' city, which he painted
With shunless destiny; aidless came off,
And with a sudden reinforcement struck
Corioles like a planet.
     (Cor II.ii.107–14)

Other examples:

Wherein I spoke… (Oth I.iii.134–69)
Doubtful it stood… (Mac I.ii.7–58)
I sit and tell… (Cym III.iii.89–98)
What she confessed… (Cym V.v.33–61)
Then have you lost a sight… (WT V.ii.46–91)

116 Chronographia—vivid reporting of events—in drama, events that occur
     off-stage (SMJ 129)

Look the world's comforter with weary gait
His day's hot task hath ended in the west;
The owl (night's herald) shrieks, 'tis very late;
The sheep are gone to fold, birds to their nest,
     And coal-black clouds that shadow heaven's light
     Do summon us to part, and bid good-night…
     (V&A 529–34)

          Look, love, what envious streaks
Do lace the severing clouds in yonder east.
Night's candles are burnt out, and jocund day
Stands tiptoe on the misty mountain tops.
     (R&J III.v.7–10)

The moon shines bright. In such a night as this,
When the sweet wind did gently kiss the trees,
And they did make no noise, in such a night
Troilus methinks mounted the Troyan walls,
And sigh'd his soul toward the Grecian tents,
Where Cressid lay that night… [etc.]
    (MV V.i.1–22)

117 Topographia—"description of places" (SMJ 129)

Or to the dreadful summit of the cliff
That beetles o'er his base into the sea…
The very place puts toys of desperation,
Without more motive, into every brain
That looks so many fadoms to the sea
And hears it roar beneath.
    (Ham I.iv.70–78)

There is a willow grows askaunt the brook,
That shows his hoary leaves in the glassy stream
    (Ham V.i.166–67)

The natural bravery of your isle, which stands
As Neptune's park, ribb'd and pal'd in
With oaks unscalable and roaring waters,
With sands that will not bear your enemies' boats,
But suck them up to th' topmast.
    (Cym III.i.18–22)

118 Topothesia—"description of imaginary places" (SMJ 130)

            Thou rememb'rest
Since once I sat upon a promontory,
And heard a mermaid on a dolphin's back
Uttering such dulcet and harmonious breath
That the rude sea grew civil at her song,
And certain stars shot madly from their spheres,
To hear the sea-maid's music?
    (MSND II.i.148–54)

I know a bank where the wild thyme blows,
Where oxlips and the nodding violet grows,
Quite over-canopied with luscious woodbine,
With sweet musk-roses and with eglantine;
There sleeps Titania sometime of the night,
Lull'd in these flowers with dances and delight;
And there the snake throws her enamell'd skin,
Weed wide enough to wrap a fairy in
      (MSND II.i.249–56)

Come on, sir, here's the place; stand still. How fearful
And dizzy 'tis, to cast one's eyes so low!
The crows and choughs that wing the midway air
Show scarce so gross as beetles. Half way down
Hangs one that gathers sampire, dreadful trade!
Methinks he seems no bigger than his head.
The fishermen that walk upon the beach
Appear like mice, and yond tall anchoring bark,
Diminish'd to her cock; her cock, a buoy
Almost too small for sight. The murmuring surge,
That on th' unnumb'red idle pebble chafes,
Cannot be heard so high. I'll look no more,
Lest my brain turn, and the deficient sight
Topple down headlong…You are now within a foot
Of th' extreme verge. For all beneath the moon
Would I not leap upright.
      (Lear IV.vi.11–27)

Contraries and Contradictories

Contraries as dramatic foils (SMJ 130)

King: Now at the latest minute of the hour,
           Grant us your loves.
Princess: A time methinks too short
           To make a world-without-end bargain in.
      (LLL V.ii.787–89)

Tut, you saw her fair, none else being by
      (R&J I.ii.94)

My reformation, glitt'ring o'er my fault,
Shall show more goodly and attract more eyes
Than that which hath no foil to set it off.
    (1H4 I.ii.213–15)

Your day's service at Shrewsbury hath a little gilded over your night's exploit
on Gadshill.
    (2H4 I.ii.148–49)

I'll be your foil, Laertes; in mine ignorance
Your skill shall like a star i' th' darkest night
Stick fiery off indeed.
    (Ham V.ii.255–57)

No contraries hold more antipathy
Than I and such a knave.
    (Lear II.ii.87–88)

Miranda: O wonder!
        How many goodly creatures are there here!
        How beauteous mankind is! O brave new world
        That has such people in't!
Prospero: 'Tis new to thee.
    (Temp V.i.181–84)

Contrary Terms—"[being] mutually repugnant, they serve to represent mental
    conflict and confusion" (SMJ 131)

To find out right with wrong—it may not be
    (R2 II.iii.145)

And in this seat of peace tumultuous wars
Shall kin with kin and kind with kind confound.
Disorder, horror, fear, and mutiny
Shall here inhabit
    (R2 IV.i.140–43)

I find myself a traitor with the rest;
For I have given here my soul's consent
T' undeck the pompous body of a king;
Made glory base, and sovereignty a slave;
Proud majesty a subject, state a peasant.
    (R2 IV.i.248–52)

> O madness of discourse,
> That cause sets up with and against itself!
> Bi-fold authority, where reason can revolt
> Without perdition, and loss assume all reason
> Without revolt. This is, and is not, Cressid!
>   (T&C V.ii.142–46)

> I am
> At war 'twixt will and will not.
>   (MM II.ii.32–33)

> By the world,
> I think my wife be honest, and think she is not;
> I think that thou art just, and think thou art not.
> I'll have some proof.
>   (Oth III.iii.383–86)

> Malcolm: Why are you silent?
> Macduff: Such welcome and unwelcome things at once
>   'Tis hard to reconcile.
>   (Mac IV.iii.137–39)

> Your knees to me? to your corrected son?
> Then let the pibbles on the hungry beach
> Fillop the stars; then let the mutinous winds
> Strike the proud cedars 'gainst the fiery sun,
> Murd'ring impossibility, to make
> What cannot be, slight work.
>   (Cor V.iii.57–62)

> Piety, and fear,
> Religion to the gods, peace, justice, truth,
> Domestic awe, night-rest, and neighborhood,
> Instruction, manners, mysteries, and trades,
> Degrees, observances, customs, and laws,
> Decline to your confounding contraries;
> And let confusion live!
>   (Timon IV.i.15–21)

Negative Terms—"contradictories of the corresponding positive terms" (including
    coinage of words beginning with un- and dis-) resulting in "vigor and
    freshness" (SMJ 133 and note)

No; first shall war unpeople this my realm
    (3H6 I.i.126)

We will untread the steps of damned flight
    (KJ V.iv.52)

My death's sad tale may yet undeaf his ear.
    (R2 II.i.16)

You have misled a prince, a royal king,
A happy gentleman in blood and lineaments,
By you unhappied and disfigured clean
    (R2 III.i.8–10)

Again uncurse their souls, their peace is made
With heads, and not with hands.
    (R2 III.ii.137–38)

God save King Henry, unking'd Richard say
    (R2 IV.i.220)

T' undeck the pompous body of a king
    (R2 IV.i.250)

Let me unkiss the oath 'twixt thee and me
    (R2 V.i.74)

Think that I am unking'd by Bullingbrook
    (R2 V.v.37)

have you any way then to unfool me again?
    (MWW IV.ii.114–15)

Thus was I, sleeping, by a brother's hand
Of life, of crown, of queen, at once dispatch'd,
Cut off even in the blossoms of my sin,
Unhous'led, disappointed, unanel'd
    (Ham I.v.74–77)

in his meed he's unfellow'd
    (Ham V.ii.142–43)

like a star disorb'd
    (T&C II.ii.46)

Why will he not upon our fair request
Untent his person and share th' air with us?
   (T&C II.iii.167–68)

but by the displanting of Cassio
   (Oth II.i.276)

As if some planet had unwitted men
   (Oth II.iii.182)

lest her body and beauty unprovide my mind again
   (Oth IV.i.205–206)

A little to disquantity your train
   (Lear I.iv.249)

Not in this land shall he remain uncaught
   (Lear II.i.57)

He's unqualited with very shame
   (A&C III.xi.44)

Dispropertied their freedoms
   (Cor II.i.248)

Unshout the noise that banish'd Martius!
   (Cor V.v.4; "unshout" Rowe conjecture for F1 "Vnshoot")

Unscissor'd shall this hair of mine remain
   (Per III.iii.29; "Unscissor'd" Steevens conjecture for Q1 "vnsisterd")

Though you would seek t' unsphere the stars with oaths
   (WT I.ii.48)

Here's such ado to make no stain a stain
   (WT II.ii.17)

Antonio: 'Tis as impossible that he's undrown'd,
        As he that sleeps here swims.
Sebastian: I have no hope
        That he's undrown'd.
Antonio: O, out of that no hope
        What great hope have you!
   (Temp II.i.237–40)

> I do beseech
> You, gracious madam, to unthink your speaking
> And to say so no more
>   (H8 II.iv.103–105)

> We come unseasonably; but when could grief
> Cull forth, as unpang'd judgment can, fitt'st time
> For best solicitation?
>   (TNK I.i.168–70)

Privative Terms—expressing "the absence or the loss of a characteristic that ought
    to be present" (SMJ 134)

> And you, my sovereign lady, with the rest,
> Causeless have laid disgraces on my head…
> And all to make away my guiltless life.
>   (2H6 III.i.161–67)

> I give you welcome with a powerless hand
>   (KJ II.i.15)

> All form is formless, order orderless,
> Save what is opposite to England's love.
>   (KJ III.i.253–54)

> The dateless limit of thy dear exile;
> The hopeless word of "never to return"
>   (R2 I.iii.151–52)

> And bootless make the breathless huswife churn
>   (MSND II.i.37)

> Cassius: Antony,
>   The posture of your blows are yet unknown;
>   But for your words, they rob the Hybla bees,
>   And leave them honeyless.
> Antony: Not stingless too?
> Brutus: O yes, and soundless too;
>   For you have stol'n their buzzing, Antony,
>   And very wisely threat before you sting.
>   (JC V.i.32–38)

> To be imprison'd in the viewless winds
> And blown with restless violence round about
> The pendant world
> > (MM III.i.123–25)

> And the strong lance of justice hurtless breaks
> > (Lear IV.vi.166)

> > How features are abroad
> I am skilless of
> > (Temp III.i.52–53)

> And ye that on the sands with printless foot
> Do chase the ebbing Neptune
> > (Temp V.i.34–35)

119 Litotes—denying the contrary or contradictory of a predicate of a subject instead of affirming it (SMJ 135)

> No, 'tis not so deep as a well, nor so wide as a
> church-door, but 'tis enough, 'twill serve.
> > (R&J III.i.96–97)

> Know, Caesar doth not wrong, nor without cause
> Will he be satisfied.
> > (JC III.i.47–48)

> True is it that we have seen better days
> > (AYLI II.vii.120)

> He hath not fail'd to pester us with message
> > (Ham I.ii.22)

> > What wouldst thou beg, Laertes,
> That shall not be my offer, not thy asking?
> > (Ham I.ii.45–46)

> > Let him fly far.
> Not in this land shall he remain uncaught
> > (Lear II.i.56–57)

<blockquote>

I did endure
Not seldom, nor no slight checks, when I have
Prompted you in the ebb of your estate
And your great flow of debts.
    (Timon II.ii.139–42)

</blockquote>

120 Synoeciosis — uniting contraries or seemingly incompatible terms (SMJ 135)

<blockquote>

I'll speak in a monstrous little voice
    (MSND I.ii.52)

</blockquote>

<blockquote>

I will roar you and 'twere any nightingale.
    (MSND I.ii.83–84)

</blockquote>

<blockquote>

Your virtues, gentle master,
Are sanctified and holy traitors to you.
O, what a world is this, when what is comely
Envenoms him that bears it!
    (AYLI II.iii.12–15)

</blockquote>

<blockquote>

they have a plentiful lack of wit
    (Ham II.ii.199)

</blockquote>

<blockquote>

I must be cruel only to be kind.
    (Ham III.iv.178)

</blockquote>

<blockquote>

A juggling trick — to be secretly open.
    (T&C V.ii.24)

</blockquote>

<blockquote>

To sue to live, I find I seek to die
And seeking death, find life.
    (MM III.i.42–43)

</blockquote>

<blockquote>

Can you make no use of nothing, nuncle?
    (Lear I.iv.130–31)

</blockquote>

<blockquote>

O monument
And wonder of good deeds evilly bestow'd!
    (Timon IV.iii.460–61)

</blockquote>

<blockquote>

Wherein I am false, I am honest; not true, to be true.
    (Cym IV.iii.42)

</blockquote>

121 Paradox — (A) self-contradiction, including Oxymoron **122**, a self-contradiction in a single phrase (not in SMJ); (B) an opinion contrary to that of most men (SMJ 136)

(A) self-contradiction, including **122** Oxymoron:

Berowne: No face is fair that is not full so black.
King: O paradox! Black is the badge of hell,
           The hue of dungeons, and the school of night…
Berowne: And therefore is she born to make black fair.
    (LLL IV.iii.249–57)

My care is loss of care…
The cares I give I have, though given away
    (R2 IV.i.196–198)

        O me! what fray was here?
Yet tell me not, for I have heard it all
    (R&J I.i.173–74)

        O brawling love! O loving hate!…
O heavy lightness, serious vanity…
Feather of lead, bright smoke, cold fire, sick health,
Still-waking sleep, that is not what it is.
This love feel I, that feel no love in this.
    (R&J I.i.176–82)

Beautiful tyrant! Fiend angelical!
Dove-feather'd raven! wolvish ravening lamb!…
A damned saint, an honorable villain!
    (R&J III.ii.75–79)

nature shows art
    (MSND II.ii.104)

A tedious brief scene…very tragical mirth
    (MSND V.i.56–57)

I am not what I am.
    (Oth I.i.65)

You undergo too strict a paradox,
Striving to make an ugly deed look fair.
    (Timon III.v.24–25)

Miranda: What foul play had we, that we came from thence?
              Or blessed was't we did?
Prospero: Both, both, my girl.
    (Temp I.ii.60–61)

(B) opinion contrary to that of most men:

Ophelia: Could beauty, my lord have better commerce than with honesty?
Hamlet: Ay, truly, for the power of beauty will sooner transform honesty from
              what it is to a bawd than the force of honesty can translate beauty into
              his likeness. This was sometime a paradox, but now the time gives it
              proof.
    (Ham III.i.108–14)

                          Better I were distract,
So should my thoughts be sever'd from my griefs,
And woes by wrong imaginations lose
The knowledge of themselves.
    (Lear IV.vi.281–84)

123 Antithesis—"setting contraries in opposition" (SMJ 137), "especially
    emphasized by the position of the contrasting words" (WNID)

Drown desperate sorrow in dead Edward's grave,
And plant your joys in living Edward's throne.
    (R3 II.ii.99–100)

For nothing hath begot my something grief,
Or something hath the nothing that I grieve
    (R2 II.ii.36–37)

Your husband, he is gone to save far off,
Whilst others come to make him lose at home
    (R2 II.ii.80–81)

My only love sprung from my only hate!
Too early seen unknown, and known too late!
    (R&J I.v.138–39)

The more my prayer, the lesser is my grace.
    (MSND II.ii.89)

Their sense thus weak, lost with their fears thus strong
    (MSND III.ii.27)

Not that I lov'd Caesar less, but that I lov'd Rome more.
  (JC III.ii.21–22)

A little more than kin, and less than kind.
  (Ham I.ii.65)

          how slow his soul sail'd on,
How swift his ship.
  (Cym I.iii.13–14)

124 Syncrisis—comparing "contrary things in contrasting clauses" (SMJ 137)

Cowards die many times before their deaths,
The valiant never taste of death but once.
  (JC II.ii.32–33)

Thorough tatter'd clothes small vices do appear;
Robes and furr'd gowns hide all. Plate sin with gold,
And the strong lance of justice hurtless breaks;
Arm it in rags, a pigmy's straw does pierce it.
  (Lear IV.vi.164–67)

Your native town you enter'd like a post,
And had no welcomes home, but he returns
Splitting the air with noise.
  (Cor V.vi.49–51)

125 Antanagoge—"balancing…an unfavorable aspect with a favorable one";
    hypothetically, "the reverse process, stating the unfavorable aspect last"
    (SMJ 138)

'Tis but a peevish boy—yet he talks well—
But what care I for words? Yet words do well
When he that speaks them pleases those that hear.
It is a pretty youth—not very pretty—
But sure he's proud—and yet his pride become him.
  (AYLI III.v.110–14)

Messenger: Caesar and he are greater friends than ever.
                              …But yet, madam—
Cleopatra: I do not like "but yet," it does allay
            The good precedence; fie upon "but yet"!
            "But yet" is as a jailer to bring forth
            Some monstrous malefactor.
    (A&C II.v.48–53)

126 Inter Se Pugnantia—pointing out hypocrisy or "discrepancy between theory
    and practice" (SMJ 138)

It is a good divine that follows his own instructions; I can easier teach twenty
what were good to be done, than to be one of the twenty to follow mine own
teaching.
    (MV I.ii.14–17)

                    But, good my brother,
Do not, as some ungracious pastors do,
Show me the steep and thorny way to heaven,
Whiles, like a puff'd and reckless libertine,
Himself the primrose path of dalliance treads,
And reaks not his own rede.
    (Ham I.iii.46–51)

The harlot's cheek, beautied with plast'ring art,
Is not more ugly to the thing that helps it
Than is my deed to my most painted word.
    (Ham III.i.50–52)

Irony—the general category containing the specific figures Irony **127**, Antiphrasis
    128, Paralipsis **129**, and Epitrope **130**, which follow (SMJ 138)

127 Irony—"naming one contrary [while intending] another, used in derision,
    mockery, jesting, dissembling" (SMJ 325); "perceived either by the
    contrariety of the matter or the manner of utterance, or both" (SMJ 325
    quoting Dudley Fenner, *Artes of Logike and Rhetorike*, 1584)

    Simple plain Clarence, I do love thee so
    That I will shortly send thy soul to heaven,
    If heaven will take the present at our hands.
        (R3 I.i.118–20)

> But Brutus says he was ambitious,
> And Brutus is an honorable man.
>   (JC III.ii.86–87)

> I am no orator, as Brutus is;
> But (as you know me all) a plain blunt man
> That love my friend, and that they know full well
> That gave me public leave to speak of him.
> For I have neither wit, nor words, nor worth,
> Action, nor utterance, nor the power of speech
> To stir men's blood; I only speak right on.
>   (JC III.ii.217–23)

> I prithee do not mock me, fellow student,
> I think it was to see my mother's wedding…
> Thrift, thrift, Horatio, the funeral bak'd-meats
> Did coldly furnish forth the marriage tables.
>   (Ham I.ii.177–81)

>   The gracious Duncan
> Was pitied of Macbeth; marry, he was dead.
> And the right valiant Banquo walk'd too late,
> Whom you may say (if't please you) Fleance kill'd,
> For Fleance fled. Men must not walk too late.
> Who cannot want the thought, how monstrous
> It was for Malcolm and for Donalbain
> To kill their gracious father? Damned fact!
> How it did grieve Macbeth! Did he not straight
> In pious rage the two delinquents tear,
> That were the slaves of drink and thralls of sleep?
> Was not that nobly done? Ay, and wisely too;
> For 'twould have anger'd any heart alive
> To hear the men deny't. So that, I say,
> He has borne all things well, and I do think
> That had he Duncan's sons under his key
> (As, an't please heaven, he shall not), they should find
> What 'twere to kill a father; so should Fleance.
>   (Mac III.vi.3–20)

128 Antiphrasis—"broad flout…irony of one word" (SMJ 139)

(For Brutus is an honorable man,
So are they all, all honorable men)…
And Brutus is an honorable man…
Yet Brutus says he was ambitious,
And Brutus is an honorable man…
And sure he is an honorable man…
I should do Brutus wrong, and Cassius wrong
Who (you all know) are honorable men.
I will not do them wrong; I rather choose
To wrong the dead, to wrong myself and you,
Than I will wrong such honorable men.
    (JC III.ii.82–127)

Some mollification for your giant, sweet lady.
    (TN I.v.204)

This is your devoted friend, sir…
    (AWEW IV.iii.235)

First let me talk with this philosopher.
    (Lear III.iv.154)

Thou, sapient sir, sit here.
    (Lear III.vi.22)

129 Paralipsis, also Paralepsis and Occupatio—"while pretending to pass over a matter, [telling] it most effectively" (SMJ 139)

But hadst thou not cross'd me, thou shouldst have heard how her horse fell, and she under her horse; thou shouldst have heard in how miry a place, how she was bemoil'd, how he left her with the horse upon her, how he beat me because her horse stumbled, how she waded through the dirt to pluck him off me; how he swore, how she pray'd that never pray'd before; how I cried, how the horses ran away, how her bridle was burst; how I lost my crupper, with many thing of worthy memory, which now shall die in oblivion, and thou return unexperienc'd to thy grave.
    (Shrew IV.i.72–84)

for what is inward between us, let it pass…and among other importunate and most serious designs, and of great import indeed too—but let that pass; for I must tell thee it will please his Grace (by the world) sometime to lean upon my poor shoulder, and with his royal finger, thus, dally with my excrement, with my mustachio; but, sweet heart, let that pass…some certain special honors it pleaseth his greatness to impart to Armado, a soldier, a man of travel, that hath seen the world; but let that pass.

> (LLL V.i.96–108)

I come to bury Caesar, not to praise him.

> (JC III.ii.74)

Let but the commons hear this testament—
Which, pardon me, I do not mean to read—
And they would go and kiss dead Caesar's wounds…
Have patience, gentle friends, I must not read it.
It is not meet you know how Caesar lov'd you…
'Tis good you know not that you are his heirs.

> (JC III.ii.130–45)

Hah? I like not that…
Nothing, my lord, or if—I know not what…
Cassio, my lord? No, sure, I cannot think it,
That he would steal away so guilty-like,
Seeing your coming…
Did Michael Cassio, when you woo'd my lady,
Know of your love? …
But for a satisfaction of my thought,
No further harm…
I did not think he had been acquainted with her…
Indeed! …
Honest, my lord? …
              Think, my lord? …
                For Michael Cassio
I dare be sworn I think that he is honest…
                    Men should be what they seem,
Or those that be not, would they might seem none!…
Why then I think Cassio's an honest man.

> (Oth III.iii.35–129)

I have done the state some service, and they know't—
No more of that.
    (Oth V.ii.339–40)

The love I bore your queen—lo, fool again!—
I'll speak of her no more, nor of your children;
I'll not remember you of my own lord,
Who is lost too. Take your patience to you,
And I'll say nothing.
    (WT III.ii.228–32)

130 Epitrope—"ironical permission" (SMJ 139)

Let the bloat king tempt you again to bed,
Pinch wanton on your cheek, call you his mouse,
And let him, for a pair of reechy kisses,
Or paddling in your neck with his damn'd fingers,
Make you to ravel all this matter out,
That I essentially am not in madness,
But mad in craft…
No, in despite of sense and secrecy,
Unpeg the basket on the house's top,
Let the birds fly, and like the famous ape,
To try conclusions in the basket creep,
And break your own neck down.
    (Ham III.iv.181–96)

Nay, pray you seek no color for your going,
But bid farewell, and go. When you sued staying,
Then was the time for words; no going then;
Eternity was in our lips and eyes
    (A&C I.iii.32–35)

Similarity and Dissimilarity

131 Homoeosis—"the general figure of similitude," its species being "Icon,
Parabola [or Parable], Paradigma [also Exemplum], and Fable [also
Apologue]" (SMJ 143), which follow below (**132–135**)

Why should the worm intrude the maiden bud?
Or hateful cuckoos hatch in sparrows' nests?
Or toads infect fair founts with venom mud?
Or tyrant folly lurk in gentle breasts?
Or kings be breakers of their own behests?
   But no perfection is so absolute,
   That some impurity does not pollute.
   (RL 848–54)

Corin:	Those that are good manners at the court are as ridiculous in the country as the behavior of the country is most mockable at the court. You told me you salute not at the court but you kiss your hands; that courtesy would be uncleanly if courtiers were shepherds.
Touchstone:	Instance, briefly; come, instance.
Corin:	Why, we are still handling our ewes, and their fells you know are greasy.
Touchstone:	Why, do not your courtier's hands sweat? And is not the grease of a mutton as wholesome as the sweat of a man? Shallow, shallow. A better instance, I say; come.

   (AYLI III.ii.45–58)

Look here upon this picture, and on this,
The counterfeit presentment of two brothers.
See what a grace was seated on this brow…
This was your husband. Look you now what follows:
Here is your husband, like a mildewed ear,
Blasting his wholesome brother…and what judgment
Would step from this to this?
   (Ham III.iv.53–71)

              'Twere all one
That I should love a bright particular star
And think to wed it, he is so above me.
In his bright radiance and collateral light
Must I be comforted, not in his sphere.
   (AWEW I.i.85–89)

If I quench thee, thou flaming minister,
I can again thy former light restore,
Should I repent me; but once put out thy light,
Thou cunning'st pattern of excelling nature,

I know not where is that Promethean heat
That can thy light relume. When I have pluck'd thy rose,
I cannot give it vital growth again,
It needs must wither. I'll smell thee on the tree.
 (Oth V.ii.8–15)

        Unnatural deeds
Do breed unnatural troubles
 (Mac V.i.71–72)

Do, villains, do, since you protest to do't.
Like workmen, I'll example you with thievery:
The sun's a thief, and with his great attraction
Robs the vast sea; the moon's an arrant thief,
And her pale fire she snatches from the sun;
The sea's a thief, whose liquid surge resolves
The moon into salt tears; the earth's a thief,
That feeds and breeds by a composture stol'n
From gen'ral excrement; each thing's a thief.
 (Timon IV.iii.434–42)

132 Icon—painting "the likeness of a person by imagery" (SMJ 143),
 "comparison of one person or thing with another, form with form, quality
 with quality" (SMJ 327)

So when this thief, this traitor Bullingbrook…
Shall see us rising in our throne, the east
 (R2 III.ii.47–50)

Down, down I come, like glist'ring Phaëton,
Wanting the manage of unruly jades.
 (R2 III.iii.178–79)

I have been studying how I may compare
This prison where I live unto the world,
And for because the world is populous,
And here is not a creature but myself,
I cannot do it; yet I'll hammer it out…
Thus play I in one person many people,
And none contented.
 (R2 V.v.1–32)

133 Parabola, or Parable—teaching a moral by means of "moral or mystical resemblance" (SMJ 143) or "by means of an extended metaphor" (RAL 70)

> So we grew together,
> Like to a double cherry, seeming parted,
> But yet an union in partition,
> Two lovely berries moulded on one stem;
> So with two seeming bodies, but one heart,
> Two of the first, like coats in heraldry,
> Due but to one, and crowned with one crest.
>   (MSND III.ii.208–14)

> Sir, I have upon a high and pleasant hill
> Feign'd Fortune to be thron'd… Amongst them all,
> Whose eyes are on this sovereign lady fix'd,
> One do I personate of Lord Timon's frame,
> Whom Fortune with her ivory hand wafts to her,
> Whose present grace to present slaves and servants
> Translates his rivals…
> All those which were his fellows but of late…
> When Fortune in her shift and change of mood
> Spurns down her late beloved, all his dependants
> Which labor'd after him to the mountain's top
> Even on their knees and hands, let him slip down,
> Not one accompanying his declining foot.
>   (Timon I.i.63–88)

> Alcibiades: How came the noble Timon to this change?
> Timon: As the moon does, by wanting light to give:
>   But then renew I could not, like the moon;
>   There were no suns to borrow of.
> (Timon IV.iii.67–70)

134 Paradigma, also Exemplum—"argument from example, judging the present from the past" (SMJ 144)

> I tell you, captain, if you look in the maps of the orld, I warrant you sall find, in the comparisons between Macedon and Monmouth, that the situations, look you, is both alike. There is a river in Macedon, and there is also moreover a river at Monmouth… [A]nd there is salmons in both. If you mark Alexander's life well, Harry of Monmouth's life is come after it

indifferent well, for there is figures in all things… I speak but in the figures
and comparisons of it: as Alexander kill'd his friend Clytus, being in his ales
and his cups; so also Harry Monmouth, being in his right wits and his good
judgments, turn'd away the fat knight with the great belly doublet.
   (H5 IV.vii.23–48)

The sense of death is most in apprehension,
And the poor beetle that we tread upon
In corporal sufferance finds a pang as great
As when a giant dies.
   (MM III.i.77–80)

135 Fable, also Apologue — "a short allegorical story that points a lesson or
   moral; the characters are frequently animals" (RAL 50) (SMJ 144)

There was a time when all the body's members
Rebell'd against the belly…
The senators of Rome are this good belly,
And you the mutinous members
   (Cor I.i.96–148)

136 Onomatopoeia — use of words or phrases that reproduce or imitate the sounds
   of what they signify (SMJ 144)

When I do count the clock that tells the time
   (Son 12.1)

But you shall shine more bright in these contents
Than unswept stone, besmear'd with sluttish time
   (Son 55.3–4)

Death's second self that seals up all in rest.
   (Son 73.8)

      rosy lips and cheeks
Within his bending sickle's compass come.
   (Son 116.9–10)

Blow, winds, and crack your cheeks! rage, blow!
You cataracts and hurricanoes, spout
Till you have drench'd our steeples, drown'd the cocks!
You sulph'rous and thought-executing fires,
Vaunt-couriers of oak-cleaving thunderbolts,
Singe my white head! And thou, all-shaking thunder,
Strike flat the thick rotundity o' th' world!
Crack nature's moulds, all germains spill at once
That makes ingrateful man!
    (Lear III.ii.1–9)

137 Simile — explicit comparison of one thing to another by the use of *like*, *as*, etc.
    (SMJ 144)

Like as the waves make towards the pibbled shore,
So do our minutes hasten to their end
    (Son 60.1–2)

He does smile his face into more lines than is in the new map, with the augmentation of the Indies
    (TN III.ii.78–80)

Heaven doth with us as we with torches do,
Not light them for themselves
    (MM I.i.32–33)

                If you should need a pin,
You could not with more tame a tongue desire it
    (MM II.ii.45–46)

Duncan: Dismay'd not this
    Our captains, Macbeth and Banquo?
Sergeant: Yes
    As sparrows eagles; or the hare the lion.
    (Mac I.ii.33–35)

                … comes in my father,
And like the tyrannous breathing of the north
Shakes all our buds from growing.
    (Cym I.iii.35–37)

> So I charm'd their ears
> That calf-like they my lowing follow'd through
> Tooth'd briers, sharp furzes, pricking goss, and thorns,
> Which ent'red their frail shins.
>   (Temp IV.i.178–81)

> to as much end
> As give a crutch to th' dead
>   (H8 I.i.171–72)

138 Metaphor—implicit comparison of one thing to another, using "a word or phrase literally denoting one kind of object or idea…in place of another to suggest a likeness or analogy between them" (MWCD) (SMJ 144)

> Let me embrace thee, good old chronicle,
> That hast so long walk'd hand in hand with time.
>   (T&C IV.v.202–203)

> a man whose blood
> Is very snow-broth
>   (MM I.iv.57–58)

> O cunning enemy, that to catch a saint,
> With saints dost bait thy hook!
>   (MM II.ii.179–80)

> Life's but a walking shadow, a poor player,
> That struts and frets his hour upon the stage,
> And then is heard no more.
>   (Mac V.v.24–26)

> I, that…o'er green Neptune's back
> With ships made cities
>   (A&C IV.xiv.57–59)

> his soaring insolence
> Shall teach the people…will be his fire
> To kindle their dry stubble; and their blaze
> Shall darken him for ever.
>   (Cor II.i.254–59)

> Look, he's winding up the watch of his wit, by and by it will strike.
>   (Temp II.i.12–13)

139 Allegory—"continu[ing] a metaphor through an entire speech" (SMJ 145)—
"the rhetorical meaning is narrower than the literary one [i.e., a story told in
symbols], though congruent with it" (RAL 3)

> All the world's a stage,
> And all the men and women merely players;
> They have their exits and their entrances,
> And one man in his time plays many parts,
> His acts being seven ages… Last scene of all…
> Is second childishness, and mere oblivion,
> Sans teeth, sans eyes, sans taste, sans every thing.
>   (AYLI II.vii.139–66)

> Our bodies are our gardens, to the which our wills are gardeners; so that if we
> will plant nettles or sow lettuce, set hyssop and weed up [thyme], supply it
> with one gender of herbs or distract it with many, either to have it sterile with
> idleness or manur'd with industry—why, the power and corrigible authority of
> this lies in our wills.
>   (Oth I.iii.320–26)

140 Catachresis—"an implied metaphor…the wrenching of a word, most often
a verb or an adjective, from its proper application to another not proper"
(SMJ 146)

> Measure his woe the length and breadth of mine
>   (Ado V.i.11)

> And let us once again assail your ears,
> That are so fortified against our story
>   (Ham I.i.31–32)

> If his occulted guilt
> Do not itself unkennel in one speech
>   (Ham III.ii.80–81)

> I will speak daggers to her, but use none
>   (Ham III.ii.396)

> For we will fetters put about this fear,
> Which now goes too free-footed.
>   (Ham III.iii.25–26)

to be demanded of a sponge…that soaks up the King's countenance, his rewards, his authorities.
    (Ham IV.ii.12–16)

                   for supple knees
Feed arrogance and are the proud man's fees.
    (T&C III.iii.48–49)

Lent him our terror, dress'd him with our love
    (MM I.i.19)

               your eye in Scotland
Would create soldiers
    (Mac IV.iii.186–87)

I have supp'd full with horrors
    (Mac V.v.13)

              we have kiss'd away
Kingdoms and provinces
    (A&C III.x.7–8)

And he will fill thy wishes to the brim
With principalities
    (A&C III.xiii.18–19)

Whose eye beck'd forth my wars and call'd them home
    (A&C IV.xii.26)

Most rich in Timon's nod
    (Timon I.i.62)

Rain sacrificial whisperings in his ear
    (Timon I.i.81)

'Tis deepest winter in Lord Timon's purse
    (Timon III.iv.14)

But now my heavy conscience sinks my knee
    (Cym V.v.413)

My favor here begins to warp.
    (WT I.ii.365)

Mine eyes, ev'n sociable to the show of thine,
Fall fellowly drops.
    (Temp V.i.63–64)

            Remember that your fame
Knolls in the ear o' th' world
    (TNK I.i.133–34)

Comparison: Greater, Equal, Less (SMJ 147ff.)

Arguments (valid and fallacious) from the greater, the equal, and the less:

For worse than Philomel you us'd my daughter,
And worse than Progne I will be reveng'd
    (Titus V.ii.194–95)

I am as woeful as Virginius was,
And have a thousand times more cause than he
To do this outrage
    (Titus V.iii.50–52)

These wrongs unspeakable, past patience,
Or more than any living man could bear
    (Titus V.iii.126–27)

Ten thousand worse than ever yet I did
Would I perform if I might have my will.
    (Titus V.iii.187–88)

But in the balance of great Bullingbrook,
Besides himself, are all the English peers,
And with that odds he weighs King Richard down.
    (R2 III.iv.87–89)

Thou knowest in the state of innocency Adam fell, and what should poor Jack
Falstaff do in the days of villainy? Thou seest I have more flesh than another
man, and therefore more frailty.
    (1H4 III.iii.164–68)

I have in equal balance justly weigh'd
What wrongs our arms may do, what wrongs we suffer,
And find our griefs heavier than our offences.
    (2H4 IV.i.67–69)

Judge me, you gods! wrong I mine enemies?
And if not so, how should I wrong a brother?
   (JC IV.ii.38–39)

Hadst thou thy wits and didst persuade revenge,
It could not move thus.
   (Ham IV.v.169–70)

Thou grumblest and railest every hour on Achilles, and thou art as full of envy
at his greatness as Cerberus is at Proserpina's beauty, ay, that thou bark'st at
him.
   (T&C II.i.32–35)

I have made my way through more impediments
Than twenty times your stop.
   (Oth V.ii.263–64)

Which of you shall we say doth love us most
   (Lear I.i.51)

Sir, I love you more than words can wield the matter,
Dearer than eyesight, space, and liberty,
Beyond what can be valued, rich or rare,
No less than life, with grace, health, beauty, honor,
As much as child e'er lov'd, or father found…
Beyond all manner of so much I love you.
   (Lear I.i.55–61)

        I'll go with thee,
Thy fifty doth double five and twenty,
And thou art twice her love.
   (Lear II.iv.258–60)

This tempest will not give me leave to ponder
On things would hurt me more.
   (Lear III.iv.24–25)

        I'll go no more.
I am afraid to think what I have done;
Look on't again I dare not.
   (Mac II.ii.47–49)

Will all great Neptune's ocean wash this blood
Clean from my hand? No; this my hand will rather
The multitudinous seas incarnadine,
Making the green one red.
   (Mac II.ii.57–60)

                        I am in blood
Stepp'd in so far that, should I wade no more,
Returning were a tedious as go o'er.
   (Mac III.iv.135–37)

                  His taints and honors
Wag'd equal with him.
   (A&C V.i.30–31)

Now, to seem to affect the malice and displeasure of the people is as bad as that
which he dislikes, to flatter them for their love.
   (Cor II.ii.21–23)

                I cannot do it to the gods,
Must I then do 't to them?
   (Cor III.ii.38–39)

Thou wrong'st a gentleman, who is as far
From thy report as thou from honor
   (Cym I.vi.145–46)

              O, this life
Is nobler than attending for a check;
Richer than doing nothing for a bable;
Prouder than rustling in unpaid-for silk
   (Cym III.iii.21–24)

                 it is I
That all th' abhorred things o' th' earth amend
By being worse than they.
   (Cym V.v.215–17)

              The gods themselves
(Humbling their deities to love) have taken
The shapes of beasts upon them. Jupiter
Became a bull and bellow'd; the green Neptune
A ram and bleated; and the fire-rob'd god,

Golden Apollo, a poor humble swain,
As I seem now. Their transformations
Were never for a piece of beauty rarer,
Nor in a way so chaste
   (WT IV.iv.25–33)

             O, she is
Ten times more gentle than her father's crabbed;
And he's compos'd of harshness.
   (Temp III.i.7–9)

141 Auxesis—"advance[ing] from lesser to greater by arranging words or clauses
    in a sequence of increasing force" (SMJ 149)

Since brass, nor stone, nor earth, nor boundless sea
   (Son 65.1)

I do affect the very ground (which is base) where her shoe (which is baser)
guided by her foot (which is basest) doth tread.
   (LLL I.ii.167–69)

This royal throne of kings, this sceptered isle,
This earth of majesty, this seat of Mars,
This other Eden, demi-paradise…
This blessed, plot, this earth, this realm, this England,
This nurse, this teeming womb of royal kings…
This land of such dear souls, this dear dear land,
Dear for her reputation through the world
   (R2 II.i.40–58)

What subject can give sentence on his king?
And who sits here that is not Richard's subject?
Thieves are not judg'd but they are by to hear,
Although apparent guilt be seen in them,
And shall the figure of God's majesty,
His captain, steward, deputy elect,
Anointed, crowned, planted many years,
Be judg'd by subject and inferior breath,
And he himself not present?
   (R2 IV.i.121–29)

I will name you the degrees. The first, the Retort Courteous; the second, the
Quip Modest; the third, the Reply Churlish; the fourth, the Reproof Valiant;
the fift, the Countercheck Quarrelsome; the sixt, the Lie with Circumstance; the
seventh, the Lie Direct.
(AYLI V.iv.91–96)

And he repell'd, a short tale to make,
Fell into a sadness, then into a fast,
Thence to a watch, thence into a weakness,
Thence to a lightness, and by this declension,
Into the madness wherein now he raves
(Ham II.ii.146–50)

Each your doing
(So singular in each particular)
Crowns what you are doing in the present deeds,
That all your acts are queens.
(WT IV.iv.143–46)

142 Hyperbole — amplification by exaggeration (SMJ 150)

this horse-back-breaker, this huge hill of flesh
(1H4 II.iv.242–43)

Thou art as valorous as Hector of Troy, worth five of Agamemnon, and ten
times better than the Nine Worthies.
(2H4 II.iv.219–21)

He brought a Grecian queen, whose youth and freshness
Wrinkles Apollo's, and makes pale the morning
(T&C II.ii.78–79)

Ross: Where sighs, and groans, and shrieks that rent the air
           Are made, not mark'd… The dead man's knell
           Is there scarce ask'd for who…
Malcolm: What's the newest grief?
Ross: That of an hour's age doth hiss the speaker;
           Each minute teems a new one.
(Mac IV.iii.168–76)

Let Rome in Tiber melt, and the wide arch
Of the rang'd empire fall! Here is my space
(A&C I.i.33–34)

th' air, which, but for vacancy,
Had gone to gaze on Cleopatra too,
And made a gap in nature.
    (A&C II.ii.216–18)

His face was as the heav'ns, and therein stuck
A sun and moon, which kept their course, and lighted
The little O, the earth…
His legs bestrid the ocean, his rear'd arm
Crested the world…realms and islands were
As plates dropp'd from his pocket.
    (A&C V.ii.79–92)

143 Meiosis — belittling, opposite of Hyperbole **142**, including by reversing
    climactic order, opposite of Auxesis **141** (SMJ 151)

This apish and unmannerly approach,
This harness'd masque and unadvised revel,
This unhair'd sauciness and boyish troops,
The King doth smile at, and is well prepar'd
To whip this dwarfish war, this pigmy arms,
From out the circle of his territories.
    (KJ V.ii.131–36)

Benvolio: What, art thou hurt?
Mercutio: Ay, ay, a scratch, a scratch, marry, 'tis enough.
    (R&J III.i.92–93)

What a frosty-spirited rogue is this!…'Zounds, and I were now by this rascal, I
could brain him with his lady's fan.
    (1H4 II.iii.20–23)

You blocks, you stones, you worse than senseless things!
    (JC I.i.35)

I found him under a tree, like a dropp'd acorn.
    (AYLI III.ii.234–35)

        What though you have no beauty—
As, by my faith, I see no more in you
Than without candle may go dark to bed
    (AYLI III.v.37–39)

> O most wicked speed: to post
> With such dexterity to incestious sheets.
> It is not, nor it cannot come to good
> (Ham I.ii.156–58)

Polonius: What do you read, my lord?
Hamlet: Words, words, words.
(Ham II.ii.191–92)

Polonius: The actors are come hither, my lord.
Hamlet: Buzz, buzz!
(Ham II.ii.392–93)

What should such fellows as I do crawling between earth and heaven?
(Ham III.i.126–28)

I am a very foolish fond old man,
Fourscore and upward, not an hour more or less;
And to deal plainly,
I fear I am not in my perfect mind…
                    I am mainly ignorant
What place this is, and all the skill I have
Remembers not these garments; nor I know not
Where I did lodge last night.
(Lear IV.vii.59–67)

Go get you home, you fragments! …
The Volsces have much corn; take these rats thither
To gnaw their garners.
(Cor I.i.222, 249–50)

Antonio: What impossible matter will he make easy next?
Sebastian: I think he will carry this island home in his pocket, and give it his
            son for an apple.
(Temp II.i.89–92)

144 Paradiastole—"extenuat[ing] in order to flatter or soothe" (SMJ 152)

Yes, lion-sick, sick of proud heart. You may call it melancholy, if you will favor
the man; but, by my head, 'tis pride.
(T&C II.iii.86–88)

Great men may jest with saints; 'tis wit in them,
But in the less foul profanation…
That in the captain's but a choleric word,
Which in the soldier is flat blasphemy.
    (MM II.ii.127–31)

145 Charientismus—"mollify[ing] threatening words by answering them with a
    smooth and appeasing mock" (SMJ 152)

Coriolanus: What's the matter, you dissentious rogues,
            That rubbing the poor itch of your opinion
            Make yourselves scabs?
1st Citizen: We have ever your good word.
    (Cor I.i.164–66)

146 Catacosmesis—"order[ing] words from greatest to least in dignity" (SMJ 152)

Write down, that they hope they serve God; and write God first, for God defend
but God should go before such villains!
    (Ado IV.ii.18–20)

Be certain what you do, sir, lest your justice
Prove violence, in the which three great ones suffer,
Yourself, your queen, your son.
    (WT II.i.127–29)

147 Epanorthosis—"correction, amend[ing] a first thought by altering it to make it
    stronger or more vehement" (SMJ 153)

By the Lord, our plot is a good plot as ever was laid, our friends true and constant: a good plot, good friends, and full of expectation; an excellent plot, very
good friends.
    (1H4 II.iii.16–20)

a good heart, Kate, is the sun and the moon, or rather the sun and not the
moon; for it shines bright and never changes, but keeps his course truly
    (H5 V.ii.162–64)

> Your brother—no, no brother, yet the son
> (Yet not the son, I will not call him son)
> Of him I was about to call his father—
> Hath heard your praises, and this night he means
> To burn the lodging where you use to lie,
> And you within it.
>   (AYLI II.iii.19–24)

> But two months dead, nay, not so much, not two
>   (Ham I.ii.138)

> "The rugged Pyrrhus, like th' Hyrcanian beast—"
> 'Tis not so, it begins with Pyrrhus:
> "The rugged Pyrrhus, he whose sable arms,
> Black as his purpose, did the night resemble…
>   (Ham II.ii.450–53)

> And when fair Cressid comes into my thoughts—
> So, traitor! "When she comes"? When is she thence?
>   (T&C I.i.30–31; Rowe substantially)

> Iago: I see, sir, you are eaten up with passion;
>   I do repent me that I put it to you.
>   You would be satisfied?
> Othello: Would? nay, and I will
>   (Oth III.iii.391–93)

> If she come in, she'll sure speak to my wife.
> My wife, my wife! what wife? I have no wife.
>   (Oth V.ii.96–97)

> I speak not out of weak surmises, but from proof as strong as my grief and as certain as I expect my revenge.
>   (Cym III.iv.23–25)

> He thinks, nay, with all confidence he swears
>   (WT I.ii.414)

>   but for the miracle
> (I mean our preservation), few in millions
> Can speak like us.
>   (Temp II.i.6–8)

Their manners are more gentle, kind, than of
Our human generation you shall find
Many, nay, almost any.
   (Temp III.iii.32–34)

148 Dirimens Copulatio—adding a point "to balance or outweigh what has
   already been said" (SMJ 153)

Harry, I do not only marvel where thou spendest thy time, but also how thou
art accompanied…for, Harry, now I do not speak to thee in drink, but in tears;
not in pleasure, but in passion; not in words only, but in woes also.
   (1H4 II.iv.398–417)

149 Emphasis—giving "prominence to a quality or trait by conceiving it as
   constituting the very substance in which it inheres" (SMJ 153), in other
   words, treating a particular person (or thing) as identical with the universal
   abstraction of a quality in order to stress his (or its) exhibition of that quality.

Farewell, fair cruelty.
   (TN I.v.288)

I am all patience
   (T&C V.ii.64)

but my brother-justice have I found so severe, that he hath forc'd me to tell him
he is indeed Justice.
   (MM III.ii.252–54)

Shrug'st thou, malice?
   (Temp I.ii.367)

              and make him
By inch-meal a disease!
   (Temp II.ii.2–3)

Bravely, my diligence.
   (Temp V.i.241)

150 Synonymia—iteration of "the same thing in many words of the same meaning to increase its force" (SMJ 154)

> the figure of God's majesty,
> His captain, steward, deputy, elect,
> Anointed, crowned, planted many years
> (R2 IV.i.125–27)

> Fluellen: What call you the town's name where Alexander the Pig was born?
> Gower: Alexander the Great
> Fluellen: Why, I pray you, is not "pig" great? The pig, or the great, or the mighty, or the huge, or the magnanimous, are all one reckonings, save the phrase is a little variations.
> (H5 IV.vii.12–18)

> But now I am cabin'd, cribb'd, confin'd, bound in
> To saucy doubts and fears.
> (Mac III.iv.23–24)

151 Exergasia, or Expolitio—repeating the same thought in many figures (SMJ 154)

> Come leave your tears… Nay, mother,
> Where is your ancient courage? You were us'd
> To say extremities was the trier of spirits,
> That common chances common men could bear,
> That when the sea was calm all boats alike
> Show'd mastership in floating; fortune's blows
> When most strook home, being gentle wounded craves
> A noble cunning. You were us'd to load me
> With precepts that would make invincible
> The heart that conn'd them.
> (Cor IV.i.1–11)

> Florizel: I take thy hand, this hand,
> As soft as dove's down and as white as it,
> Or Ethiopian's tooth, or the fann'd snow that's bolted
> By th' northern blasts twice o'er.
> Polixenes: What follows this?
> How prettily th' young swain seems to wash
> The hand was fair before!
> (WT IV.iv.362–67)

152 Paradiegesis—introductory narrative to open a speech (SMJ 155)

> Hear me, grave fathers! noble tribunes, stay!
> For pity of mine age, whose youth was spent
> In dangerous wars whilst you securely slept;
> For all my blood in Rome's great quarrel shed,
> For all the frosty nights that I have watch'd,
> And for these bitter tears which now you see
> Filling the aged wrinkles in my cheeks,
> Be pitiful to my condemned sons…
>   (Titus III.i.1–8)

153 Parecbasis—digression (SMJ 155, 333)

> You speak, Lord Mowbray, now you know not what.
> The Earl of Herford was reputed then
> In England the most valiant gentleman.
> Who knows on whom fortune would then have smil'd?
> But if your father had been victor there,
> He ne'er had borne it out of Coventry;
> For all the country in a general voice
> Cried hate upon him; and all their prayers and love
> Were set on Herford, whom they doted on
> And bless'd and grac'd and did, more than the King–
> But this is mere digression from my purpose.
>   (2H4 IV.i.128–38)

> Sir, we had but two in the house, which at that very distant time stood, as it
> were, in a fruit-dish, a dish of some threepence—your honors have seen such
> dishes; they are not china dishes, but very good dishes.
>   (MM II.i.91–94)

154 Reditus ad Propositum—return from digression (SMJ 155, 333)

> But this is mere digression from my purpose.
> Here come I from our princely general
> To know your griefs, to tell you from his Grace
> That he will give you audience
>   (2H4 IV.i.138–41)

Cause and Effect, Antecedent and Consequent (SMJ 156ff.)

Cause and Effect

Arguments of Efficient Cause:

> the remembrance of my former love
> Is by a newer object quite forgotten…
> Methinks my zeal to Valentine is cold…
> If I can check my erring love, I will;
> If not, to compass her I'll use my skill.
> (TGV II.iv.194–214)

> The cause is in my will, I will not come
> (JC II.ii.71)

> Poor lord, is't I
> That chase thee from thy country, and expose
> Those tender limbs of thine to the event
> Of the none-sparing war?…[T]o be the mark
> Of smoky muskets?…
> Whoever shoots at him, I set him there;
> Whoever charges on his forward breast,
> I am the caitiff that do hold him to't;
> And though I kill him not, I am the cause
> His death was so effected.
> (AWEW III.ii.102–16)

Argument of Material and Formal Cause:

> his…spirit lent a fire
> Even to the dullest peasant in his camp…
> For from his metal was his party steeled,
> Which once in him abated, all the rest
> Turn'd on themselves, like dull and heavy lead.
> (2H4 I.i.112–18)

Arguments of Final Cause:

> tell
> Why thy canoniz'd bones, hearsed in death,
> Have burst their cerements; why the sepulchre,
> Wherein we saw the quietly inurn'd,
> Hath op'd his ponderous and marble jaws
> To cast thee up again. What may this mean…
> Say why is this? wherefore? what should we do?
>   (Ham I.iv.46–57)

> for any thing so o'erdone is from the purpose of playing, whose end, both
> at the first and now, was and is, to hold as 'twere the mirror up to nature: to
> show virtue her feature, scorn her own image, and the very age and body of
> the time his form and pressure.
>   (Ham III.ii.19–24)

> We may carry it thus, for our pleasure and his penance, till our very pastime,
> tir'd out of breath, prompt us to have mercy on him
>   (TN III.iv.137–39)

> What was't
> That mov'd pale Cassius to conspire? And what
> Made all-honor'd, honest, Roman Brutus,
> With the arm'd rest, courtiers of beauteous freedom,
> To drench the Capitol, but that they would
> Have one man but a man?
>   (A&C II.vi.14–19)

> They being penitent,
> The sole drift of my purpose doth extend
> Not a frown further.
>   (Temp V.i.28–30)

Argument from Effect to Cause:

> Helen must needs be fair,
> When with your blood you daily paint her thus.
>   (T&C I.i.90–91)

107B Metonymy (B)—substitution of cause for effect or effect for cause (SMJ 158); for **107A** Metonymy (A) (substitution of subject for adjunct or adjunct for subject) see under *Logos*: Topics of Invention: Artificial Arguments: Division (A): Subjects and Adjuncts

Of the Efficient Cause (substitution of author's name for his work):

Or so devote to Aristotle's checks
As Ovid be an outcast quite abjur'd.
    (Shrew I.i.32–33)

Of the Material Cause:

                    he tilts
With piercing steel at bold Mercutio's breast
    (R&J III.i.158–59)

Is it not strange that sheep's guts should hale souls out of men's bodies?
    (Ado II.iii.59–60)

Substitution of Effect for Cause:

I think the honey guarded with a sting
    (RL 493)

We see the ground whereon these woes do lie
    (R&J V.iii.179)

I have made my way through more impediments
Than twenty times your stop.
    (Oth V.ii.263–64)

All torment, trouble, wonder, and amazement
Inhabits here.
    (Temp V.i.104–105)

155 Metalepsis—attributing "a present effect to a remote cause" (SMJ 158)

To what base uses we may return, Horatio! Why may not imagination trace the noble dust of Alexander, till 'a find it stopping a bunghole?…Alexander died, Alexander was buried, Alexander returneth to dust, the dust is earth, of earth we make loam, and why of that loam whereto he was converted might they not stop a beer barrel?
    (Ham V.i.202–12)

> There spake my brother; there my father's grave
> Did utter forth a voice.
>> (MM III.i.85–86)

Antecedent and Consequent (SMJ 159ff.)

Arguments from Antecedents and Consequents:

> But when we in our viciousness grow hard
> (O misery on't!), the wise gods seel our eyes,
> In our own filth drop our clear judgments, make us
> Adore our errors, laugh at 's while we strut
> To our confusion.
>> (A&C III.xiii.111–15)

> Ah, when the means are gone that buy this praise,
> The breath is gone whereof this praise is made.
> Feast-won, fast-lost
>> (Timon II.ii.169–71)

Arguments from Consequents:

> Proof enough to misuse the Prince, to vex Claudio, to undo Hero, and kill
> Leonato.
>> (Ado II.ii.28–30)

> Marry, this well carried shall on her behalf
> Change slander to remorse; that is some good…
> But on this travail look for greater birth:
> She dying…
> Shall be lamented, pitied, and excus'd
> Of every hearer [etc.]
>> (Ado IV.i.210–39)

> It were not for your quiet nor your good,
> Nor for my manhood, honesty, and wisdom,
> To let you know my thoughts.
>> (Oth III.iii.152–54)

> Yet she must die, else she'll betray more men.
>> (Oth V.ii.6)

This peace is nothing but to rust iron, increase tailors, and breed ballad-makers.
(Cor IV.v.219–20)

Argument from Necessary Consequents:

It seems to me most strange that men should fear,
Seeing that death, a necessary end,
Will come when it will come.
(JC II.ii.35–37)

Argument from Contingent Consequents:

It must be by his death… He would be crown'd:
How that might change his nature, there's the question…
Crown him that,
And then I grant we put a sting in him
That at his will he may do danger with.
Th' abuse of greatness is when it disjoins
Remorse from power… So Caesar may;
Then lest he may, prevent.
(JC II.i.10–28)

156 Hypothetical Proposition—An "if A…then B" statement (SMJ 159)

And if you crown him, let me prophesy,
The blood of English shall manure the ground,
And future ages groan for this foul act.
(R2 IV.i.136–38)

If I suspect without cause, why then make sport at me, then let me be your jest.
(MWW III.iii.149–51)

If we can do this, Cupid is no longer an archer; his glory shall be ours
(Ado II.i.384–86)

If I see any thing to-night why I should not marry her, to-morrow in the congregation, where I should wed, there will I shame her.
(Ado III.ii.123–25)

If they make you not then the better answer, you may say they are not the
men you took them for.
  (Ado III.iii.46–48)

          If his occulted guilt
Do not itself unkennel in one speech,
It is a damned ghost that we have seen
  (Ham III.ii.80–82)

Lady, you are the cruell'st she alive
If you will lead these graces to the grave,
And leave the world no copy.
  (TN I.v.241–43)

If in his death the gods have us befriended,
Great Troy is ours, and our sharp wars are ended.
  (T&C V.ix.9–10)

If chance will have me king, why, chance may crown me
Without my stir.
  (Mac I.iii.143–44)

157 Antisagoge—joining a promise of reward to a precept and a promise of
    punishment to its violation (SMJ 160)

Do't, and thou hast the one half of my heart;
Do't not, thou split'st thine own.
  (WT I.ii.348–49)

But that the good mind of Camillo tardied
My swift command, though I with death and with
Reward did threaten and encourage him,
Not doing it and being done.
  (WT III.ii.162–65)

The following example is "A travesty of this figure" (SMJ 161):

Dogberry: …you are to bid any man stand, in the Prince's name.
2nd Watch: How if 'a will not stand?
Dogberry: Why then take no note of him, but let him go, and presently call
the rest of the watch together, and thank God you are rid of a
knave.
Verges: If he will not stand when he is bidden, he is none of the Prince's
subjects.
Dogberry: True, and they are to meddle with none but the Prince's
subjects… [Y]ou are to call at all the alehouses, and bid those
that are drunk get them to bed.
2nd Watch: How if they will not?
Dogberry: Why then let them alone till they are sober. If they make you
not then the better answer, you may say they are not the men
you took them for
(Ado III.iii.25–48)

Notation and Conjugates—words "regarded as words…in their relation to things
and to each other" (SMJ 162): *Notation* refers to words as names of things,
Conjugates to words of the same derivation differing in form (as *just, justice,
justly, justify*, etc.)

66 Polyptoton—repetition of conjugates, words having the same derivation but
different terminations (SMJ 162) (for a fuller list see also under Grammar:
Figures of Repetition)

If it were so, it was a grievous fault,
And grievously hath Caesar answer'd it
(JC III.ii.79–80)

        This woman's answer sorts,
For womanish it is to be from thence.
(T&C I.i.106–107)

Spirits are not finely touch'd
But to fine issues
(MM I.i.35–36)

The loyalty well held to fools does make
Our faith mere folly
(A&C III.xiii.42–43)

158 Etymology—use of a word's etymology or derivation to illuminate meaning
(SMJ 162)

> My gentle babe Marina, whom,
> For she was born at sea, I have nam'd so
> (Per III.iii.12–13)

> Thou, Leonatus, art the lion's whelp;
> The fit and apt construction of thy name,
> Being *Leo-natus*, doth import so much.
> [*To Cymbeline*]
> The piece of tender air, thy virtuous daughter,
> Which we call *mollis aer*, and *mollis aer*
> We term it *mulier*; [*to Posthumus*] which *mulier* I divine
> Is this most constant wife
> (Cym V.v.443–49)

> and for the babe
> Is counted lost for ever, Perdita
> I prithee call't.
> (WT III.iii.32–34)

> Admir'd Miranda,
> Indeed the top of admiration! worth
> What's dearest to the world!
> (Temp III.i.37–39)

Relation of Name to Thing (SMJ 163):

> Make but my name thy love, and love that still,
> And then thou lovest me, for my name is Will.
> (Son 136.13–14)

> 'Tis but thy name that is my enemy…
> O, be some other name!
> What's in a name? That which we call a rose
> By any other name [Q1, "word" Q2] would smell as sweet
> (R&J II.ii.38–44)

'Tis only title thou disdain'st in her, the which
I can build up... If she be
All that is virtuous—save what thou dislik'st,
A poor physician's daughter—thou dislik'st
Of virtue for the name... Good alone
Is good, without a name; vileness is so:
The property by what it is should go,
Not by the title... The mere word's a slave...
If thou canst like this creature as a maid,
I can create the rest. Virtue and she
Is her own dower; honor and wealth from me.
    (AWEW II.iii.117–44)

                He was my son,
But I do wash his name out of my blood,
And thou art all my child.
    (AWEW III.ii.66–68)

King: Is't real that I see?
Helena: No, my good lord,
      'Tis but the shadow of a wife you see,
      The name, and not the thing.
Bertram: Both, both. O, pardon!
    (AWEW V.iii.306–308)

Ambiguity—play on words and puns (SMJ 164ff.)

159 Antanaclasis—"repeating a word [with a shift] from one of its meanings to another" (SMJ 165) (with or without a different spelling), "homonymic pun" (RAL 9)

Armado: By the north pole, I do challenge thee.
Costard: I will not fight with a pole like a Northren man; I'll slash, I'll do it by the sword.
    (LLL V.ii.693–95)

Hubert: And with hot irons must I burn them out.
Arthur: Ah, none but in this iron age would do it!
    (KJ IV.i.59–60)

King Richard: What comfort, man? how is't with aged Gaunt?
Gaunt: O how that name befits my composition!
                 Old Gaunt indeed, and gaunt in being old…
                 Gaunt am I for the grave, gaunt as a grave,
                 Whose hollow womb inherits nought but bones.
   (R2 II.i.72–83)

Queen: For his designs crave haste, his haste good hope.
            Then wherefore dost thou hope he is not shipp'd?
Green: That he, our hope, might have retir'd his power,
            And driven into despair an enemy's hope
   (R2 II.ii.44–47)

Swell'st thou, proud heart? I'll give thee scope to beat,
Since foes have scope to beat both thee and me.
   (R2 III.iii.140–41)

In the base court? Base court, where kings grow base,
To come at traitors' calls and do them grace.
In the base court, come down? Down court! Down king!
   (R2 III.iii.180–82)

My legs can keep no measure in delight,
When my poor heart no measure keeps in grief
   (R2 III.iv.7–8)

                     Was this the face
That like the sun, did make beholders wink?
Is this the face which fac'd so many follies,
That was at last out-fac'd by Bullingbrook?
A brittle glory shineth in this face,
As brittle as the glory is the face
   (R2 IV.i.283–88)

But let them measure us by what they will,
We'll measure them a measure and be gone.
   (R&J I.iv.9–10)

Some say the lark and loathed toad change eyes;
O now I would they had chang'd voices too,
Since arm from arm that voice doth us affray,
Hunting thee hence with hunt's-up to the day.
   (R&J III.v.31–34)

We see the ground whereon these woes do lie,
But the true ground of all these piteous woes
We cannot without circumstance descry.
    (R&J V.iii.179–81)

With faining voice verses of faining love
    (MSND I.i.31, with a pun on *feigning*)

Thou toldst me they were stol'n unto this wood;
And here am I, and wode within this wood
    (MSND II.i.192)

It is no mean happiness therefore to be seated in the mean
    (MV I.ii.7–8)

Not on thy sole, but on thy soul, harsh Jew,
Thou mak'st thy knife keen
    (MV IV.i.123–24)

Give you a reason on compulsion? if reasons were as plentiful a blackberries, I
would give no man a reason upon compulsion, I.
    (1H4 II.iv.238–40, with a pun on *raisin*[s])

No quips now, Pistol! Indeed I am in the waist two yards about; but I am now
about no waste; I am about thrift.
    (MWW I.iii.41–43)

Shallow: …Use his men well, Davy, for they are arrant knaves, and will back-
          bite.
Davy: No worse than they are backbitten, sir, for they have marvail's foul
          linen.
Shallow: Well conceited, Davy.
    (2H4 V.i.31–36)

To England will I steal, and there I'll steal
    (H5 V.i.87)

O world! thou wast the forest to this hart,
And this indeed, O world, the heart of thee.
    (JC III.i.207–208)

1 Page: You are deceiv'd, sir, we kept time, we lost not our time.
Touchstone: By my troth, yes; I count it but time lost to hear such a foolish song.
    (AYLI V.iii.37–40)

Fabian: This is a dear manikin to you, Sir Toby.
Sir Toby: I have been dear to him, lad, some two thousand strong, or so.
    (TN III.ii.53–55)

                    She speaks, and 'tis
Such sense that my sense breeds with it.
    (MM II.ii.141–42)

With Conjugates:

              You have made fair hands,
You and your crafts! You have crafted fair!
    (Cor IV.vi.117–18)

22B Syllepsis (B) — using "a word having simultaneously two different meanings, although it is not repeated" (SMJ 166); for **22A** Syllepsis (A) (using one verb to govern a number of clauses with at least one of whose subjects it lacks grammatical congruence) see under Grammar: Schemes of Grammar: Schemes of Construction: Omission

I say, without characters fame lives long.
[*Aside*.] Thus, like the formal Vice, Iniquity,
I moralize two meanings in one word.
    (R3 III.i.81–83)

Am I so round with you, as you with me,
That like a football you do spurn me thus? …
If I last in this service, you must case me in leather.
    (CE II.i.82–85)

'Twill make me think the world is full of rubs,
And that my fortune runs against the bias
    (R2 III.iv.4–5)

O, I am press'd to death through want of speaking!
    (R2 III.iv.72)

Ask for me to-morrow, and you shall find me a grave man.
    (R&J III.i.97–98)

Belike for want of rain; which I could well
Beteem them from the tempest of my eyes.
    (MSND I.i.130–31)

Falstaff: My honest lads, I will tell you what I am about.
Pistol: Two yards, and more.
   (MWW I.iii.38–40)

At a word, hang no more about me, I am no gibbet for you.
   (MWW II.ii.16–17)

For all the soil of the achievement goes
With me into the earth.
   (2H4 IV.v.189–90)

If the Prince be too important, tell him there is measure in every thing, and so
dance out the answer.
   (Ado II.i.70–72)

Kill the poys and the luggage!
   (H5 IV.vii.1)

O, let us have him, for his silver hairs
Will purchase us a good opinion
   (JC II.i.144–45)

Jaques: I am ambitious for a motley coat.
Duke Senior: Thou shalt have one.
Jaques: It is my only suit—
         Provided that you weed your better judgments
         Of all opinion that grows rank in them
         That I am wise.
   (AYLI II.vii.43–47)

here in the skirts of the forest, like fringe upon a petticoat.
   (AYLI III.ii.335–37)

Vex not his ghost. O, let him pass, he hates him
That would upon the rack of this tough world
Stretch him out longer.
   (Lear V.iii.314–16)

Thou seest the heavens, as troubled with man's act,
Threaten his bloody stage.
   (Mac II.iv.5–6)

> having both the key
> Of officer and office, set all hearts i' th' state
> To what tune pleas'd his ear
> > (Temp I.ii.83–85)

160 Paronomasia — using a word that sounds similar to but not exactly like a
preceding word, differing from Antanaclasis **159** "in that the words repeated
are nearly but not precisely alike in sound" (SMJ 166)

We are the Queen's abjects, and must obey.
> (R3 I.i.106)

Thou little valiant, great in villainy!
> (KJ III.i.116)

They might have live'd to bear and he to taste
Their fruits of duty. Superfluous branches
We lop away, that bearing boughs may live;
Had he done so, himself had borne the crown
> (R2 III.iv.62–65)

And palm to palm is holy palmers' kiss
> (R&J I.v.100)

The one I'll slay, the other slayeth me.
> (MSND II.i.190; "slay…slayeth" Thirlby conjecture for "stay…stayeth"
> Q1–2, F1, cf., R&J IV.i.72)

For lying so, Hermia, I do not lie
> (MSND II.ii.52)

were it not here apparent that thou art heir apparent
> (1H4 I.ii.57–58)

Turning the word to sword and life to death.
> (2H4 IV.ii.10)

Messenger: And a good soldier too, lady.
Beatrice: And a good soldier to a lady, but what is he to a lord?
> (Ado I.i.53–55)

Now is it Rome indeed and room enough,
When there is in it but one only man.
> (JC I.ii.156–57)

I am here with thee and thy goats as the most capricious poet, honest Ovid, was
among the Goths.
    (AYLI III.iii.7–9)

> I cannot say "whore."
> It does abhor me now I speak the word
>   (Oth IV.ii.161–62)

> If he do bleed,
> I'll gild the faces of the grooms withal,
> For it must seem their guilt.
>   (Mac II.ii.52–54)

> for now
> All length is torture; since the torch is out,
> Lie down and stray no farther
>   (A&C IV.xiv.45–47)

out, sword, and to a sore purpose!
    (Cym IV.i.22–23)

I should leave grazing, were I of your flock,
And only live by gazing
    (WT IV.iv.109–10)

Arcite: Dear Cousin Palamon—
Palamon: Cozener Arcite, give me language such
         As thou hast show'd me feat.
    (TNK III.i.43–45)

161 Asteismus—"a figure of reply in which the answerer catches a certain word
and throws it back to the first speaker with an unexpected twist, an unlooked
for meaning" (SMJ 167); "a facetious or mocking answer that plays on a
word" (RAL 18)

Bullingbrook: Go some of you, convey him to the Tower.
King Richard: O, good! convey! Conveyers are you all
    (R2 IV.i.316–17)

Queen: Which art a lion and the king of beasts?
King Richard: A king of beasts indeed—if aught but beasts,
         I had been still a happy king of men
    (R2 V.i.34–36)

Mercutio: And soar with them above a common bound.
Romeo: I am too sore enpiercèd with his shaft
            To soar with his light feathers, and so bound
            I cannot bound a pitch above dull woe
   (R&J I.iv.18–21)

Hermia: It cannot be but thou hast murd'red him;
            So should a murtherer look—so dead, so grim.
Demetrius: So should the murthered look, and so should I
   (MSND III.ii.56–58)

Jaques: By my troth, I was seeking for a fool when I found you.
Orlando: He is drown'd in the brook; look but in, and you shall see him.
   (AYLI III.ii.285–88)

Rosalind: Well, in her person, I say I will not have you.
Orlando: Then in mine own person, I die.
Rosalind: No, faith, die by attorney.
   (AYLI IV.i.91–94)

Doctor: Well, well, well.
Gentlewoman: Pray God it be, sir.
   (Mac V.i.57–58)

Timon: Whither art going?
Apemantus: To knock out an honest Athenian's brains.
Timon: That's a deed thou't die for.
Apemantus: Right, if doing nothing be death by th' law.
   (Timon I.i.191–94)

1. Lord: What time a' day is't, Apemantus?
Apemantus: Time to be honest.
1 Lord: That time serves still.
Apemantus: The more accursèd thou that still omit'st it.
   (Timon I.i.256–59)

Varro's Servant: How dost, fool?
Apemantus: Dost dialogue with thy shadow?
Varro's Servant: I speak not to thee.
Apemantus: No, 'tis to thyself.
   (Timon II.ii.50–53)

Cloten: Would he had been one of my rank!
2. Lord: [*Aside*] To have smell'd like a fool.
   (Cym II.i.15–16)

Combination of **159** Antanaclasis, **160** Paronomasia, and **161** Asteismus (SMJ
   167ff.):

Falstaff: My honest lads, I will tell you what I am about.
Pistol: Two yards, and more.
Falstaff: No quips now, Pistol! Indeed I am in the waist two yards about; but I
           am now about no waste: I am about thrift.
   (MWW I.iii.38–43)

Not a penny… I have grated upon my good friends for three reprieves for you
and your coach-fellow Nym; or else you had look'd through the grate, like a
geminy of baboons.
   (MWW II.ii.5–9)

Polonius: I did enact Julius Caesar. I was kill'd i' th' Capitol; Brutus kill'd me.
Hamlet: It was a brute part of him to kill so capital a calf there.
   (Ham III.ii.108)

162 Distinctio, Distinction—removing the ambiguity of words (SMJ 171)

Let me give light, but let me not be light,
For a light wife doth make a heavy husband
   (MV V.i.129–30)

Deliberate Obscurity—employing words "rather to veil meaning than to reveal it
   openly" (SMJ 171)

163 Enigma—riddle, "the meaning of which is to be discovered or guessed" and
   which "hides its meaning under obscure or ambiguous allusions" (WNID)
   (SMJ 171)

4. Citizen: You have deserv'd nobly of your country, and you have not
              deserv'd nobly.
Coriolanus: Your enigma?
4. Citizen: You have been a scourge to her enemies, you have been a rod to
              her friends; you have not indeed lov'd the common people.
   (Cor II.iii.88–93)

When as a lion's whelp shall, to himself unknown, without seeking find, and be embrac'd by a piece of tender air; and when from a stately cedar shall be lopp'd branches, which, being dead many years, shall after revive, be jointed to the old stock, and freshly grow; then shall Posthumus end his miseries, Britain be fortunate and flourish in peace and plenty.
    (Cym V.iv.138–44, solved at V.v.443–58)

164 Noema — "obscure and subtle speech" (SMJ 171)

King: How fares our cousin Hamlet?
Hamlet: Excellent, i' faith, of the chameleon's dish: I eat the air, promise-
          cramm'd—you cannot feed capons so.
    (Ham III.ii.92–95)

You that way and you this; but two in company;
Each man apart, all single and alone,
Yet an arch-villain keeps him company.
[*To one*.] If, where thou art, two villains shall not be,
Come not near him. [*To the other*.] If thou wouldst not reside
But where one villain is, then him abandon.
    (Timon V.i.106–11)

165 Schematismus — "circuitous speech" (SMJ 172)

1. Amb.:   May't please your Majesty to give us leave
            Freely to render what we have in charge?
            Or shall we sparingly show you far off
            The Dauphin's meaning and our embassy?
               [i.e., engage in Schematismus]
King Henry: We are no tyrant, but a Christian king,
            Unto whose grace our passion is as subject
            As are our wretches fett'red in our prisons;
            Therefore with frank and with uncurbèd plainness
            Tell us the Dauphin's mind.
    (H5 I.ii.237–45)

> Alcibiades: I am an humble suitor to your virtues;
> For pity is the virtue of the law,
> And none but tyrants use it cruelly.
> …O my lords,
> As you are great, be pitifully good.

(Timon III.v.7–52)

Logos
Logical Argumentation

Logical Argumentation

> Unless my study and my books be false,
> The argument you held was wrong in you
> > (1H6 II.iv.56–57)

> Full well hath Clifford play'd the orator,
> Inferring arguments of mighty force.
> > (3H6 II.ii.43–44)

> Well have you argued, sir, and, for your pains,
> Of capital treason we arrest you here.
> > (R2 IV.i.150–51)

> Now, could I come to her with any detection in my hand, my desires had
> instance and argument to commend themselves.
> > (MWW II.ii.245–47)

Conjunction—one of the three simple "arguable relations of propositions" (the others
being contradiction and contrariety—see under *Logos*: Topics of Invention:
Artificial Arguments: Division [A]: Contraries and Contradictories): "A
conjunction of propositions is true only if all of its parts are true. It is false if
any part is false" (SMJ 174)

> Armado: Pretty and apt.
> Moth: How mean you, sir? I pretty, and my saying apt? or I apt, and my
> saying pretty?
> > (LLL I.ii.18–20)

Leontes: How cam't, Camillo,
       That he did stay?
Camillo: At the good Queen's entreaty.
Leontes: At the Queen's be't; "good" should be pertinent,
       But so it is, it is not.
    (WT I.ii.219–22)

Camillo: I dare not know, my lord.
Polixenes: How, dare not? Do not? Do you know, and dare not?
          Be intelligent to me
    (WT I.ii.376–78)

          One of these is true:
I think affliction may subdue the cheek,
But not take in the mind.
    (WT IV.iv.575–77)

Adrian: Tunis was never grac'd before with such a paragon to their queen.
Gonzalo: Not since widow Dido's time…
Adrian: "Widow Dido" said you? You make me study of that. She was of
          Carthage, not of Tunis.
Gonzalo: This Tunis, sir, was Carthage.
    (Temp II.i.75–84)

          I advise you…that you read
The Cardinal's malice and his potency
Together
    (H8 I.i.102–106)

Syllogistic Reasoning—"a conjunction of propositions related not merely materially
       but formally as premises from which a conclusion spontaneously follows"
       (SMJ 176)

Examples of "sustained and closely knit syllogistic reasoning" (SMJ 182):

Proposition   So mak'st thou faith an enemy to faith
                     And like a civil war set'st oath to oath,
                     Thy tongue against thy tongue.

Major premise   O, let thy vow
                     First made to heaven, first be to heaven perform'd,
                     That is, to be the champion of our church!

Minor premise	What since thou swor'st is sworn against thyself,
Conclusion	And may not be performèd by thyself,
Minor is proved	For that which thou has sworn to do amiss
Major	Is not amiss when it is truly done;
Minor	And being not done, where doing tends to ill,
Conclusion	The truth is then most done not doing it.
	(KJ III.i.263–73)

Major	It is religion that doth make vows kept,
Minor	But thou has sworn against religion,
	By what thou swear'st against the thing thou swear'st,
Explanation	And mak'st an oath the surety for thy truth
of minor	Against an oath;
Minor is proved	the truth thou art unsure
	To swear, swears only not to be forsworn,
Major	Else what a mockery should it be to swear!
Minor	But thou dost swear only to be forsworn,
	And most forsworn, to keep what thou dost swear;
Conclusion	Therefore thy later vows, against thy first,
	Is in thyself rebellion to thyself
	(KJ III.i.279–89)

Proposition	All places that the eye of heaven visits
	Are to a wise man ports and happy havens.
	Teach thy necessity to reason thus:
Minor	There is no virtue like necessity.
Minor is proved	(1) Think not the King did banish thee
	But thou the King… (2) or suppose
	Devouring pestilence hangs in our air…
	(3) Look what thy soul holds dear, imagine it
	To lie that way thou goest…
Conclusion	For gnarling sorrow hath less power to bite
	The man that mocks at it and sets it light.
	(R2 I.iii.275–93)

	Claudio:	I have hope to live, and am prepar'd to die.
Proposition	Duke:	Be absolute for death: either death or life
		Shall thereby be the sweeter. Reason thus with life:
Minor Premise		If I do lose thee, I do lose a thing
		That none but fools would keep.
Minor Premise		(1) A breath thou art…
proved		(2) Merely, thou art death's fool…
		(3) Thou art not noble…
		(4) Thou'rt by no means valiant…
		(5) Thou art not thyself…
		(6) Happy thou art not…
		(7) Thou art not certain…
		(8) If thou art rich, thou'rt poor…
		(9) Friend hast thou none…
		(10) Thou hast nor youth nor age…
		(11) Yet in this life
		Lie hid moe thousand deaths; yet death we fear
		That makes these odds all even.
	Claudio:	I humbly thank you
Conclusion		To sue to live, I find I seek to die,
		And seeking death, find life. Let it come on.

(MM III.i.4–43)

Valid Syllogistic Reasoning — "If the premises are true, valid syllogistic reasoning
yields true conclusions" (SMJ 176)

Simple Syllogism

Armado: Boy, what sign is it when a man of great spirit grows melancholy?
Moth: A great sign, sir, that he will look sad…
Armado: Sing, boy, my spirit grows heavy in love.
Moth: And that's great marvel, loving a light wench.
   (LLL I.ii.1–3, 122–24)

I deny your major.
   (1H4 II.iv.495)

Prince: Sirrah, do I owe you a thousand pound?
Falstaff: A thousand pound, Hal? a million, thy love is worth a million; thou
          owest me thy love.
   (1H4 III.iii.135–37)

Conclude, conclude, he is in love.
    (Ado III.ii.62)

If that this simple syllogism will serve, so; if it will not, what remedy?
    (TN I.v.50–51)

Viola/Cesario: Cesario is your servant's name, fair princess.
Olivia: My servant sir?…
                 Y'are servant to the Count Orsino, youth.
Viola/Cesario: And he is yours, and his must needs be yours:
                 Your servant's servant is your servant, madam.
    (TN III.i.97–102)

Timon: Why dost thou call them knaves? thou know'st them not.
Apemantus: Are they not Athenians?
Timon: Yes.
Apemantus: Then I repent not.
    (Timon I.i.181–84)

Flavius: Have you forgot me, sir?
Timon: Why dost ask that? I have forgot all men.
          Then, if thou grant'st th'art a man, I have forgot thee.
    (Timon IV.iii.472–74)

She being none of your flesh and blood, your flesh and blood has not offended
the King, and so your flesh and blood is not to be punish'd by him.
    (WT IV.iv.693–95)

Enthymeme—"an abridged syllogism" in which "only two of the three
    propositions…are expressed, while one is merely implicit" (SMJ 177)

If to be fat be to be hated, then Pharaoh's lean kine are to be lov'd.
    (1H4 II.iv.472–74)

Had you rather Caesar were living, and die all slaves, than that Caesar were
dead, to live all freemen?
    (JC III.ii.23–25)

Mark'd ye his words? He would not take the crown,
Therefore 'tis certain he was not ambitious.
    (JC III.ii.112–13)

"I may command where I adore." Why, she may command me: I serve her,
she is my lady. Why, this is evident to any formal capacity
>   (TN II.v.115–17)

The amity that wisdom knits not, folly may easily untie.
>   (T&C II.iii.101–102)

Wouldst thou have laugh'd had I come coffin'd home,
That weep'st to see me triumph?
>   (Cor II.i.176–77)

>   O, she is
Ten times more gentle than her father's crabbed;
And he's composed of harshness.
>   (Temp III.i.7–9)

>   Look, the good man weeps!
He's honest, on mine honor. God's blest Mother!
I swear he is true-hearted
>   (H8 V.i.152–54)

>   'tis your passion
That thus mistakes, the which to you being enemy,
Cannot to me be kind.
>   (TNK III.i.48–50)

166 Aetiologia—"the most usual form of the enthymeme or abridged
syllogism,…which states the conclusion first, supported by the major or
the minor premise…a reason given for a sentence uttered" (SMJ 178)

let them be well us'd, for they are the abstract and brief chronicles of the
time
>   (Ham II.ii.523–25)

167 Syllogismus—a "more abridged…form [of the *Enthymeme*], present[ing]
a single vivid suggestion, from which the mind leaps to the desired
inference without adverting to the process of reasoning which underlies
it" (SMJ 179)

Eight yards of uneven ground is threescore and ten miles afoot with me, and
the stony-hearted villains know it well enough.
>   (1H4 II.ii.24–27)

Fool: Sirrah, you were best take my coxcomb. ["The full implication is:
      You are a fool. A fool wears a coxcomb. Therefore you should wear a
      coxcomb." (SMJ 179)]
Kent: Why, Fool?
Fool: Why? for taking one's part that's out of favor.
    (Lear I.iv.97–100)

He had rather see the swords and hear a drum than look upon his
schoolmaster.
    (Cor I.iii.55–56)

But I am not to say it is a sea, for it is now the sky, betwixt the firmament
and it you cannot thrust a bodkin's point.
    (WT III.iii.84–86)

Sorites — "a chain of reasoning, a series of abridged syllogisms or enthymemes"
    (SMJ 180), with or without **65** Climax

65 Climax, also Gradation — Anadiplosis **64** carried through three or more
    clauses (SMJ 83); here, a sorites involving "repetition of the last word of
    each sentence or clause at the beginning of the next, [marking] the degrees
    or steps in the argument" (SMJ 180); see also under Grammar: Figures of
    Repetition

My conscience hath a thousand several tongues,
And every tongue brings in a several tale,
And every tale condemns me for a villain.
    (R3 V.iii.193–95)

The love of wicked men converts to fear,
That fear to hate, and hate turns one or both
To worthy danger and deservèd death.
    (R2 V.i.66–68)

If thou would have such a one, take me! and take me, take a soldier; take a
soldier, take a king. And what say'st thou then to my love?
    (H5 V.ii.165–67)

> For your brother and my sister no sooner met but they look'd; no sooner
> look'd but they lov'd; no sooner lov'd but they sigh'd; no sooner sigh'd
> but they ask'd one another the reason; no sooner knew the reason but they
> sought the remedy: and in these degrees have they made a pair of stairs to
> marriage
>   (AYLI V.ii.32–38)

> I'll see before I doubt; when I doubt, prove;
> And on the proof there is no more but this—
> Away at once with love or jealousy!
>   (Oth III.iii.190–92)

Sorites without Climax **65**:

>   My noble father,
> I do perceive here a divided duty:
> To you I am bound for life and education;
> My life and education both do learn me
> How to respect you; you are the lord of duty;
> I am hitherto your daughter. But here's my husband;
> And so much duty as my mother show'd
> To you, preferring you before her father,
> So much I challenge that I may profess
> Due to the Moor, my lord.
>   (Oth I.iii.180–89)

> If you have poison for me, I will drink it.
> I know you do not love me, for your sisters
> Have (as I do remember) done me wrong:
> You have some cause, they have not.
>   (Lear IV.vii.71–74)

> Put him to choler straight…
> Being once chaf'd…he speaks
> What's in his heart, and that is there which looks
> With us to break his neck.
>   (Cor III.iii.25–30)

Compound Syllogism

Hypothetical Syllogism—a syllogism "that has for its major premise a
    hypothetical proposition" (SMJ 185)

But if you do refuse to marry me,
You'll give yourself to this most faithful shepherd?
   (AYLI V.iv.13–14)

I knew when seven justices could not take up a quarrel, but when the parties
were met themselves, one of them thought but of an If, as, "If you said so, then
I said so"; and they shook hands and swore brothers. Your If is the only peace-
maker; much virtue in If.
   (AYLI V.iv.98–103)

And now I'll do't—and so 'a goes to heaven,
And so am I reveng'd. That would be scann'd:
A villain kills my father, and for that
I, his sole son, do this same villain send
To heaven.
Why, this is hire and salary, not revenge.
   (Ham III.iii.74–79—"Hamlet's assumption in this hypothetical syllogism is
      false: If I kill him now, he will go to heaven" SMJ 187)

"I would be consul," says he; "aged custom,
But by your voices, will not so permit me;
Your voices therefore."
   (Cor II.iii.168–70)

168 Epilogus –"Inferring what will follow from what has been spoken or done
      before" (RAL 43) (SMJ 185, 362)

                  when he had no power,
   But was a petty servant to the state,
   He was your enemy, ever spake against
   Your liberties and the charters that you bear
   I' th' body of the weal; and now, arriving
   A place of potency and sway o' th' state,
   If he should still malignantly remain
   Fast foe to th' plebeii, your voices might
   Be curses to yourselves?…Did you perceive
   He did solicit you in free contempt
   When he did need your loves; and do you think
   That his contempt shall not be bruising to you
   When he hath power to crush?
      (Cor II.iii.177–203)

Disjunctive Syllogism—a syllogism that "has for its major premise a disjunctive [either/or] proposition, expressing alternatives, one of which the minor premise affirms or denies, while the conclusion in consequence affirms or denies the other" (SMJ 186)

Touchstone: …You do love this maid?
William: I do, sir.
Touchstone: Give me your hand. Art thou learned?
William: No, sir.
Touchstone: Then learn this of me: to have, is to have. For it is a figure in rhetoric that drink, being pour'd out of a cup into a glass, by filling the one doth empty the other. For all your writers do consent that ipse is he: now, you are not ipse, for I am he.
William: Which he, sir?
Touchstone: He, sir, that must marry this woman.
   (AYLI V.i.36–46)

             If his occulted guilt
Do not itself unkennel in one speech,
It is a damned ghost that we have seen,
And my imaginations are as foul
As Vulcan's stithy…
O good Horatio, I'll take the ghost's word for a thousand pound. Didst perceive?…Upon the talk of the pois'ning?
   (Ham III.ii.80–84, 286–89)

And what's in prayer but this twofold force,
To be forestallèd ere we come to fall,
Or pardon'd being down? then I'll look up.
My fault is past, but, O, what form of prayer
Can serve my turn? "Forgive me my foul murther"?
That cannot be, since I am still possess'd
Of those effects for which I did the murther:
My crown, mine own ambition, and my queen.
May one be pardon'd and retain th' offense? …
Try what repentance can. What can it not?
Yet what can it, when one can not repent?
   (Ham III.iii.48–66)

169 Apophasis, also Expeditio—rejection of all alternatives except one (SMJ
187–88), akin to the Disjunctive Syllogism

For we are peremptory to dispatch
This viperous traitor. To eject him hence
Were but one danger, and to keep him here
Our certain death; therefore it is decreed
He dies to-night.
  (Cor III.i.284–88)

170 Prosapodosis—arguing in support of each of several alternatives (SMJ
188), akin to the Disjunctive Syllogism

    Now, whether he kill Cassio,
Or Cassio him, or each do kill the other,
Every way makes my gain [F1, "game" Q1].
  (Oth V.i.12–14)

Miranda: What foul play had we, that we came from thence?
      Or blessed was't we did?
Prospero: Both, both, my girl.
      By foul play (as thou say'st) were we heav'd thence,
      But blessedly holp hither.
  (Temp I.ii.60–63)

Dilemma—"the most complex form of reasoning…a compound syllogism having
    for its major premise a compound hypothetical proposition and for its
    minor premise a disjunctive proposition" (SMJ 188)

171 Dialysis, or Dilemma—"an abridged form [of Dilemma] with only the
    major premise stated and the rest implied" (SMJ 188)

If we are mark'd to die, we are enow
To do our country loss; and if to live,
The fewer men, the greater share of honor.
God's will, I pray thee wish not one man more.
  (H5 IV.iii.20–23)

Redeem thy brother
By yielding up thy body to my will,
Or else he must not only die the death,
But thy unkindness shall his death draw out
To ling'ring sufferance.
    (MM II.iv.163–67)

thou barr'st us
Our prayers to the gods, which is a comfort
That all but we enjoy. For how can we,
Alas! how can we, for our country pray,
Whereto we are bound, together with thy victory,
Whereto we are bound? Alack, or we must lose
The country, our dear nurse, or else thy person,
Our comfort in the country. We must find
An evident calamity, though we had
Our wish, which side should win; for either thou
Must as a foreign recreant be led
With manacles through our streets, or else
Triumphantly tread on thy country's ruin,
And bear the palm for having bravely shed
Thy wife and children's blood.
    (Cor V.iii.104–118)

If it were so that our request did tend
To save the Romans, thereby to destroy
The Volsces whom you serve, you might condemn us,
As poisonous of your honor. No, our suit
Is that you reconcile them
    (Cor V.iii.132–36) [escape from the horns of the dilemma by a third option]

Say my request's unjust,
And spurn me back; but if it be not so,
Thou art not honest, and the gods will plague thee
That thou restrain'st from me the duty which
To a mother's part belongs.
    (Cor V.iii.164–68)

What case stand I in? I must be the poisoner
Of good Polixenes, and my ground to do't
Is the obedience to a master, one
Who, in rebellion with himself, will have
All that are his so too. To do this deed,
Promotion follows. If I could find example
Of thousands that had struck anointed kings
And flourish'd after, I'ld not do't; but since
Nor brass nor stone nor parchment bears not one,
Let villainy itself forswear't. I must
Forsake the court. To do't, or no, is certain
To me a break-neck.
    (WT I.ii.352–63) [escape from the horns of the dilemma by flight]

Fallacious Reasoning—"Fallacious reasoning, which has only the appearance of
    validity, may draw false conclusions even from true premises" (SMJ 176);
    "The sophist employs the outward forms of logic to hide the fallacy in his
    specious reasoning" (SMJ 190). Fallacies are either formal or material (SMJ
    191).

Whiles Warwick…smooths the wrong,
Inferreth arguments of mighty strength
    (3H6 III.i.48–49)

Until I know this sure uncertainty,
I'll entertain the offer'd fallacy.
    (CE II.ii.185–86)

                folly, in wisdom hatch'd,
Hath wisdom's warrant and the help of school,
And wit's own grace to grace a learned fool.
    (LLL V.ii.70–72)

Formal Fallacy—"Formal fallacies are those which violate the rules of the
    syllogism and therefore yield no valid conclusion, even when the
    premises are true. The most common formal fallacy is that which ignores
    the necessity of using the middle term in its full extension in at least one
    of the premises" (SMJ 191)

Well, "set thee down, sorrow!" for so they say the fool said, and so say I, and I
the fool: well prov'd, wit! By the Lord, this love is as mad as Ajax. It kills sheep;
it kills me, I a sheep: well prov'd again
  (LLL IV.iii.3–7) [implied syllogisms: The fool said this. I say this. Therefore
    I am a fool. Ajax was mad. Ajax killed sheep. Love is as mad as Ajax.
    Therefore Love kills sheep. Love kills me. Therefore I am a sheep.]

I will do any thing, Nerissa, ere I will be married to a sponge.
  (MV I.ii.98–99) [implied syllogism: A sponge drinks. He drinks. Therefore he
    is a sponge.]

Material Fallacy—"Material fallacies are those which have their root in the
    matter, that is, in the terms of a syllogism which appears to be formally
    correct. Logicians distinguish thirteen material fallacies, six occasioned
    by the ambiguity of language and seven by a false assumption hidden
    in the thought" (SMJ 191); in addition, captious arguments form seven
    more material fallacies, six of which may be illustrated by Shakespeare
    (SMJ 199)

Fallacies of ambiguity of language:

172 Equivocation, also Antistasis—use of the middle term in two different
    senses, involving the figures of Ambiguity (SMJ 191), see also under *Logos*:
    Topics of Invention: Artificial Arguments: Division (A): Notation and
    Conjugates, especially **159** Antanaclasis

Speed: … What news then in your paper?
Launce: The blackest news that ever thou heard'st.
Speed: Why, man? how black?
Launce: Why, as black as ink.
  (TGV III.i.285–88)

I wasted time, and now doth time waste me
  (R2 V.v.49)

Lady Capulet: And then I hope thou wilt be satisfied.
Juliet: Indeed I never shall be satisfied
               With Romeo, till I behold him—dead—
               Is my poor heart…
  (R&J III.v.92–95)

1 Clown: There is no ancient gentlemen but gard'ners, ditchers, and grave-makers; they hold up Adam's profession.
2 Clown: Was he a gentleman?
1 Clown: 'A was the first that ever bore arms.
2 Clown: Why, he had none.
1 Clown: What, art a heathen? How dost thou understand the Scripture? The Scripture says Adam digg'd; could he dig without arms?
    (Ham V.i.29–37, F1)

Viola/Cesario: 'Save thee, friend, and thy music! Dost thou live by thy tabor?
Feste: No, sir, I live by the church.
Viola/Cesario: Art thou a churchman?
Feste: No such matter, sir. I do live by the church; for I do live at my house, and my house doth stand by the church.
    (TN III.i.1)

Alexander: They say he is a very man per se and stands alone.
Cressida: So do all men, unless th' are drunk, sick, or have no legs.
    (T&C I.ii.15–18)

Provost: Come hither, sirrah; can you cut off a man's head?
Pompey: If the man be a bachelor, sir, I can; but if he be a married man, he's his wive's head, and I can never cut off a woman's head.
    (MM IV.ii.1–5)

Desdemona: Do you know, sirrah, where Lieutenant Cassio lies?
Clown: I dare not say he lies any where.
Desdemona: Why, man?
Clown: He's a soldier, and for me to say a soldier lies, 'tis stabbing.
    (Oth III.iv.1–6)

41 Amphibologia, or Amphibology—ambiguity in grammatical construction (SMJ 193)—see also under Grammar: Vices of Language

The duke yet lives that Henry shall depose
    (2H6 I.iv.30)

But I was a gentleman born before my father; for the King's son took me by the hand, and call'd me brother; and then the two kings call'd my father brother
    (WT V.ii.139–42)

Dramatic ambiguity:

> I pull in resolution, and begin
> To doubt th' equivocation of the fiend
> That lies like truth. "Fear not, till Birnam wood
> Do come to Dunsinane," and now a wood
> Comes toward Dunsinane…
> And be these juggling fiends no more believ'd,
> That palter with us in a double sense,
> That keep the word of promise to our ear,
> And break it to our hope.
> (Mac V.v.41–45, V.viii.19–22)

173 Compositio, or Composition—attributing to a group what is applicable to individual members of the group (SMJ 193), joining of things that are to be severed (as asserting that five is both even and odd because it is made of two, which is even, and three, which is odd)

> Dost thou think because thou art virtuous there shall be no more cakes and ale?
> (TN II.iii.114–16)

174 Division (B), or Divisio—severing things that are to be joined, the reverse of **173** Compositio—"No instance of Shakespeare's use of [this figure] has been observed by the present writer" (SMJ 194); for Division (A) see under *Logos*: Topics of Invention: Artificial Arguments

175 Form of Speech—ambiguity in a verb phrase (SMJ 194)

> Pisanio: I thought you would not back again.
> Imogen: Most like,
>   Bringing me here to kill me.
> (Cym III.iv.116–17) [Pisanio's "would" meaning wish construed as an auxiliary by Imogen]

176 Accent—alteration of the true significance of a word by pronunciation, leading to a wrong conclusion (SMJ 194)

> Frenchman: *O, prenez miséricorde! ayez pitié de moi!*
> Piston: Moy shall not serve. I will have forty moys,
>   Or I will fetch thy rim out at thy throat
>   In drops of crimson blood.

Frenchman: *Est-il impossible d'éschapper la force de ton bras?*
Piston: Brass, cur? ...
                   Offer'st me brass?
   (H5 IV.iv.12–20)

Fallacies of false hidden assumption:

177 Accident — "the false assumption that something which belongs only to a substance may be attributed to an accident or adjunct of that substance, or contrariwise" (SMJ 194)

Henry VI: I was anointed king at nine months old,
                   My father and my grandfather were kings;
                   And you were sworn true subjects unto me;
                   And tell me then, have you not broke your oaths?
1. Keeper: No.
                   For we were subjects but while you were king.
Henry VI: Why? Am I dead? Do I not breathe a man?
   (3H6 III.i.76–82) [loyalty to man/substance vs. to kingship/accident]

Prince Hal: I say 'tis copper. Darest thou be as good as thy word now?
Falstaff: Why, Hal! thou knowest, as thou art but man, I dare, but as thou
                   art Prince, I fear thee as I fear the roaring of the lion's whelp.
   (1H4 III.iii.143–47)

178 Secundum Quid — assuming that what is true of a subject in a qualified sense is true of it absolutely or vice versa (SMJ 195)

Cade: I am able to endure much.
Dick: [*Aside.*] No question of that; for I have seen him whipt three market-
             days together.
Cade: I fear neither sword nor fire.
Smith: [*Aside.*] He need not fear the sword, for his coat is of proof.
Dick: [*Aside.*] But methinks he should stand in fear of fire, being burnt i'
             th' hand for stealing of sheep.
   (2H6 IV.ii.56–63)

["In The Arte of Logick Thomas Blundeville quotes as a common jest a sorites vitiated by taking in an absolute sense what is true only in respect to a particular time.

> Whoso drinketh well, sleepeth well,
> Whoso sleepeth well, sinneth not,
> Whoso sinneth not, shall be blessed:
> *Ergo*, Whoso drinketh well, shall be blessed. (p. 177)

…Two of Shakespeare's characters [Berowne and Parolles] employ this specious reasoning" (SMJ 196)]:

And then to sleep but three hours in the night,
And not be seen to wink of all the day—
When I was wont to think no harm all night,
And make a dark night too of half the day—
   (LLL I.i.42–45)

but doth not the appetite alter? A man loves the meat in his youth that he cannot endure in his age. Shall quips and sentences and these paper bullets of the brain awe a man from the career of his humor? No, the world must be peopled. When I said I would die a bachelor, I did not think I should live till I were married.
   (Ado II.iii.238–44)

Pistol: Base Troyan, thou shalt die.
Fluellen: You say very true, scald knave, when God's will is.
   (H5 V.i.31–33)

Truly, shepherd, in respect of itself, it is a good life; but in respect that it is a shepherd's life, it is naught. In respect that it is solitary, I like it very well; but in respect that it is private, it is a very vild life. Now in respect it is in the fields, it pleaseth me well; but in respect it is not in the court, it is tedious. As it is a spare life (look you) it fits my humor well; but as there is no more plenty in it, it goes much against my stomach.
   (AYLI III.ii.13–21)

Hamlet: What man dost thou dig it for?
1. Clown: For no man, sir.
Hamlet: What woman then?
1. Clown: For none neither.
Hamlet: Who is to be buried in't?

1. Clown: One that was a woman, sir, but, rest her soul, she's dead.
   Hamlet: How absolute the knave is! we must speak by the card, or
              equivocation will undo us.
   (Ham V.i.130–38)

Not to be a-bed after midnight is to be up betimes…To be up after midnight
and to go to bed then, is early; so that to go to bed after midnight is to go to
bed betimes.
   (TN II.iii.1–9)

Drunkenness is his best virtue, for he will be swine-drunk, and in his sleep
he does little harm
   (AWEW IV.iii.255–56)

179 Ignoratio Elenchi—literally, ignorance of the nature of refutation: an
   unnoticed change in the argument (SMJ 197), specifically, "falsely
   assuming that the point at issue has been disproved when one merely
   resembling it has been disproved" (Triv 202)

Touchstone: No, by mine honor…
Rosalind: Where learn'd you that oath, fool?
Touchstone: Of a certain knight, that swore by his honor they were good
             pancakes, and swore by his honor the mustard was naught.
             Now I'll stand to it, the pancakes were naught, and the mus-
             tard was good, and yet was not the knight forsworn.
Celia: How prove you that, in the great heap of your knowledge?…
Touchstone: Stand you both forth now. Stroke your chins, and swear by
             your beards that I am a knave.
Celia: By our beards (if we had them) thou art.
Touchstone: By my knavery (if I had it) then I were. But if you swear by
             that that is not, you are not forsworn. No more was this knight,
             swearing by his honor, for he never had any; or if he had, he
             had sworn it away before ever he saw those pancakes or that
             mustard.
   (AYLI I.ii.60–80)

180 Consequent—the fallacy of assuming "that a proposition is convertible simply when it is not," that is, that the subject and predicate may be reversed, as "All those at the court have good manners; therefore all who have good manners are at the court" (SMJ 197), or of assuming that the contrary of the antecedent must yield the contrary of the consequent, as "It is a man: *Ergo*, It is a sensible body. It is no man: *Ergo*, it is no sensible body" (SMJ 371, quoting Thomas Blundeville, *Arte of Logick* [1599], 1617)

Rosalind: The Duke my father lov'd his father dearly.
Celia: Doth it therefore ensue that you should love his son dearly? By this kind of chase, I should hate him, for my father hated his father dearly; yet I hate not Orlando.
  (AYLI I.iii.29–34)

Why, if thou never wast at court, thou never saw'st good manners; if thou never saw'st good manners, then thy manners must be wicked, and wickedness is sin, and sin is damnation. Thou art in a parlous state, shepherd.
  (AYLI III.ii.40–44)

181 False Cause—"putting for a cause that which is not a cause" (SMJ 198)

Williams: Now, if these men do not die well, it will be a black matter for the King that led them to it…
King Henry: So, if a son that is by his father sent about merchandise do sinfully miscarry upon the sea, the imputation of his wickedness, by your rule, should be impos'd upon his father that sent him; or if a servant, under his master's command transporting a sum of money, be assail'd by robbers and die in many irreconcil'd iniquities, you may call the business of the master the author of the servant's damnation. But this is not so. The King is not bound to answer the particular endings of his soldiers, the father of his son, nor the master of his servant; for they purpose not their death when they purpose their services. Besides, there is no king, be his cause never so spotless, if it come to the arbitrement of swords, can try it out with all unspotted soldiers…Then if they die unprovided, no more is the King guilty of their damnation than he was before guilty of those impieties for the which they are now visited. Every subject's duty is the King's, but every subject's soul is his own.
  (H5 IV.i.144–77)

182 Begging the Question—using the conclusion to be proved as one of the
premises in the proof; circular reasoning (SMJ 198)

I have no other but a woman's reason:
I think him so, because I think him so.
    (TGV I.ii.23–24)

Aeneas: How now, Prince Troilus, wherefore not a-field?
Troilus: Because not there. This woman's answer sorts,
       For womanish it is to be from thence.
    (T&C I.i.105–107)

Fool: The reason why the seven stars are no moe than seven is a pretty
       reason.
Lear: Because they are not eight.
Fool: Yes indeed, thou wouldst make a good Fool.
    (Lear I.v.34–38)

183 Many Questions—"demanding a simple answer to a complex question"
(SMJ 199)

Somerset: Was not thy father, Richard Earl of Cambridge,
       For treason executed in our late king's days?
       And by his treason, stand'st not thou attainted,
       Corrupted, and exempt from ancient gentry? …
Plantagenet: My father was attached, not attainted,
       Condemn'd to die for treason, but no traitor
    (1H6 II.iv.90–97)

Interpreter: "You shall demand of him, whether one Captain Dumaine be i'
       th' camp, a Frenchman; what his reputation is with the Duke;
       what his valor, honesty, and expertness in wars; or whether he
       thinks it were not possible with well-weighing sums of gold to
       corrupt him to a revolt." What say you to this? What do you
       know of it?
Parolles: I beseech you let me answer to the particular of the
       inter'gatories. Demand them singly.
    (AWEW IV.iii.175–83)

Captious Arguments (SMJ 199ff.):

184 Antistrephon—an "argument which turns that which serves the
opponent's purpose to one's own" (SMJ 199)

> Bassanio: This is no answer, thou unfeeling man,
>   To excuse the current of thy cruelty.
> Shylock: I am not bound to please thee with my answers.
> Bassanio: Do all men kill the things they do not love?
> Shylock: Hates any man the thing he would not kill?
> Bassanio: Every offense is not a hate at first.
> Shylock: What, wouldst thou have a serpent sting thee twice?
>   (MV IV.i.63–69)

> Must he needs trouble me in't—hum!—'bove all others?
> He might have tried Lord Lucius or Lucullus;
> And now Ventidius is wealthy too,
> Whom he redeem'd from prison. All these
> Owes their estates unto him…
> Must I be his last refuge?…I see no sense for't,
> But his occasions might have wooed me first;
> For, in my conscience, I was the first man
> That e'er received gift from him;
> And does he think so backwardly of me now,
> That I'll requite it last? No!
> So it may prove an argument of laughter
> To th' rest, and 'mongst lords I be thought a fool…
> Who bates mine honor shall not know my coin.
>   (Timon III.iii.1–26)

185 Cacosistaton—"an argument [that] serves as well for the one side as for the
other" (SMJ 200)

> Audrey: Would you not have me honest?
> Touchstone: No, truly, unless thou wert hard-favor'd; for honesty coupled
>   to beauty is to have honey a sauce to sugar…
> Audrey: Well, I am not fair, and therefore I pray the gods make me
>   honest.
> Touchstone: Truly, and to cast away honesty upon a foul slut were to put
>   good meat into an unclean dish.
>   (AYLI III.iii.28–37)

2. Clown: Will you ha' the truth an't? If this had not been a gentlewoman,
           she should have been buried out a' Christian burial.
1. Clown: Why, there thou say'st, and the more pity that great folk should
           have count'nance in this world to drown or hang themselves,
           more than their even-Christen.
   (Ham V.i.23–29)

186 Pseudomenos—putting "another into such a position that whatever he
    says must needs be said amiss…as to ask whether a Cretan should be
    believed when he says, All Cretans are liars" (SMJ 201)

Romeo: I dreamt a dream to-night.
Mercutio: And so did I.
Romeo: Well, what was yours?
Mercutio: That dreamers often lie.
   (R&J I.iv.50–51)

187 Assistaton—"a kind of caviling, as to remark of one who has just said he
    holds his peace, 'He that holds his peace speaks'" (SMJ 201)

Antonio: Fie, what a spendthrift he is of his tongue!
Alonso: I prithee spare.
Gonzalo: Well, I have done. But yet—
Sebastian: He will be talking
   (Temp II.i.24–27)

188 Ceratin—"the horned argument," which "puts a matter in such terms that
    the propounder will win his point either way" (SMJ 201)

Every true man's apparel fits your thief. If it be too little for your thief, your
true man thinks it big enough. If it be too big for your thief, your thief thinks
it little enough; so every true man's apparel fits your thief.
   (MM IV.ii.43–47)

189 Crocodilites (Crocodile's Argument)—which "harms the opponent either
    way" (SMJ 202), named for the "ancient illustration of the dilemma: A boy
    has been stolen by a crocodile, which promises to restore him if the boy's
    father answers truly the crocodile's question 'Am I going to return this
    boy or not?' If he replies in the affirmative, the crocodile keeps the boy,
    and thus the father answers falsely; if in the negative, should the crocodile
    restore the boy the father will have answered falsely" (WNID)

> Prince Hal: Sir John stands to his word, the devil shall have his bargain, for
> he was never yet a breaker of proverbs. He will give the devil
> his due.
> Poins: Then art thou damn'd for keeping thy word with the devil.
> Prince Hal: Else he had been damn'd for cozening the devil.
>   (1H4 I.ii.117–23)

> The man's undone for ever, for if Hector break not his neck i' th' combat,
> he'll break't himself in vainglory.
>   (T&C III.iii.258–59)

> Fool: Prithee, nuncle, keep a schoolmaster that can teach thy Fool to lie—I
> would fain learn to lie.
> Lear: And you lie, sirrah, we'll have you whipt.
> Fool: I marvel what kin thou and thy daughters are. They'll have me whipt
> for speaking true; thou'lt have me whipt for lying; and sometimes I
> am whipt for holding my peace.
>   (Lear I.iv.179–85)

190 Utis—(A) an argument in which the proof is as uncertain as the thing to
be proved: "No example has been noticed [in Shakespeare]" (SMJ 199);
(B) the same as **182** Begging the Question (SMJ 372)

Disputation—syllogistic reasoning exercised in "building up both sides of an
argument," whether with oneself or with an opponent, using either valid
syllogistic reasoning, fallacious reasoning, or both (SMJ 176, 203)

Rhetorical Figures of Disputation:

191 Aporia—"doubting or deliberating with oneself" (SMJ 214), real or feigned
(RAL 15)

> I cannot tell if to depart in silence,
> Or bitterly to speak in your reproof,
> Best fitteth my degree or your condition.
>   (R3 III.vii.141–43)

> I cannot tell, I make it breed as fast.
>   (MV I.iii.96)

> Hath not a Jew eyes? [etc.]
>   (MV III.i.59ff.)

I and my bosom must debate awhile,
And then I would no other company.
   (H5 IV.i.31–32)

Did this in Caesar seem ambitious?
        … Was this ambition?
   (JC III.ii.90–97)

Why, what an ass am I! This is most brave,
That I, the son of a dear father murthered,
Prompted to my revenge by heaven and hell,
Must like a whore unpack my heart with words,
And fall a-cursing like a very drab,
A stallion. Fie upon't, foh!
About, my brains! Hum—
   (Ham II.ii.582–88)

To be, or not to be… To die, to sleep—
No more, and by a sleep to say we end
The heart-ache and the thousand natural shocks
That flesh is heir to; 'tis a consummation
Devoutly to be wish'd. To die, to sleep—
To sleep, perchance to dream—ay, there's the rub,
For in that sleep of death what dreams may come,
When we have shuffled off this mortal coil,
Must give us pause…who would fardels bear,
To grunt and sweat under a weary life,
But that the dread of something after death,
The undiscover'd country, from whose bourn
No traveller returns, puzzles the will,
And makes us rather bear those ills we have,
Than fly to others that we know not of?
   (Ham III.i.55–81)

Then live, Macduff; what need I fear of thee?
But yet I'll make assurance double sure,
And take a bond of fate: thou shalt not live…
   (Mac IV.i.82–84)

192 Anthypophora—"reasoning with self, asking questions and answering them oneself" (SMJ 214)

What do I fear? Myself? There's none else by.
Richard loves Richard, that is, I am I.
Is there a murderer here? No. Yes, I am.
Then fly. What, from myself? Great reason why—
Lest I revenge. What, myself upon myself?
Alack, I love myself. Wherefore? For any good
That I myself have done unto myself?
O no!
   (R3 V.iii.182–89)

Say that she rail, why then I'll tell her plain
She sings as sweetly as a nightingale;
Say that she frown, I'll say she looks as clear
As morning roses newly wash'd with dew;
Say she be mute, and will not speak a word,
Then I'll commend her volubility,
And say she uttereth piercing eloquence;
If she do bid me pack, I'll give her thanks,
As though she bid me stay by her a week;
If she deny to wed, I'll crave the day
When I shall ask the banes, and when be married.
   (Shrew II.i.170–80)

What must the King do now? Must he submit?
The King shall do it. Must he be depos'd?
The King shall be contented. Must he lose
The name of king? a' God's name let it go.
   (R2 III.iii.143–46)

O Romeo, Romeo, wherefore art thou Romeo? …
What's Montague? It is nor hand nor foot,
Nor arm nor face, nor any other part
Belonging to a man…
What's in a name? That which we call a rose
By any other word would smell as sweet…
   (R&J II.ii.33–44)

What says this leaden casket?
"Who chooseth me must give and hazard all he hath."
Must give—for what? for lead, hazard for lead?
This casket threatens. Men that hazard all
Do it in hope of fair advantages…
What says the silver with her virgin hue?
"Who chooseth me shall get as much as he deserves."
As much as he deserves! Pause there, Morocco…
Thou dost deserve enough…
Is't like that lead contains her? 'Twere damnation
To think so base a thought.
    (MV II.vii.15–50)

What need I be so forward with him that calls not on me? Well, 'tis no matter,
honor pricks me on. Yea, but how if honor prick me off when I come on? how
then? Can honor set to a let? No. Or an arm? No. Or take away the grief of a
wound? No. Honor hath no skill in surgery then? No. What is honor? A word.
What is in that word honor? What is that honor? Air. A trim reckoning! Who
hath it? He that died a' Wednesday. Doth he feel it? No. Doth he hear it? No.
'Tis insensible then? Yea, to the dead. But will't not live with the living? No.
Why? Detraction will not suffer it. Therefore I'll none of it, honor is a mere
scutcheon. And so ends my catechism.
    (1H4 V.i.128–41)

Show men dutiful?

Why, so didst thou. Seem they grave and learned?
Why, so didst thou. Come they of noble family?
Why, so didst thou. Seem they religious?
Why, so didst thou. Or are they spare in diet,
Free from gross passion, or of mirth or anger,
Constant in spirit, not swerving with the blood,
Garnish'd and deck'd in modest complement,
Not working with the eye without the ear,
And but in purged judgment trusting neither?
Such and so finely bolted didst thou seem.
    (H5 II.ii.127–37)

If then that friend demand why Brutus rose against Caesar, this is my answer:
Not that I lov'd Caesar less, but that I lov'd Rome more.
    (JC III.ii.20–22)

To be, or not to be, that is the question:
Whether 'tis nobler in the mind to suffer
The slings and arrows of outrageous fortune,
Or to take arms against a sea of troubles,
And by opposing, end them…
For who would bear the whips and scorns of time…?
…who would fardels bear…
But that the dread of something after death,
                    …puzzles the will,
And makes us rather bear those ills we have,
Than fly to others that we know not of?
    (Ham III.i.55–81)

Was't Hamlet wrong'd Laertes? Never Hamlet!…
Who does it then? His madness.
    (Ham V.ii.233–37)

What's this? what's this? Is this her fault, or mine?
The tempter, or the tempted, who sins most, ha?
                  …Can it be
That modesty may more betray our sense
Than woman's lightness? Having waste ground enough,
Shall we desire to raze the sanctuary
And pitch our evils there? O fie, fie, fie!
What dost thou? Or what art thou, Angelo?
Dost thou desire her foully for those things
That make her good?…What, do I love her,
That I desire to hear her speak again?
And feast upon her eyes? What is't I dream on?
    (MM II.ii.162–78)

… and what delight shall she have to look on the devil? When the blood is
made dull with the act of sport, there should be, again to inflame it and to give
satiety a fresh appetite, loveliness in favor, sympathy in years, manners, and
beauties—all which the Moor is defective in… Now, sir, this granted…who
stands so eminent in the degree of this fortune as Cassio does? a knave very
voluble; no further conscionable than in putting on the mere form of civil and
humane seeming, for the better compass of his salt and most hidden loose
affection? Why, none, why, none—
    (Oth II.i.225–41)

193 Anacoenosis—asking counsel of one's hearers (SMJ 215)

Brutus: Who is here so base that would be a bondman? If any, speak, for him
have I offended. Who is here so rude that would not be a Roman? If
any, speak, for him have I offended. Who is here so vile that will not
love his country? If any, speak, for him have I offended. I pause for a
reply.
All: None, Brutus, none.
Brutus: Then none have I offended.
   (JC III.ii.29–36)

… and I charge you, O men, for the love you bear to women (as I perceive by
your simp'ring, none of you hates them), that between you and the women the
play may please…[A]nd I am sure, as many as have good beards, or good faces,
or sweet breaths, will for my kind offer, when I make curtsy, bid me farewell.
   (AYLI Epi. 14–23)

               Now, my liege,
Tell me what blessings I have here alive,
That I should fear to die?
   (WT III.ii.106–108)

194 Synchoresis—trusting so strongly in his own cause that the speaker freely
gives his questioner leave to judge him (SMJ 215)

And here I stand. Judge, my masters.
   (1H4 II.iv.439)

Our reasons are so full of good regard
That were you, Antony, the son of Caesar,
You should be satisfied.
   (JC III.i.224–26)

Make choice of whom your wisest friends you will,
And they shall hear and judge 'twixt you and me.
   (Ham IV.v.205–206)

If you suspect my husbandry or falsehood,
Call me before th' exactest auditors,
And set me on the proof.
   (Timon II.ii.155–57)

195 Procatalepsis—confuting the objection that one's opponent is likely to make
even before he has uttered it (SMJ 215)

You'll ask me why I rather choose to have
A weight of carrion flesh than to receive
Three thousand ducats. I'll not answer that;
But say it is my humor…
   (MV IV.i.40–43)

If it were so that our request did tend
To save the Romans, thereby to destroy
The Volsces whom you serve, you might condemn us,
As poisonous of your honor. No, our suit
Is that you reconcile them: while the Volsces
May say, "This mercy we have show'd," the Romans,
"This we receiv'd"; and each in either side
Give the all-hail to thee, and cry, "Be blest
For making up this peace!"
   (Cor V.iii.132–40)

196 Paromologia—conceding a point unfavorable to one's own position and then
bringing in a point that overthrows what was granted (SMJ 216)

Sicinius: He's a disease that must be cut away.
Menenius: O, he's a limb that has but a disease:
                  Mortal, to cut it off; to cure it, easy.
   (Cor III.i.293–95)

197 Concessio—granting a point that hurts the opponent to whom it is granted
(SMJ 216)

Nay, do not pause: for I did kill King Henry—
But 'twas thy beauty that provoked me.
Nay, now dispatch: 'twas I that stabb'd young Edward,
But 'twas thy heavenly face that set me on.
   (R3 I.ii.179–82)

Portia: A pound of that same merchant's flesh is thine,
           The court awards it, and the law doth give it…
           And you must cut this flesh from off his breast,
           The law allows it, and the court awards it.
Shylock: Most learned judge, a sentence! Come prepare!
Portia: Tarry a little, there is something else.
           This bond doth give thee here no jot of blood;
           The words expressly are "a pound of flesh."
           Take then thy bond, take thou thy pound of flesh,
           But in the cutting it, if thou dost shed
           One drop of Christian blood, thy lands and goods
           Are by the laws of Venice confiscate
           Unto the state of Venice…
Shylock: Is that the law?
Portia: Thyself shall see the act;
           For as thou urgest justice, be assur'd
           Thou shalt have justice more than thou desir'st.
      (MV IV.i.299–316)

Falstaff: Boy, tell him I am deaf.
Page: You must speak louder, my master is deaf.
Chief Justice: I am sure he is, to the hearing of any thing good.
      (2H4 I.ii.66–69)

198 Metastasis—turning back an objection against the one who made it (SMJ 217)

An excellent device! so if any of the audience hiss, you may cry, "Well done,
Hercules, now thou crushest the snake!" That is the way to make an offense
gracious, though few have the grace to do it.
      (LLL V.i.137–41)

The mercy that was quick in us but late,
By your own counsel is suppress'd and kill'd.
You must not dare (for shame) to talk of mercy,
For your own reasons turn into your bosoms,
As dogs upon their masters, worrying you.
      (H5 II.ii.79–83)

Oliver: Get you with him, you old dog.
Adam: Is "old dog" my reward? Most true, I have lost my teeth in your
           service.
      (AYLI I.i.81–83)

> King Lear: Kent, on thy life, no more.
> Kent: My life I never held but as a pawn
>   To wage against thine enemies, ne'er fear'd to lose it,
>   Thy safety being motive.
> King Lear: Out of my sight!
> Kent: See better, Lear, and let me still remain
>   The true blank of thine eye.
>   (Lear I.i.154–59)

> Fare thee well, King; sith thus thou wilt appear,
> Freedom lives hence, and banishment is here.
>   (Lear I.i.180–81)

199 Apodioxis—rejection of the argument of an opponent (SMJ 218), with
indignation at its impertinence or absurdity (RAL 13)

> 1. Senator: To revenge is no valor, but to bear.
> Alcibiades: …Why do fond men expose themselves to battle,
>   And not endure all threats? sleep upon't,
>   And let the foes quietly cut their throats
>   Without repugnancy? If there be
>   Such valor in the bearing, what make we
>   Abroad? Why then, women are more valiant
>   That stay at home, if bearing carry it;
>   And the ass more captain than the lion, the fellow
>   Loaden with irons wiser than the judge,
>   If wisdom be in suffering.
>   (Timon III.v.39–51)

200 Diasyrmus—using a base similitude to disparage an opponent's argument or
make it appear ridiculous (SMJ 218)

> Falstaff: …you starveling, you eel-skin, you dried neat's tongue, you bull's
>   pizzle, you stock-fish!…[Y]ou tailor's yard, you sheath, you bowcase,
>   you vile standing tuck—
> Prince: Well, breathe a while, and then to it again, and when thou hast tir'd
>   thyself in base comparisons, hear me speak but this—
>   (1H4 II.iv.244–51)

<pre>
Nestor: Ajax…sets Thersites,
           A slave whose gall coins slanders like a mint,
           To match us in comparisons with dirt,
           To weaken or discredit our exposure,
           How rank soever rounded in with danger.
Ulysses: They tax our policy, and call it cowardice,
           Count wisdom as no member of the war,
           Forestall prescience, and esteem no act
           But that of hand. The still and mental parts…
           Why, this hath not a finger's dignity.
           They call this bed-work, mapp'ry, closet-war
     (T&C I.iii.188–205)
</pre>

All the argument is a whore and a cuckold, a good quarrel to draw emulous
factions and bleed to death upon.
    (T&C II.iii.72–74)

<pre>
Aufidius: …He has betray'd your business, and given up,
               For certain drops of salt, your city Rome,
               I say "your city," to his wife and mother,
               Breaking his oath and resolution like
               A twist of rotten silk, never admitting
               Counsel a' th' war; but at his nurse's tears
               He whin'd and roar'd away your victory…
Coriolanus: Hear'st thou, Mars?
Aufidius: Name not the god, thou boy of tears! …
Coriolanus: Measureless liar, thou hast made my heart
               Too great for what contains it. "Boy"? …
                                   …"Boy," false hound!
               If you have writ your annals true, 'tis there,
               That, like an eagle in a dovecote, I
               Flutter'd your Volscians in Corioles.
               Alone I did it. "Boy"!
     (Cor V.vi.91–116)
</pre>

201 Antirrhesis—rejection of "an opponent's argument or opinion because of its
error or wickedness" (SMJ 219)

Away, I do condemn mine ears that have
So long attended thee. If thou wert honorable,
Thou wouldst have told this tale for virtue, not
For such an end thou seek'st—as base as strange.
Thou wrong'st a gentleman, who is as far
From thy report as thou from honor, and
Solicits here a lady that disdains
Thee and the devil alike.
    (Cym I.vi.141–48)

202 Aphorismus (B)—reprehending "by raising a question about the proper
application of a word" (SMJ 220)—for Aphorismus (A), see **74** Proverb under
Logos: Topics of Invention: Inartificial Arguments: Testimony of Men

I saw the man to-day, if man he be.
    (AWEW V.iii.203)

        if I shall be condemn'd
Upon surmises…I tell you
'Tis rigor and not law.
    (WT III.ii.111–14)

203 Commoratio—insistent repetition of one's strongest point (SMJ 220), often
joined to **204** Epimone

To have the due and forfeit of my bond…
        I would have my bond…
Till thou canst rail the seal from off my bond,
Thou but offend'st thy lungs…
         I crave the law,
The penalty and forfeit of my bond…
There is no power in the tongue of man
To alter me: I say here on my bond…
So says it in the bond, doth it not, noble judge?…
Is it so nominated in the bond?…
I cannot find it, 'tis not in the bond…
    (MV IV.i.37, 87, 139–40, 206–207, 241–42, 253, 259, 262)

O that this too too sallied flesh would melt,
Thaw, and resolve itself into a dew!
    (Ham I.ii.129–30)

How weary, stale, flat, and unprofitable
Seem to me all the uses of this world!
    (Ham I.ii.133–34)

204 Epimone—repetition of the same point in the same words, somewhat in the
    manner of a refrain, often joined to **203** Commoratio (SMJ 220)

A horse, a horse! my kingdom for a horse!
    (R3 V.iv.13)

let him look to his bond. He was wont to call me usurer, let him look to his
bond. He was wont to lend money for a Christian cur'sy, let him look to his
bond.
    (MV III.i.47–50)

Who is here so base that would be a bondman? If any, speak, for him have I
offended. Who is here so rude that would not be a roman? If any, speak, for him
have I offended. Who is here so vile that will not love his country? If any, speak,
for him have I offended.
    (JC III.ii.29–34)

(For Brutus is an honorable man,
So are they all, all honorable men)…
And Brutus is an honorable man…
And Brutus is an honorable man…
And sure he is an honorable man…
Who (you all know) are honorable men…
Than I will wrong such honorable men…
I fear I wrong the honorable men…
They that have done this deed are honorable…
            …They are wise and honorable…
    (JC III.ii.82–83, 87, 94, 99, 124, 127, 151, 212, 214)

Put money in thy purse; follow thou the wars; defeat thy favor with an usurped
beard. I say put money in thy purse. It cannot be long that Desdemona should
continue her love to the Moor—put money in thy purse—nor he his to her.
It was a violent commencement in her, and thou shalt see an answerable
sequestration—put but money in thy purse.
    (Oth I.iii.339–46) [cf., Proverbs 4:5–7]

Reputation, reputation, reputation! O, I have lost my reputation! I have lost the immortal part of myself, and what remains is bestial. My reputation, Iago, my reputation!
    (Oth II.iii.262–65)

Desdemona: Pray you let Cassio be receiv'd again.
Othello: Fetch me the handkerchief, my mind misgives.
Desdemona: Come, come;
             You'll never meet a more sufficient man.
Othello: The handkerchief!
Desdemona: I pray talk me of Cassio.
Othello: The handkerchief!
Desdemona: A man that all his time
             Hath founded his good fortunes on your love,
             Shar'd dangers with you—
Othello: The handkerchief!
    (Oth III.iv.88–96)

Sicinius: …I' th' people's name,
          I say it shall be so.
All [Plebeians]: It shall be so, it shall be so. Let him away!
          He's banish'd, and it shall be so…
Brutus: There's no more to be said, but he is banish'd
          As enemy to the people and his country.
          It shall be so.
All [Plebeians]:   It shall be so, it shall be so.
    (Cor III.iii.104–119)

Cloten: "His garments"?…"His garment"?…"His meanest garment"?…
       "His mean'st garment"?
    (Cym II.iii.137, 139, 150, 156)

205 Apoplanesis—evading "the issue by digressing to another matter" (SMJ 221)

Justice: Sir John, I sent for you before your expedition to Shrewsbury.
Flastaff: An't please your lordship, I hear his Majesty is return'd with some
        discomfort from Wales.
Justice: I talk not of his Majesty. You would not come when I sent for you.
Falstaff: And I hear, moreover, his Highness is fall'n into this same whoreson
        apoplexy. [etc.]
    (2H4 I.ii.101–117)

206 Proecthesis — giving as excuse a defense of what one has said or done and a reason why he ought not to be blamed (SMJ 221)

> Mine eyes
> Were not in fault, for she was beautiful;
> Mine ears, that heard her flattery, nor my heart,
> That thought her like her seeming. It had been vicious
> To have mistrusted her; yet, O my daughter,
> That it was folly in me, thou mayst say,
> And prove it in thy feeling. Heaven mend all!
>   (Cym V.v.62–68)

207 Dicaeologia, or Anangeon — excusing one's word or action by pleading necessity (SMJ 221)

> Hear me, Queen:
> The strong necessity of time commands
> Our services awhile…Our Italy
> Shines o'er with civil swords…
>   (A&C I.iii.41–45)

208 Pareuresis — using an excuse of such might as to vanquish all objections (SMJ 222)

> If Hamlet from himself be ta'en away,
> And when he's not himself does wrong Laertes,
> Then Hamlet does it not, Hamlet denies it.
> Who does it then? His madness. If't be so,
> Hamlet is of the faction that is wronged,
> His madness is poor Hamlet's enemy.
>   (Ham V.ii.234–39)

209 Pysma — asking "many questions requiring diverse answers, in order to gain attention, to provoke, to confirm, or to confute" (SMJ 222)

> Where is thy husband now? Where be thy brothers?
> Where be thy two sons? Wherein dost thou joy?
> Who sues, and kneels, and says, "God save the Queen"?
> Where be the bending peers that flattered thee?
> Where be the thronging troops that followed thee?
> Decline all this, and see what now thou art…
>   (R3 IV.iv.92–97)

> Cornwall: Come, sir, what letters had you late from France?…
>   And what confederacy have you with the traitors
>   Late footed in the kingdom?…
>   Where hast thou sent the King?…
> Gloucester: To Dover.
> Regan: Wherefore to Dover? Wast thou not charg'd at peril—
> Cornwall: Wherefore to Dover? Let him first answer that.
>   (Lear III.vii.42–53) [Cornwall's interruption prevents Regan from
>   committing the fallacy **177** Many Questions]

>   Why, good fellow,
> What shall I do the while? where bide? how live?
> Or in my life what comfort, when I am
> Dead to my husband?
>   (Cym III.iv.127–30)

210 Dehortatio — dissuasion, which combines many figures to achieve its effect
   (SMJ 223)

> Andromache: Unarm, unarm, and do not fight to-day…
>   My dreams will sure prove ominous to the day…
> Cassandra: No notes of sally, for the heavens, sweet brother…
>   The gods are deaf to hot and peevish vows;
>   They are polluted off'rings, more abhorr'd
>   Than spotted livers in the sacrifice.
> Andromache: O, be persuaded! do not count it holy
>   To hurt by being just; it is as lawful,
>   For we would give much, to use violent thefts,
>   And rob in the behalf of charity.
> Cassandra: It is the purpose that makes strong the vow,
>   But vows to every purpose must not hold;
>   Unarm, sweet Hector…
>   Lay hold upon him, Priam, hold him fast,
>   He is thy crutch. Now if thou lose thy stay,
>   Thou on him leaning, and all Troy on thee,
>   Fall all together.
> Priam: Come, Hector, come, go back.
>   Thy wife hath dreamt, thy mother hath had visions,
>   Cassandra doth foresee, and I myself
>   Am like a prophet suddenly enrapt

> To tell thee that this day is ominous.
> Therefore come back…
> Ay, but thou shalt not go…
Cassandra: O Priam, yield not to him.
Andromache: Do not, dear father.
>   (T&C V.iii.3–25, 62–76)

>   Now the good gods forbid
> That our renowned Rome, whose gratitude
> Towards her deserved children is enroll'd
> In Jove's own book, like an unnatural dam
> Should now eat up her own!…
> O, he's a limb that has but a disease:
> Mortal, to cut it off; to cure it, easy.
> What has he done to Rome that's worthy death?
> Killing our enemies, the blood he hath lost
> (Which, I dare vouch, is more than that he hath
> By many an ounce) he dropp'd it for his country;
> And what is left, to lose it by his country
> Were to us all that do't, and suffer it
> A brand to th' end a' th' world…
>   The service of the foot,
> Being once gangren'd, is not then respected
> For what before it was…
>   One word more, one word:
> This tiger-footed rage, when it shall find
> The harm of unscann'd swiftness, will (too late)
> Tie leaden pounds to 's heels. Proceed by process,
> Lest parties (as he is belov'd) break out,
> And sack great Rome with Romans…
> Consider this: he has been bred i' th' wars
> Since 'a could draw a sword, and is ill school'd
> In bolted language; meal and bran together
> He throws without distinction. Give me leave,
> I'll go to him, and undertake to bring him
> Where he shall answer, by a lawful form
> (In peace), to his utmost peril.
>   (Cor III.i.288–324)

211 Protrope—persuasion "by joining promises, threats, and commands with mighty reasons to move the mind to the course desired" (SMJ 223)

> Be brave then, for your captain is brave, and vows reformation. There shall be in England seven halfpenny loaves sold for a penny; the three-hoop'd pot shall have ten hoops, and I will make it a felony to drink small beer. All the realm shall be in common, and in Cheapside shall my palfrey go to grass…
> For I am rightful heir unto the crown…
> Edmund Mortimer, Earl of March,
> Married the Duke of Clarence' daughter, did he not?…
> By her he had two children at one birth…
> The elder of them, being put to nurse,
> Was by a beggar-woman stol'n away,
> And ignorant of his birth and parentage,
> Became a bricklayer when he came to age.
> His son am I, deny it if you can…
> Fellow kings, I tell you that that Lord Say hath gelded the commonwealth, and made it an eunuch; and more than that, he can speak French, and therefore he is a traitor… Nay, answer if you can. The Frenchmen are our enemies. Go to then, I ask but this: can he that speaks with the tongue of an enemy be a good counsellor, or no?…
> And you that love the commons, follow me.
> Now show yourselves men, 'tis for liberty,
> We will not leave one lord, one gentleman;
> Spare none but such as go in clouted shoon,
> For they are thrifty honest men, and such
> As would (but that they dare not) take our parts.
> (2H6 IV.ii.64–69, 131, 136–46, 164–72, 182–87)

> Once more unto the breach, dear friends, once more;
> Or close the wall up with our English dead… [etc.]
> Follow your spirit; and upon this charge
> Cry, "God for Harry, England, and Saint George!"
> (H5 III.i.1–34)

No, my fair cousin.
If we are mark'd to die, we are enow
To do our country loss; and if to live,
The fewer men, the greater share of honor.
God's will, I pray thee wish not one man more…[etc.]
For he to-day that sheds his blood with me
Shall be my brother; be he ne'er so vile,
This day shall gentle his condition;
And gentlemen in England, now a-bed,
Shall think themselves accurs'd they were not here;
And hold their manhoods cheap whiles any speaks
That fought with us upon Saint Crispin's day.
    (H5 IV.iii.19–67)

Seeming, seeming!
I will proclaim thee, Angelo, look for't!
Sign me a present pardon for my brother,
Or with an outstretch'd throat I'll tell the world aloud
What man thou art.
    (MM II.iv.150–54)

Confess yourself to heaven,
Repent what's past, avoid what is to come,
And do not spread the compost on the weeds
To make them ranker…
O, throw away the worser part of it,
And live the purer with the other half.
Good night, but go not to my uncle's bed—
Assume a virtue, if you have it not…
Refrain to-night,
And that shall lend a kind of easiness
To the next abstinence, the next more easy
And when you are desirous to be blest,
I'll blessing beg of you.
    (Ham III.iv.149–72)

Now put your shields before your hearts, and fight
With hearts more proof than shields. Advance, brave Titus!
They do disdain us much beyond our thoughts,
Which makes me sweat with wrath. Come on, my fellows!
He that retires, I'll take him for a Volsce,
And he shall feel mine edge…
All the contagion of the south light on you,
You shames of Rome! you herd of—Biles and plagues
Plaster you o'er, that you may be abhorr'd
Farther than seen, and one infect another
Against the wind a mile! You souls of geese,
That bear the shapes of men, how have you run
From slaves that apes would beat! Pluto and hell!
All hurt behind! backs red, and faces pale
With flight and agued fear! Mend and charge home,
Or, by the fires of heaven, I'll leave the foe
And make my wars on you. Look to't; come on!
If you'll stand fast, we'll beat them to their wives,
As they us to our trenches. Follow 's.
So, now the gates are ope; now prove good seconds:
'Tis for the followers fortune widens them,
Not for the fliers. Mark me, and do the like.
    (Cor I.iv.24–45)

        If any such be here
(As it were sin to doubt) that love this painting
Wherein you see me smear'd; if any fear
Lesser his person than an ill report;
If any think brave death outweighs bad life,
And that his country's dearer than himself;
Let him alone, or so many so minded,
Wave thus to express his disposition,
And follow Martius.
O, me alone! make you a sword of me?
If these shows be not outward, which of you
But is four Volsces? None of you but is
Able to bear against the great Aufidius
A shield as hard as his…
    (Cor I.vi.67–80); see also Cor III.ii.16–110, Cor V.iii.87–182, TNK I.i.25–205

Examples of delight in disputation (SMJ 209–13):

TGV I.i.81–93
LLL V.i.46–61
LLL V.ii.18–29
R&J II.iv.88–91
R&J III.v.146–51
R&J IV.i.18–21
1H4 II.iv.221–75
Ado I.i.61–64
Ado V.ii.42–46
H5 III.ii.94–98
Ham V.i.41–59
TN I.v.57–72
TN III.i.60–66
T&C I.ii.99–104
T&C II.iii.58–68, F1
T&C III.i.17–30
Timon I.i.235–39

Examples of Shakespeare's "earnest and weighty" dramatic use of disputation (SMJ 224–40):

3H6 I.i.72–163, 190
3H6 I.ii.22–35
R3 I.ii.70–139
R3 I.iv.109–41, 163–66, 195–98, 244–48
R3 III.i.46–56
R3 IV.iv.294–431
KJ II.i.104–107
KJ III.i.184–90
R2 II.i.195–208
R2 II.iii.113–14, 133–36, 140–47
R2 III.iii.75–81
T&C I.iii.1–137
T&C II.ii
T&C III.iii.115–84
MM I.ii.184–86
MM II.ii.37–142
MM II.iv.50–170

Oth II.i.218–80
Oth II.iii.314–33, 336–62
Oth III.iii.368–426
Oth IV.i.1–45, 146–213
Lear I.i.51–181
Mac I.vii

Pathos

Pathos—the "form of persuasion by which one endeavors to put the auditor into whatever frame
of mind is favorable to one's purpose" (SMJ 242), "the temper of mind induced in the
hearers by the speaker" (SMJ 243)

Examples of the value of *pathos* (figures of vehemence) in argument:

Is it not monstrous that this player here,
But in a fiction, in a dream of passion,
Could force his soul so to his own conceit
That from her working all the visage wann'd,
Tear in his eyes, distraction in his aspect,
A broken voice, an' his whole function suiting
With forms to his conceit? And all for nothing,
For Hecuba!
What's Hecuba to him, or he to Hecuba,
That he should weep for her? What would he do
Had he the motive and the cue for passion
That I have? He would drown the stage with tears,
And cleave the general ear with horrid speech,
Make mad the guilty, and appall the free,
Confound the ignorant, and amaze indeed
The very faculties of eyes and ears.
   (Ham II.ii.551–66)

The best persuasions to the contrary
Fail not to use, and with what vehemency
Th' occasion shall instruct you.
   (H8 V.i.147–49)

212 Exuscitatio—showing deep emotion by which hearers are stirred to the like
feeling (SMJ 244)

York: O Tiger's heart wrapp'd in a woman's hide!
                   How couldst thou drain the life-blood of the child,
                   To bid the father wipe his eyes withal,
                   And yet be seen to wear a woman's face?…
                   These tears are my sweet Rutland's obsequies,
                   And every drop cries vengeance for his death
                   'Gainst thee, fell Clifford, and thee, false Frenchwoman.
Northumberland: Beshrew me, but his passions moves me so
                   That hardly can I check my eyes from tears…
York: This cloth thou dipp'dst in blood of my sweet boy,
                   And I with tears do wash the blood away.
        (3H6 I.iv.137–58)

                    Bear with me,
My heart is in the coffin there with Caesar,
And I must pause till it come back to me.
        (JC III.ii.105–107)

213 Correctio—advance warning of an unpleasant statement to come (RAL 28, not
    in SMJ)

Let not your ears despise my tongue for ever,
Which shall possess them with the heaviest sound
That ever yet they heard.
        (Mac IV.iii.201–203)

214 Aposiopesis—the "sudden breaking off of a speech" (SMJ 245). Related
    to this figure are Anacoluthon **215**, Anapodoton **216**, and the neologism
    Paraprosdokian **217**, which follow, none of which appears in SMJ

Richard: Some light-foot friend post to the Duke of Norfolk;
           Ratcliff, thyself—or Catesby—where is he?
Catesby: Here, my good lord.
Richard: Catesby, fly to the Duke.
Catesby: I will, my lord, with all convenient haste.
Richard: Ratcliff, come hither. Post to Salisbury;
           When thou com'st thither—[*to Catesby*] Dull unmindful villain,
           Why stay'st thou here, and go'st not to the Duke?
Catesby: First, mighty liege, tell me your Highness' pleasure,
           What from your Grace I shall deliver to him.
        (R3 IV.iv.440–48)

       and yet, within a month—
Let me not think on't—
    (Ham I.ii.145–46)

Ay, sir, but "While the grass grows"—the proverb is
something musty.
    (Ham III.ii.343–44)

But for the handkerchief—
    (Oth IV.i.18)

Othello: What hath he said?
Iago: Faith, that he did—I know not what he did.
Othello: What? what?
Iago: Lie—
    (Oth IV.i.31–34)

I will have such revenges on you both
That all the world shall—I will do such things—
What they are yet I know not, but they shall be
The terrors of the earth!
    (Lear II.iv.279–82)

215 Anacoluthon—"ending a sentence with a different structure from that with
    which it began" (RAL 7, not in SMJ), see Aposiopesis **214**

Rather proclaim it, Westmoreland, through my host,
That he which hath no stomach to this fight,
Let him depart
    (H5 IV.iii.34–36)

              To die, to sleep—
No more, and by a sleep to say we end
The heart-ache and the thousand natural shocks
That flesh is heir to… To die, to sleep—
To sleep, perchance to dream—ay, there's the rub
    (Ham III.i.59–64)

216 Anapodoton—"omitting a main clause from a conditional sentence" (RAL 8, not in SMJ), see Aposiopesis **214**

Ay, sir, but "While the grass grows"—the proverb is
something musty.
    (Ham III.ii.343–44)

217 Paraprosdokian—a recent coinage for the surprise or unexpected ending of a phrase, series, or sentence (not in SMJ), see Aposiopesis **214**

Queen Marg.: …Thou slander of thy heavy mother's womb!
               Thou loathed issue of thy father's loins!
               Thou rag of honor! thou detested—
Gloucester: Margaret.
    (R3 I.iii.230–33)

Duchess: God bless thee, and put meekness in thy breast,
           Love, charity, obedience, and true duty!
Gloucester: Amen!—[*aside*] and make me die a good old man!
           I marvel that her Grace did leave it out.
    (R3 II.ii.107–111)

218 Ecphonesis—"exclamation, the most widely used figure of vehemence and one expressing every species of emotion" (SMJ 245)

O judgment! thou art fled to brutish beasts,
And men have lost their reason.
    (JC III.ii.104–105)

O villainy!…Treachery!
    (Ham V.ii.311–312)

Treason! treason!
    (Ham V.ii.323)

Darkness and devils!
    (Lear I.iv.22)

Vengeance! plague! death! confusion!
    (Lear II.iv.95)

> O sun,
> Burn the great sphere thou mov'st in! darkling stand
> The varying shore o' th' world! O Antony,
> Antony, Antony!
>   (A&C IV.xv.9–12)

219 Thaumasmus—"exclamation of wonder" (SMJ 245)

> O you gods!
> Is yond despis'd and ruinous man my lord?
> Full of decay and failing? O monument
> And wonder of good deeds evilly bestow'd!
>   (Timon IV.iii.458–61)

> This is a lord! O noble misery,
> To be i' th' field, and ask "what news?" of me!
> To-day how many would have given their honors
> To have sav'd their carcasses! took heel to do't,
> And yet died too!
>   (Cym V.iii.64–68)

> O, she's warm!
> (WT V.iii.109)

> (O you wonder!)
> (Temp I.ii.427)

> O wonder!
> How many goodly creatures are there here!
> How beauteous mankind is! O brave new world
> That has such people in't!
>   (Temp V.i.181–84)

220 Erotema, or Erotesis or Interrogatio—"rhetorical question" (SMJ 246)

> What, is my Richard both in shape and mind
> Transform'd and weak'ned? Hath Bullingbrook depos'd
> Thine intellect? Hath he been in thy heart?
>   (R2 V.i.26–28)

> What if I stray'd no farther, but chose here?
>   (MV II.vii.35)

How many then should cover that stand bare?
How many be commanded that command?
How much low peasantry would then be gleaned
From the true seed of honor? and how much honor
Pick'd from the chaff and ruin of the times
To be new varnish'd?
    (MV II.ix.44–49)

Is there not my father, my uncle, and myself? Lord
Edmund Mortimer, my Lord of York, and Owen
Glendower? Is there not besides the Douglas? Have I
not all their letters to meet me in arms by the ninth of
the next month? and are they not some of them set
forward already?
    (1H4 II.iii.23–29)

O heavens, is't possible a young maid's wits
Should be as mortal as an old man's life?
    (Ham IV.v.160–61)

Why should a dog, a horse, a rat, have life,
And thou no breath at all?
    (Lear V.iii.307–308)

                  What the hope drunk
Wherein you dress'd yourself? Hath it slept since?
And wakes it now to look so green and pale
At what it did so freely?…Art thou afeard
To be the same in thine own act and valor
As thou art in desire? Wouldst thou have that
Which thou esteem'st the ornament of life,
And live a coward in thine own esteem,
Letting "I dare not" wait upon "I would,"
Like the poor cat i' th' adage?
    (Mac I.vii.35–45)

221 Apostrophe — "a turning of speech from the persons previously addressed to another, sometimes to a thing or an abstraction personified" (SMJ 246)

Grim death, how foul and loathsome is thine image!
    (Shrew Ind. i. 35)

Arise, fair sun, and kill the envious moon
    (R&J II.ii.4)

O churl, drunk all, and left no friendly drop
To help me after?…O happy dagger,
This is thy sheath; there rust, and let me die.
    (R&J V.iii.163–70)

And what art thou, thou idol Ceremony?
What kind of god art thou, that suffer'st more
Of mortal griefs than do thy worshippers?
What are thy rents? what are thy comings-in?
O Ceremony, show me but thy worth!…
          O, be sick, great greatness,
And bid thy ceremony give thee cure!…
          No, thou proud dream…
I am a king that find thee…thrice-gorgeous ceremony
    (H5 IV.i.240–66)

That I did love thee, Caesar, O, 'tis true;
If then thy spirit look upon us now,
Shall it not grieve thee dearer than thy death
To see thy Antony making his peace,
Shaking the bloody fingers of thy foes,
Most noble! in the presence of thy corse?
    (JC III.i.194–99)

O, pardon me, thou bleeding piece of earth,
That I am meek and gentle with these butchers!
Thou art the ruins of the noblest man
That ever lived in the tide of times.
    (JC III.i.254–57)

For Brutus, as you know, was Caesar's angel.
Judge, O you gods, how dearly Caesar lov'd him!
    (JC III.ii.181–82)

O God, God,
How weary, stale, flat, and unprofitable
Seem to me all the uses of this world!…
Heaven and earth,
Must I remember?…
Frailty, thy name is woman!—
(Ham I.ii.132–46)

O all you host of heaven! O earth! What else?
And shall I couple hell? O fie, hold, hold, my heart,
And you, my sinows, grow not instant old,
But bear me stiffly up. Remember thee!
Ay, thou poor ghost…
(Ham I.v.92–96)

Work on,
My medicine, work!
(Oth IV.i.44–45)

You see me here, you gods, a poor old man…
(Lear II.iv.272)

Blow, winds, and crack your cheeks! rage, blow!
You cataracts and hurricanoes, spout
Till you have drench'd our steeples, drown'd the cocks!
You sulph'rous and thought-executing fires,
Vaunt-couriers of oak-cleaving thunderbolts,
Singe my white head! And thou, all-shaking thunder,
Strike flat the thick rotundity o' th' world!
Crack nature's moulds, all germains spill at once
That makes ingrateful man!
(Lear III.ii.1–9)

I tax not you, you elements, with unkindness…
But yet I call you servile ministers,
That will with two pernicious daughters join
Your high-engender'd battles 'gainst a head
So old and white as this.
(Lear III.ii.16–24)

Poor naked wretches, wheresoe'er you are,
That bide the pelting of this pitiless storm…
    (Lear III.iv.28–29)

I might have sav'd her, now she's gone for ever!
Cordelia, Cordelia, stay a little. Ha!
What is't thou say'st? Her voice was ever soft,
Gentle, and low, an excellent thing in woman.
I kill'd the slave that was a-hanging thee…
                    Did I not, fellow?
    (Lear V.iii.271–76)

                  Come, you spirits
That tend on mortal thoughts, unsex me here,
And fill me from the crown to the toe topful
Of direst cruelty!…Come to my woman's breasts,
And take my milk for gall, you murth'ring ministers,
Wherever in your sightless substances
You wait on nature's mischief! Come, thick night,
And pall thee in the dunnest smoke of hell
    (Mac I.v.40–51)

Is this a dagger which I see before me,
The handle toward my hand? Come, let me clutch thee:
I have thee not, and yet I see thee still.
Art thou not, fatal vision, sensible
To feeling as to sight?…
                Thou sure and firm-set earth,
Hear not my steps, which way they walk, for fear
The very stones prate of my whereabout,
and take the present horror from the time,
Which now suits with it…
Hear it not, Duncan, for it is a knell,
That summons thee to heaven or to hell.
    (Mac II.i.33–64)

            Come, seeling night,
Scarf up the tender eye of pitiful day,
And with thy bloody and invisible hand
Cancel and tear to pieces that great bond
Which keeps me pale!
    (Mac III.ii.46–50)

[*To the gold.*] O thou sweet king-killer, and dear divorce
'Twixt natural son and sire! thou bright defiler
Of Hymen's purest bed! thou valiant Mars!
Thou ever young, fresh, lov'd, and delicate wooer,
Whose blush doth thaw the consecrated snow
That lies on Dian's lap! thou visible god,
That sold'rest close impossibilities,
And mak'st them kiss! that speak'st with every tongue
To every purpose! O thou touch of hearts,
Think thy slave man rebels, and by thy virtue
Set them into confounding odds, that beasts
May have the world in empire!
    (Timon IV.iii.381–92)

All of her that is out of door most rich!
If she be furnish'd with a mind so rare,
She is alone th' Arabian bird, and I
Have lost the wager. Boldness be my friend;
Arm me audacity from head to foot
    (Cym I.vi.15–19)

222 Anamnesis—"recital of matters past, most often of woes or injuries" (SMJ
    247–48)

Tell over your woes again by viewing mine:
I had an Edward, till a Richard kill'd him;
I had a Harry, till a Richard kill'd him;
Thou hadst an Edward, till a Richard kill'd him;
Thou hadst a Richard, till a Richard kill'd him. [etc.]
    (R3 IV.iv.39–70)

I remember when I was in love, I broke my sword upon a stone, and bid him
take that for coming a-night to Jane Smile; and I remember the kissing of her
batler and the cow's dugs that her pretty chopp'd hands had milk'd; and I
remember the wooing of a peascod instead of her, from whom I took two cods,
and giving her them again, said with weeping tears, "Wear these for my sake."
    (AYLI II.iv.46–54)

My brother and thy uncle, call'd Antonio—
I pray thee mark me—that a brother should
Be so perfidious!—he whom next thyself
Of all the world I lov'd, and to him put
The manage of my state… [etc.]
   (Temp I.ii.66–168)

Caliban: …When thou cam'st first,
      Thou strok'st me and made much of me, wouldst give me
      Water with berries in't, and teach me how
      To name the bigger light, and how the less,
      That burn by day and night; and then I lov'd thee
      And show'd thee all the qualities o' th' isle…
Prospero: I have us'd thee
      (Filth as thou art) with human care, and lodg'd thee
      In mine own cell, till thou didst seek to violate
      The honor of my child.
Caliban:…Thou didst prevent me…
Miranda: …I pitied thee,
      Took pains to make thee speak, taught thee each hour
      One thing or other… [etc.]
   (Temp I.ii.332–64)

                      I have bedimm'd
The noontide sun, call'd forth the mutinous winds,
And 'twixt the green sea and the azur'd vault
Set roaring war; to the dread rattling thunder
Have I given fire, and rifted Jove's stout oak
With his own bolt; the strong-bas'd promontory
Have I made shake, and by the spurs pluck'd up
The pine and cedar. Graves at my command
Have wak'd their sleepers, op'd, and let 'em forth
By my so potent art.
   (Temp V.i.41–50)

223 Threnos—"a lament" (SMJ 248)

Be it lawful that I invocate thy ghost
To hear the lamentations of poor Anne,
Wife to thy Edward, to thy slaught'red son,
Stabb'd by the self-same hand that made these wounds!
Lo, in these windows that let forth thy life
I pour the helpless balm of my poor eyes.
  (R3 I.ii.8–13)

Ah! who shall hinder me to wail and weep,
To chide my fortune, and torment myself?
I'll join with black despair against my soul,
And to myself become an enemy.
  (R3 II.ii.34–37)

Queen Elizabeth: Was never widow had so dear a loss.
Children: Were never orphans had so dear a loss.
Duchess of York: Was never mother had so dear a loss.
                         Alas! I am the mother of these griefs:
                         Their woes are parcell'd, mine is general.
                         She for an Edward weeps, and so do I;
                         I for a Clarence weep, so doth not she;
                         These babes for Clarence weep, and so do I;
                         I for an Edward weep, so do not they.
                         Alas! you three on me, threefold distress'd,
                         Pour all your tears. I am your sorrow's nurse,
                         And I will pamper it with lamentation.
  (R3 II.ii.77–88)

[*Titus Andronicus* passim]

Nurse: O woe! O woeful, woeful, woeful day!
             Most lamentable day, most woeful day
             That ever, ever, I did yet behold!
             O day, O day, O day, O hateful day!
             Never was seen so black a day as this.
             O woeful day, O woeful day!
Paris: Beguil'd, divorced, wronged, spited, slain!…

Capulet: Despis'd, distressed, hated, martyr'd, kill'd!...
                        Alack, my child is dead,
            And with my child my joys are buried.
      (R&J IV.v.49–64)

                  it made this threne
To the Phoenix and the Dove,
Co-supremes and stars of love,
A chorus to their tragic scene.
            THRENOS
Beauty, Truth, and Rarity,
Grace in all simplicity,
Here enclos'd, in cinders lie… [etc.]
      (P&T 49–67)

Howl, howl, howl! O, you are men of stones!
Had I your tongues and eyes, I'ld use them so
That heaven's vault should crack. She's gone for ever!
                  …Thou'lt come no more,
Never, never, never, never, never.
      (Lear V.iii.258–60, 308–309)

224 Apocarteresis — "the casting away of all hope in one direction and turning to
      another for aid" (SMJ 249)

                        it shall scarce boot me
To say "Not guilty." Mine integrity,
Being counted falsehood, shall (as I express it)
Be so receiv'd. But thus, if pow'rs divine
Behold our human actions (as they do),
I doubt not then but innocence shall make
False accusation blush, and tyranny
Tremble at patience.
      (WT III.ii.25–32)

225 Optatio — "ardent wish or prayer" (SMJ 249)

A horse, a horse! my kingdom for a horse!
      (R3 V.iv.7, 13)

O that the slave had forty thousand lives!
One is too poor, too weak for my revenge…
Arise, black vengeance, from the hollow hell!
Yield up, O love, thy crown and hearted throne
To tyrannous hate! Swell, bosom, with thy fraught,
For 'tis of aspics' tongues!
    (Oth III.iii.442–50)

O heaven, that such companions thou'dst unfold,
And put in every honest hand a whip
To lash the rascals naked through the world
Even from the east to th' west!
    (Oth IV.ii.141–44)

                Let the great gods,
That keep this dreadful pudder o'er our heads,
Find out their enemies now. Tremble, thou wretch
That has within thee undivulged crimes
Unwhipt of justice! Hide thee, thou bloody hand,
Thou perjur'd, and thou simular of virtue
That art incestuous! Caitiff, to pieces shake,
That under covert and convenient seeming
Has practic'd on man's life! Close pent-up guilts,
Rive your concealing continents, and cry
These dreadful summoners grace.
    (Lear III.ii.49–60)

The Jove of power make me most weak, most weak,
Your reconciler! Wars 'twixt you twain would be
As if the world should cleave, and that slain men
Should solder up the rift
    (A&C III.iv.29–32)

226 Deesis, also Obtestatio—"vehement supplication" (SMJ 250)

              O you kind gods!
Cure this great breach in his abused nature,
Th' untun'd and jarring senses, O, wind up
Of this child-changed father!
    (Lear IV.vii.13–16)

> Come, you spirits
> That tend on mortal thoughts, unsex me here,
> And fill me from the crown to the toe topful
> Of direst cruelty! Make thick my blood,
> Stop up th' access and passage to remorse,
> That no compunctious visitings of nature
> Shake my fell purpose, nor keep peace between
> Th' effect and it! Come to my woman's breasts,
> And take my milk for gall, you murth'ring ministers,
> Wherever in your sightless substances
> You wait on nature's mischief!
>   (Mac I.v.40–50)

>   But, gentle heavens,
> Cut short all intermission. Front to front
> Bring thou this fiend of Scotland and myself;
> Within my sword's length set him
>   (Mac IV.iii.231–34)

Additional examples:
    Rutland: 3H6 I.iii.35–45
    Clarence: R3 I.iv.181–267
    Tamora: Titus I.i.104- 20
    Lavinia: Titus II.iii.136–78
    Titus: Titus III.i.1 –26
    Arthur: KJ IV.i.41–120
    Duchess of York and Aumerle: R2 V.iii.30–135
    Arcite to Mars: TNK V.i.49–61
    Palamon to Venus: TNK V.i.77–97, 126–29
    Emilia to Diana: TNK V.i.137–62

227 Mempsis—"a complaint against injuries and a craving for redress" (SMJ 251)

> I hate him for he is a Christian;
> But more, for that in low simplicity
> He lends out money gratis, and brings down
> The rate of usance here in Venice.
> If I can catch him once upon the hip,
> I will feed fat the ancient grudge I bear him.
>   (MV I.iii.42–47)

He hath disgrac'd me, and hind'red me half a million,
laugh'd at my losses, mock'd at my gains, scorn'd my
nation, thwarted my bargains, cool'd my friends, heated
mine enemies… And if you wrong us, shall we not
revenge?…The villainy you teach me, I will execute, and
it shall go hard but I will better the instruction.
    (MV III.i.54–73)

[We] have the summary of all our griefs
(When time shall serve) to show in articles;
Which long ere this we offer'd to the King,
And might by no suit gain our audience.
When we are wrong'd and would unfold our griefs,
We are denied access unto his person
Even by those men that most have done us wrong…
Then take, my Lord of Westmerland, this schedule,
For this contains our general grievances:
Each several article herein redress'd…
We come within our aweful banks again,
And knit our powers to the arm of peace.
    (2H4 IV.i.73–79, 166–75)

I cannot think but your age has forgot me,
It could not else be I should prove so base
To sue and be denied such common grace.
My wounds ache at you…
                I have kept back their foes,
While they have told their money, and let out
Their coin upon large interest—I myself
Rich only in large hurts. All those, for this?
Is this the balsom that the usuring Senate
Pours into captains' wounds? Banishment!
    (Timon III.v.92–110)

228 Paramythia—"seeking to console or diminish sorrow" (SMJ 252)

Why, foolish Lucius, dost thou not perceive
That Rome is but a wilderness of tigers?
Tigers must prey, and Rome affords no prey
But me and mine. How happy art thou then,
From these devourers to be banished!
    (Titus III.i.53–57)

Teach thy necessity to reason thus:
There is no virtue like necessity.
Think not the King did banish thee,
But thou the King. Woe doth the heavier sit
Where it perceives it is but faintly borne.
Go, say I sent thee forth to purchase honor,
And not the King exil'd thee; or suppose
Devouring pestilence hangs in our air,
And thou art flying to a fresher clime.
Look what thy soul holds dear, imagine it
To lie that way thou goest, not whence thou com'st.
Suppose the singing birds musicians,
The grass whereon thou tread'st the presence strow'd,
The flowers fair ladies, and they steps no more
Than a delightful measure or a dance,
For gnarling sorrow hath less power to bite
The man that mocks at it and sets it light.
    (R2 I.ii.277–93)

                       Sir, he may live.
I saw him beat the surges under him,
And ride upon their backs. He trod the water,
Whose enmity he flung aside, and breasted
The surge most swoll'n that met him. His bold head
'Bove the contentious waves he kept, and oared
Himself with his good arms in lusty stroke
To th' shore, that o'er his wave-worn basis bowed,
As stooping to relieve him. I not doubt
He came alive to land.
    (Temp II.i.114–23)

229 Medela — seeking "to palliate by conciliatory words the offenses of a friend when they can [be neither] defended nor denied" (SMJ 253)

> Consider this: he has been bred i' th' wars
> Since 'a could draw a sword, and is ill school'd
> In bolted language; meal and bran together
> He throws without distinction.
>   (Cor III.i.318–21)

> To kill, I grant, is sin's extremest gust,
> But in defense, by mercy, 'tis most just.
> To be in anger is impiety;
> But who is man that is not angry?
> Weigh but the crime with this.
>   (Timon III.v.54–58)

230 Philophronesis — "seeking to mitigate by gentle speech and humble submission the anger of an adversary whose might is too great to be overcome" (SMJ 253)

> Why, look you how you storm!
> I would be friends with you, and have your love,
> Forget the shames that you have stain'd me with,
> Supply your present wants, and take no doit
> Of usance for my moneys, and you'll not hear me.
> This is kind I offer.
>   (MV I.iii.137–42)

> Thus, Brutus, did my master bid me kneel;
> Thus did Mark Antony bid me fall down;
> And being prostrate, thus he bade me say:
> Brutus is noble, wise, valiant, and honest;
> Caesar was mighty, bold, royal, and loving.
> Say, I love Brutus, and I honor him;
> Say, I fear'd Caesar, honor'd him, and lov'd him.
> If Brutus will vouchsafe that Antony
> May safely come to him, and be resolv'd
> How Caesar hath deserv'd to lie in death,
> Mark Antony shall not love Caesar dead
> So well as Brutus living; but will follow

The fortunes and affairs of noble Brutus
Thorough the hazards of this untrod state
With all true faith. So says my master Antony.
    (JC III.i.123–37)

                    my master and my lord
I must obey…Sole sir o' th' world…
                            'tis yours, and we,
Your scutcheons and your signs of conquest, shall
Hang in what place you please.
    (A&C V.ii.116–36)

231 Mycterismus — "a scornful mock, sometimes accompanied by a facial gesture,
    as drawing the lip awry" (SMJ 254)

When we have match'd our rackets to these balls,
We will in France, by God's grace, play a set
Shall strike his father's crown into the hazard…
And tell the pleasant prince this mock of his
Hath turn'd his balls to gun-stones
    (H5 I.ii.261–82)

Thrift, thrift, Horatio, the funeral bak'd-meats
Did coldly furnish forth the marriage tables.
    (Ham I.ii.180–81)

Sir Toby: Sot, dids't see Dick surgeon, sot?
Feste: O, he's drunk, Sir Toby, an hour agone; his eyes were set at eight i' th'
           morning.
                (TN V.i.197–99)

Cleopatra: Celerity is never more admir'd
           Than by the negligent.
Antony: A good rebuke,
           Which might have well becom'd the best of men
           To taunt at slackness.
    (A&C III.vii.24–27)

Sicinius: When we were chosen tribunes for the people—
Brutus: Mark'd you his lip and eyes?
Sicinius: Nay, but his taunts.
Brutus: Being mov'd, he will not spare to gird the gods.
Sicinius: Bemock the modest moon.
    (Cor I.i.254–57)

Apemantus: Canst not read?
Page: No.
Apemantus: There will little learning die then that day thou art hang'd.
    (Timon II.ii.80–83)

Apemantus: There is no leprosy but what thou speak'st.
Timon: If I name thee.
    (Timon IV.iii.362–63)

232 Sarcasmus—"a more bitter taunt than mycterismus [**231**], a more open mock"
    (SMJ 255)

Demetrius: So now go tell, and if thy tongue can speak,
              Who 'twas that cut thy tongue and ravish'd thee.
Chiron: Write down thy mind, bewray thy meaning so,
               And if thy stumps will let thee play the scribe.
Demetrius: See how with signs and tokens she can scrowl…
Chiron: And 'twere my cause, I should go hang myself.
Demetrius: If thou hadst hands to help thee knit the cord.
    (Titus II.iv.1–10)

Constance: … And hang a calve's-skin on those recreant limbs.
Austria: O that a man should speak those words to me!
Bastard: And hang a calve's-skin on those recreant limbs.
Austria: Thou dar'st not say so, villain, for thy life.
Bastard: And hang a calve's-skin on those recreant limbs. [etc.]
    (KJ III.i.129–33, 199, 220, 299)

Brutus: Good words are better than bad strokes, Octavius.
Antony: In your bad strokes, Brutus, you give good words;
           Witness the hole you made in Caesar's heart,
           Crying, "Long live! hail, Caesar!"
    (JC V.i.29–32)

<pre>
1. Watch: Now, sir, is your name Menenius?
2. Watch: 'Tis a spell, you see, of much power. You
            know the way home again.
1. Watch: Do you hear how we are shent for keeping
            your greatness back?
2. Watch: What cause do you think I have to swound?
   (Cor V.ii.95–101)
</pre>

233 Epiplexis, also Percontatio—asking questions in order to chide or reprehend
(SMJ 256)

<pre>
                    Are these your herd?
Must these have voices, that can yield them now,
And straight disclaim their tongues? What are your offices?
You being their mouths, why rule you not their teeth?
Have you not set them on?
   (Cor III.i.33–37)
</pre>

234 Onedismus—"upbraiding another for ingratitude or impiety" (SMJ 256)

<pre>
And you degenerate, you ingrate revolts,
You bloody Neroes, ripping up the womb
Of your dear Mother England, blush for shame
   (KJ V.ii.151–53)
</pre>

<pre>
What shall I say to thee, Lord Scroop, thou cruel,
Ingrateful, savage, and inhuman creature? …
For this revolt of thine, methinks, is like
Another fall of man.
   (H5 II.ii.94–142)
</pre>

<pre>
Suspend thy purpose, if you didst intend
To make this creature fruitful.
Into her womb convey sterility,
Dry up in her the organs of increase…
                        If she must teem
Create her child of spleen, that it may live
And be a thwart disnatur'd torment to her…
Turn all her mother's pains and benefits
To laughter and contempt, that she may feel
</pre>

How sharper than a serpent's tooth it is
To have a thankless child!
    (Lear I.iv.276–89)

                      He that trusts to you,
Where he should find you lions, finds you hares;
Where foxes, geese. You are no surer, no,
Than is the coal of fire upon the ice
Or hailstone in the sun…He that depends
Upon your favors swims with fins of lead,
And hews down oak with rushes. Hang ye! Trust ye?
With every minute you do change a mind,
And call him noble, that was now your hate;
Him vild, that was your garland.
    (Cor I.i.170–84)

235 Categoria—"lay[ing] open the secret wickedness of another before his face"
    (SMJ 257)

                      Such an act
That blurs the grace and blush of modesty,
Calls virtue hypocrite, takes off the rose
From the fair forehead of an innocent love
And sets a blister there, makes marriage vows
As false as dicers' oaths…
Could you on this fair mountain leave to feed,
And batten on this moor?…What devil was't
That thus hath cozen'd you at hoodman-blind?
               …O shame, where is thy blush?
    (Ham III.iv.40–81)

                      I wrote to you,
When rioting in Alexandria you
Did pocket up my letters; and with taunts
Did gibe my missive out of audience.
    (A&C II.ii.71–74)

236 Proclees—"provok[ing or goading] an adversary to the conflict by a vehement accusation or by a confident offer of justification" (SMJ 257)

A heart unspotted is not easily daunted.
The purest spring is not so free from mud
As I am clear from treason to my sovereign.
Who can accuse me? Wherein am I guilty?
   (2H6 III.i.100–103)

Look what I speak, my life shall prove it true:
That Mowbray hath receiv'd eight thousand nobles
In name of lendings for your Highness' soldiers,
The which he hath detain'd for lewd employments,
Like a false traitor and injurious villain;
Besides I say, and will in battle prove,
Or here or elsewhere to the furthest verge
That ever was surveyed by English eye,
That all the treasons for these eighteen years,
Complotted and contrived in this land,
Fetch from false Mowbray their first head and spring.
Further I say, and further will maintain
Upon his bad life to make all this good,
That he did plot the Duke of Gloucester's death,
Suggest his soon-believing adversaries,
And consequently, like a traitor coward,
Sluic'd out his innocent soul through streams of blood,
Which blood…cries…
To me for justice and rough chastisement;
And, by the glorious worth of my descent,
This arm shall do it, or this life be spent.
   (R2 I.i.87–108)

Sicinius: We charge you, that you have contriv'd to take
              From Rome all season'd office, and to wind
              Yourself into a power tyrannical,
              For which you are a traitor to the people.
Coriolanus: How? traitor?…
              The fires i' th' lowest hell fold in the people!
              Call me their traitor, thou injurious tribune!
              Within thine eyes sate twenty thousand deaths,
              In thy hands clutch'd as many millions, in
              Thy lying tongue both numbers, I would say
              "Thou liest" unto thee with a voice as free
              As I do pray the gods.
    (Cor III.iii.63–74)

Aufidius: Name not the god, thou boy of tears!
Coriolanus: Ha?…
              Measureless liar, thou hast made my heart
              Too great for what contains it. "Boy"? O slave!…
              Cut me to pieces, Volsces, men and lads,
              Stain all your edges on me. "Boy," false hound!
              If you have writ your annals true, 'tis there
              That, like an eagle in a dove-cote, I
              Flutter'd your Volscians in Corioles.
              Alone I did it. "Boy"!
    (Cor V.vi.100–116)

237 Bdelygmia, or Bdelygma—expressing "hate or abhorrence, usually in a few
    words" (SMJ 258)

                       Fie, fie, my brother!
Weigh you the worth and honor of a king
So great as our dread father in a scale
Of common ounces? Will you with compters sum
The past-proportion of his infinite,
And buckle in a waist most fathomless
With spans and inches so diminutive
As fears and reasons? Fie, for godly shame!
    (T&C II.ii.25–32)

> O gull, O dolt,
> As ignorant as dirt!
>> (Oth V.ii.163–64)

Out, varlet, from my sight!
> (Lear II.iv.187)

You shames of Rome! you herd of—Biles and plagues
Plaster you o'er, that you may be abhorr'd
Farther than seen…You souls of geese,
That bear the shapes of men, how have you run
From slaves that apes would beat! Pluto and hell!
All hurt behind! backs red, and faces pale
With flight and agued fear!
> (Cor I.iv.31–38)

238 Cataplexis—threatening plagues or punishments (SMJ 258)

Yet know, my master, God omnipotent,
Is mustering in his clouds on our behalf
Armies of pestilence, and they shall strike
Your children yet unborn and unbegot,
That lift your vassal hands against my head,
And threat the glory of my precious crown.
> (R2 III.iii.85–90)

And you be mine, I'll give you to my friend;
And you be not, hang, beg, starve, die in the streets,
For, by my soul, I'll ne'er acknowledge thee,
Nor what is mine shall never do thee good.
> (R&J III.v.191–94)

> Hence,
Horrible villain, or I'll spurn thine eyes
Like balls before me; I'll unhair thy head,
Thou shalt be whipp'd with wire, and stew'd in brine,
Smarting in ling'ring pickle.
> (A&C II.v.62–66)

For this, be sure, to-night thou shalt have cramps,
Side-stitches, that shall pen thy breath up; urchins
Shall, for that vast of night that they may work,
All exercise on thee; thou shalt be pinch'd
As thick as honeycomb, each pinch more stinging
Than bees that made 'em.
    (Temp I.ii.325–30)

239 Ara—"cursing" (SMJ 259)

If ever he have wife, let her be made
More miserable by the life of him
Than I am made by my young lord and thee!
    (R3 I.ii.26–28) [unwittingly cursing herself]

Why then give way, dull clouds, to my quick curses!
Though not by war, by surfeit die your king,
As ours by murther, to make him a king!
Edward thy son, that now is Prince of Wales,
For Edward our son, that was Prince of Wales,
Die in his youth by like untimely violence!
Thyself a queen, for me that was a queen,
Outlive thy glory like my wretched self!
Long may'st thou live to wail thy children's death,
And see another, as I see thee now,
Deck'd in thy rights as thou art stall'd in mine!
Long die thy happy days before thy death,
And after many length'ned hours of grief,
Die neither mother, wife, nor England's queen.
                …God, I pray him
That none of you may live his natural age,
But by some unlook'd accident cut off!…
            Stay, dog, for thou shalt hear me.
If heaven have any grievous plague in store
Exceeding those that I can wish upon thee,
O, let them keep it till thy sins be ripe,
And then hurl down their indignation
On thee, the troubler of the poor world's peace!
    (R3 I.iii.195–220)

Therefore take with thee my most grievous curse,
Which in the day of battle tire thee more
Than all the complete armor that thou wear'st!
My prayers on the adverse party fight,
And there the little souls of Edward's children
Whisper the spirits of thine enemies
And promise them success and victory.
    (R3 IV.iv.188–94)

Thou ceaseless lackey to eternity,
With some mischance cross Tarquin in his flight.
Devise extremes beyond extremity,
To make him curse this cursed crimeful night.
Let ghastly shadows his lewd eyes affright,
    And the dire thought of his committed evil
    Shape every bush a hideous shapeless devil.
Disturb his hours of rest with restless trances…
Let him have time to tear his curled hair…
Let him have time to see his friend his foes…
O Time, thou tutor both to good and bad,
Teach me to curse him that thou taught'st this ill.
At his own shadow let the thief run mad,
Himself himself seek every hour to kill.
    (RL 967–98)

                        O you gods divine,
Make Cressid's name the very crown of falsehood,
If ever she leave Troilus!
    (T&C IV.ii.99–101) [unwittingly cursing herself]

Whip me, ye devils,
From the possession of this heavenly sight!
Blow me about in winds! roast me in sulphur!
Wash me in steep-down gulfs of liquid fire!
    (Oth V.ii.277–80)

Infected be the air whereon they ride,
And damn'd all those that trust them!
    (Mac IV.i.138–39) [unintentionally cursing himself]

May these add to the number that may scald thee!
Let molten coin be thy damnation,
Thou disease of a friend, and not himself!…
O, may diseases only work upon't!
And when he's sick to death, let not that part of nature
Which my lord paid for, be of any power
To expel sickness, but prolong his hour!
    (Timon III.i.51–63)

Now the gods keep you old enough that you may live
Only in bone, that none may look on you!
    (Timon III.v.103–104)

O blessed breeding sun, draw from the earth
Rotten humidity; below thy sister's orb
Infect the air!…be abhorr'd
All feasts, societies, and throngs of men!…
Destruction fang mankind!
    (Timon IV.iii.1–23)

The gods confound them all in thy conquest,
And thee after, when thou hast conquer'd!…
Be as a planetary plague when Jove
Will o'er some high-vic'd city hang his poison
In the sick air.
    (Timon IV.iii.104–111)

a plague consume you, wicked caitiffs left!
    (Timon V.iv.71)

                          Pisanio,
All curses madded Hecuba gave the Greeks,
And mine to boot, be darted on thee!
    (Cym IV.ii.313–14)

240 Eulogia—pronouncing a blessing (SMJ 261)

The gods to their dear shelter take thee, maid
    (Lear I.i.182)

If Edgar live, O, bless him!
    (Lear IV.vi.40)

> Hearty thanks,
> The bounty and the benison of heaven
> To boot, and boot!
>   (Lear IV.vi.224–26)

> God's benison go with you, and with those
> That would make good of bad, and friends of foes!
>   (Mac II.iv.40–41)

> The benediction of these covering heavens
> Fall on their heads like dew! for they are worthy
> To inlay heaven with stars.
>   (Cym V.v.350–52)

241 Paeanismus — expressing exuberance of joy (SMJ 261)

> And, father, do but think
> How sweet a thing it is to wear a crown,
> Within whose circuit is Elysium
> And all that poets feign of bliss and joy.
>   (3H6 I.ii.28–31)

> O love, be moderate, allay thy ecstasy,
> In measure rain thy joy, scant this excess!
> I feel too much thy blessing; make it less,
> For fear I surfeit.
>   (MV III.ii.111–14)

> Do you see this? Look on her! Look her lips.
> Look there, look there!
>   (Lear V.iii.311–12)

> O Helicanus, strike me, honored sir,
> Give me a gash, put me to present pain,
> Lest this great sea of joys rushing upon me
> O'erbear the shores of my mortality,
> And drown me with their sweetness.
>   (Per V.i.190–94)

Ethos

Ethos—"the persuasion exerted upon the minds and hearts of the audience by the personal character of the speaker, causing them to believe in his sincerity, his truth, his ability, his good will toward them" (SMJ 272)

Example of *pathos* engendering *ethos*:

> Macduff, this noble passion,
> Child of integrity, hath from my soul
> Wip'd the black scruples, reconcil'd my thoughts
> To thy good truth and honor. Devilish Macbeth
> By many of these trains hath sought to win me
> Into his power, and modest wisdom plucks me
> From over-credulous haste. But God above
> Deal between thee and me! for even now
> I put myself to thy direction, and
> Unspeak mine own detraction, here abjure
> The taints and blames I laid upon myself,
> For strangers to my nature.
> (Mac IV.iii.114–25)

242 Comprobatio—commending "the good [the speaker] sees in the judges whose confidence he wishes to win" (SMJ 273)

> Honor, health, and compassion to the Senate!…
> I am an humble suitor to your virtues;
> For pity is the virtue of the law…
> O my lords,
> As you are great, be pitifully good.
> (Timon III.v.5–52)

243 Parrhesia—showing humble respect "or, if necessity demands, [being] courageously outspoken in addressing those whom [one] ought to reverence or fear on a matter that concerns them or those near to them" (SMJ 273)

Royal Lear,

Whom I have ever honor'd as my king,
Lov'd as my father, as my master follow'd,
As my great patron thought on in my prayers…

be Kent unmannerly

When Lear is mad. What wouldest thou do, old man?
Think'st thou that duty shall have dread to speak
When power to flattery bows? To plainness honor's bound,
When majesty falls to folly. Reserve thy state,
And in thy best consideration check
This hideous rashness. Answer my life my judgment,
Thy youngest daughter does not love thee least,
Nor are those empty-hearted whose low sounds
Reverb no hollowness…
My life I never held but as a pawn
To wage against thine enemies, ne'er fear'd to lose it,
Thy safety being motive…
See better, Lear, and let me still remain
The true blank of thine eye…
Kill thy physician, and the fee bestow
Upon the foul disease. Revoke thy gift,
Or whilst I can vent clamor from my throat,
I'll tell thee thou dost evil.

    (Lear I.i.139–66)

Good my liege, I come—

And I beseech you hear me, who professes
Myself your loyal servant, your physician,
Your most obedient counsellor; yet that dares
Less appear so, in comforting your evils,
Than such as most seem yours—I say, I come
From your good queen…

I'll not call you tyrant;
But this most cruel usage of your queen
(Not able to produce more accusation
Than your own weak-hing'd fancy) something savors
Of tyranny, and will ignoble make you,
Yea, scandalous to the world.
    (WT II.iii.52–58, 116–21)

244 Eucharistia — giving thanks for benefits received (SMJ 274)

I can no other answer make but thanks,
And thanks; and ever oft good turns
Are shuffled off with such uncurrent pay;
But were my worth as is my conscience firm,
You should find better dealing.
    (TN III.iii.14–18)

Most honor'd Cleon…You and your lady
Take from my heart all thankfulness! The gods
Make up the rest upon you!
    (Per III.iii.1–5)

        My recompense is thanks, that's all,
Yet my good will is great, though the gift small.
    (Per III.iv.17–18)

245 Syngnome — forgiving injuries (SMJ 274)

        No cause, no cause.
    (Lear IV.vii.74)

            Kneel not to me.
The pow'r that I have on you is to spare you;
The malice towards you, to forgive you. Live,
And deal with others better.
    (Cym V.v.417–20)

> For you, most wicked sir, whom to call brother
> Would even infect my mouth, I do forgive
> Thy rankest fault—all of them
> (Temp V.i.130–32)

Brief illustration of *Logos*, *Pathos*, and *Ethos*:

Logos: Methinks there is much reason in his sayings.

Pathos: Poor soul, his eyes are red as fire with weeping.

Ethos: There's not a nobler man in Rome than Antony.
(JC III.ii.108, 115, 116)

Glossary

Note: The numbers in **boldface** in the following glossary refer to the rhetorical figures listed in the Outline of Shakespeare's Rhetorical Figures with Examples. Included here, along with those rhetorical figures, are many of the terms for categories of figures used in the works of the grammarians and rhetoricians and identified by Sister Miriam Joseph in *Shakespeare's Use of the Arts of Language*. They are given in italics to distinguish them from the rhetorical figures themselves. The pronunciation guide (in parentheses) indicates only major stresses and some long vowels. Definitions quoted from *Shakespeare's Use of the Arts of Language* are indicated by Sister Miriam Joseph's initials (SMJ) and a page number. For other references see the List of Abbreviations.

Accent **176**—alteration of the true significance of a word by pronunciation, leading to a wrong conclusion—a material fallacy of ambiguity of language

Accident **177**—"the false assumption that something which belongs only to a substance may be attributed to an accident or adjunct of that substance, or contrariwise" (SMJ 194)—a material fallacy of hidden assumption

Acyrologia (a-ce-ro-LO-gi-a), or Acyron (A-cy-ron) **53**—"use of a word repugnant or contrary to what is meant" (SMJ 77)

Acyron—see Acyrologia **53**

Adage—see Proverb **74**

Adjunct—the property or attribute of a *Subject*, see under *Logos*: Topics of Invention: Artificial Arguments: Division (A): Subjects and Adjuncts

Aetiologia (ae-ti-o-LO-gi-a) **166**—"the most usual form of the enthymeme or abridged syllogism,…which states the conclusion first, supported by the major or the minor premise…a reason given for a sentence uttered" (SMJ 178)

Aischrologia—see Cacemphaton **43**

Allegory (AL-le-go-ry) **139**—"continu[ing] a metaphor through an entire speech" (SMJ 145)—"the rhetorical meaning is narrower than the literary one [which is a story told in symbols], though congruent with it" (RAL 3)

Alliteration (al-lit-ter-A-tion), also Paroemion (pa-ROEM-i-on) or Paromoeion **54**—repetition of initial sounds of words (SMJ 78–79)

Ambiguity—(A) of words (play on words and puns) (SMJ 164), see under *Logos*: Topics of Invention: Artificial Arguments: Division (A): Notation and Conjugates: Ambiguity; (B) of language (SMJ 191–94), see under *Logos*: Logical Argumentation: Syllogistic Reasoning: Fallacious Reasoning: Material Fallacy: Ambiguity of Language

Amphibologia (am-phi-bo-LO-gi-a), or Amphibology (am-phi-BOL-o-gy) **41**—"ambiguity of grammatical structure, often occasioned by mispunctuation" (SMJ 66)—a material fallacy of ambiguity of language, see under Grammar: Vices of Language and also under *Logos*: Logical Argumentation: Syllogistic Reasoning: Fallacious Reasoning: Material Fallacy: Ambiguity of Language

Amphibology—see Amphibologia **41**

Anacoenosis (a-na-se-NO-sis) **193**—asking counsel of one's hearers (SMJ 215)—a figure of *Disputation*

Anacoluthon (a-na-co-LU-thon) **215**—"ending a sentence with a different structure from that with which it began" (RAL 7, not in SMJ), see Aposiopesis **214**

Anadiplosis (a-na-di-PLO-sis) **64**—"repetition of the last word of one clause or sentence at the beginning of the next" (SMJ 82), see also Climax **65**

Anamnesis (a-nam-NĒ-sis) **222**—"recital of matters past, most often of woes or injuries" (SMJ 247–48)—a figure of *Pathos*

Anangeon—see Dicaeologia **207**

Anaphora (a-NAPH-or-a) **59**—"beginning a series of clauses with the same word" (SMJ 79)

Anapodoton (a-na-PO-do-ton) **216**—"omitting a main clause from a conditional sentence" (RAL 8, not in SMJ), see Aposiopesis **214**

Anastrophe (a-NAS-tro-phē) **14**—unusual word order, a species of Hyperbaton **13** (SMJ 54)

Antanaclasis (an-tan-AC-la-sis) **159**—"repeating a word [with a shift] from one of its meanings to another" (SMJ 165) (with or without a different spelling), "homonymic pun" (RAL 9)

Antanagoge (an-ta-na-GO-ge) **125**—"balancing...an unfavorable aspect with a favorable one"; hypothetically, "the reverse process, stating the unfavorable aspect last" (SMJ 138)

Antecedent—that which leads to a consequent temporally rather than productively (see *Cause*). The hypothetical (or conditional) proposition states the relation of antecedent and consequent—if A...then B—and the relation between antecedent and consequent may be either necessary (yielding knowledge) or contingent (yielding opinion) (SMJ 159–60, 336 substantially), see *Hypothetical Proposition*

Anthimeria (an-thi-MER-i-a) **36**—"substitution of one part of speech for another" (SMJ 62)

Anthypophora (an-thy-PO-pho-ra) **192**—"reasoning with self, asking questions and answering them oneself" (SMJ 214)—a figure of *Disputation*

Antimetabole (an-ti-me-TAB-o-lē), also Chiasmus (chi-AS-mus) **63**—repeating the words of a phrase in reverse order to produce a contrasting sense, the A-B-B-A or mirror image structure of a phrase or clause in sound or in meaning: Technically, Antimetabole is the "repetition of the same words in transposed order" and Chiasmus is the inversion of the syntactical order of words in parallel phrases or clauses (WNID), but the two are "virtual synonyms" (RAL10), cf., Epanalepsis **62**

Antiphrasis (an-TIPH-ra-sis) **128**—"broad flout...irony of one word" (SMJ 139), see *Irony*

Antirrhesis (an-tir-RHE-sis) **201**—rejection of "an opponent's argument or opinion because of its error or wickedness" (SMJ 219)—a figure of *Disputation*

Antisagoge (an-tis-a-GO-ge) **157**—joining a promise of reward to a precept and a promise of punishment to its violation (SMJ 160)

Antistasis— see Equivocation **172**

Antisthecon (an-TIS-the-con) **11**—exchange of one sound for another in a word, "as *wrang* for *wrong*, usually for the sake of rhyme" (SMJ 53)

Antistrephon (an-TIS-tre-phon) **184**—an argument that "turns that which serves the opponent's purpose to one's own" (SMJ 199)—a *Captious Argument*

Antistrophe—see Epistrophe **60**; see also Ploce **68**

Antithesis (an-TITH-e-sis) **123**—"setting contraries in opposition" (SMJ 137), "especially emphasized by the position of the contrasting words" (WNID)

Antonomasia (an-ton-o-MĀ-si-a) **105**—(A) substituting "a descriptive phrase for a proper name"; (B) substituting "a proper name for a quality associated with it" (SMJ 125)

Aphaeresis (a-FER-e-sis) **4**—subtracting a syllable from the beginning of a word, "as *round* for *around* and *coon* for *raccoon*" (MWCD)

Aphorismus (A) (a-phor-IS-mus)—see Proverb **74**

Aphorismus (B) **202**—reprehending "by raising a question about the proper application of a word" (SMJ 220)—a figure of *Disputation*

Aphorism—see Proverb **74**

Apocarteresis (a-po-car-tar-E-sis) **224**—"the casting away of all hope in one direction and turning to another for aid" (SMJ 249)—a figure of *Pathos*

Apocope (a-POC-o-pē) **7**—subtraction of the last syllable of a word, "as *bet* for *better*" (SMJ 53)

Apodioxis (a-po-di-OX-is) **199**—rejection of the argument of an opponent (SMJ 218), with indignation at its impertinence or absurdity (RAL 13)—a figure of *Disputation*

Apodixis (a-po-DIX-is) **72**—argument based on the experience of many

Apologue—see Fable **135**

Apomnemonysis (a-po-[m]ne-mo-NĒ-sis) **76**—quoting "for authority the testimony of approved authors" (SMJ 104)

Apophasis (a-POPH-a-sis), also Expeditio (ex-pe-DI-ti-o) **169**—rejection of all alternatives except one (SMJ 187–88), akin to the *Disjunctive Syllogism*

Apoplanesis (a-po-pla-NE-sis) **205**—evading "the issue by digressing to another matter" (SMJ 221)—a figure of *Disputation*

Aporia (a-por-I-a) **191**—"doubting or deliberating with oneself" (SMJ 214), real or feigned (RAL 15)—a figure of *Disputation*

Aposiopesis (ap-o-si-o-PĒ-sis) **214**—the "sudden breaking off of a speech" (SMJ 245)—a figure of *Pathos*: Related to this figure are Anacoluthon **215**, Anapodoton **216**, and the neologism Paraprosdokian **217**, none of which appears in SMJ

Apostrophe (a-POS-tro-phē) **221**—"a turning of speech from the persons previously addressed to another, sometimes to a thing or an abstraction personified" (SMJ 246)—a figure of *Pathos*

Apothegm (A-po-the[g]m)—see Proverb **74**

Appositio—see Epergesis **19**

Ara (A-ra) **239**—"cursing" (SMJ 259)—a figure of *Pathos*

Artificial Argument—an argument "derived from a subject by the art of topical investigation," that is by the artifice of the speaker or writer, as opposed to *Inartificial Argument*, the testimony of another independent of artifice in the speaker or writer, see under *Logos*: Topics of Invention: Artificial Argument, cf., *Topics* and *Invention*

Aschrologia—see Cacemphaton **43**

Asphalia (as-pha-LI-a) **82**—the offer of surety for another (SMJ 105)

Assistaton (as-SIS-ta-ton ?) **187**—"a kind of caviling, as to remark of one who has just said he holds his peace, 'He that holds his peace speaks'" (SMJ 201)—a *Captious Argument*

Assonance **55**—repetition of internal vowel sounds (not included in SMJ)

Asteismus (a-ste-IS-mus) **161**—"a figure of reply in which the answerer catches a certain word and throws it back to the first speaker with an unexpected twist, an unlooked for meaning" (SMJ 167); "a facetious or mocking answer that plays on a word" (RAL 18)

Asyndeton (a-SYN-de-ton) **26**—"omitting conjunctions between clauses" (SMJ 59)

Auxesis (aus-ES-is) **141**—"advanc[ing] from lesser to greater by arranging words or clauses in a sequence of increasing force" (SMJ 149), cf., Meiosis **143**

Barbarismus (bar-bar-IS-mus) **38**—mispronunciation of words, especially by a foreign speaker (SMJ 65)

Bdelygma—see Bdelygmia **237**

Bdelygmia (bdel-YG-mi-a), or Bdelygma (bdel-YG-ma) **237**—expressing "hate or abhorrence, usually in a few words" (SMJ 258)—a figure of *Pathos*

Begging the Question **182**—using the conclusion to be proved as one of the premises in the proof, circular reasoning—a *Material Fallacy* of hidden assumption: N.B., it does *not* mean calling for a certain question to be asked, a common but erroneous usage at present, see also Utis (B) **190**

Bomphiologia (bom-phi-o-LO-gi-a) **51**—"bombastic speech" (SMJ 70), speech exhibiting braggadocio

Brachylogia (brach-y-LO-gi-a) **25**—"omission of conjunctions between words" (SMJ 59)

Cacemphaton (cac-EM-pha-ton), or Aischrologia (ais-chro-LO-gi-a) (also spelled Aschrologia) **43**—(A) foul, scurrilous, or lewd speech, or (B) "an unpleasing combination of sounds such as results from excessive alliteration" (SMJ 68)

Cacosistaton (cac-o-SIS-ta-ton) **185**—"an argument [that] serves as well for the one side as for the other" (SMJ 200)—a *Captious Argument*

Cacosyntheton (cac-o-SYN-the-ton) **44**—awkward or misleading placement of words, "as when an adjective improperly follows a noun or when there is any other unpleasing order of words" (SMJ 68)

Cacozelia (ca-co-ZĒ-li-a) **52**—(A) "Affected diction, especially the coining of fine words out of Latin" (SMJ 72); (B) "ignorant misapplication of words...malapropism" (SMJ 75), including mistaking a word in one language for a word in another

Captious Arguments—seven forms of *Material Fallacy*, including Antistrephon **184**, Cacosistaton **185**, Pseudomenos **186**, Assistaton **187**, Ceratin **188**, Crocodilites **189**, and Utis **190**—see under *Logos*: Logical Argumentation: Syllogistic Reasoning: Fallacious Reasoning: Material Fallacy

Catachresis (cat-a-CHRĒ-sis) **140**—"an implied metaphor...the wrenching of a word, most often a verb or an adjective, from its proper application to another not proper" (SMJ 146)

Catacosmesis (ca-ta-cos-ME-sis) **146**—"order[ing] words from greatest to least in dignity" (SMJ 152)

Cataplexis (cat-a-PLEX-is) **238**—threatening plagues or punishments (SMJ 258)—a figure of *Pathos*

Categoria (cat-e-go-RI-a) **235**—laying "open the secret wickedness of another before his face" (SMJ 257)—a figure of *Pathos*

Cause—whatever contributes in any way to produce an effect. Logicians distinguish four causes: The Efficient Cause is constituted of the agent and his instruments, as a carpenter and his axe, hammer, and saw. The Material Cause is that out of which a thing is made, as wood and stone in a house. The Formal Cause is that which makes a thing to be what it is and thereby different from something else. A thing's form may be either internal (not perceivable by the senses) or external (perceivable by the senses) and either natural (occurring naturally without artifice) or artificial (made or performed by human art). The form is at the root of both identity and change—universal alteration of the form changes the thing to another thing (as a house pulled down and rebuilt from the same materials is a different house); particular alteration does not (as a house on which repairs are made remains the same house). The Final Cause is the end, purpose, or intent of the agent that leads him to produce the effect, as one causes a house to be built in order to live in it. It is the first in intention but the last in realization. Cause and effect are related productively, whereas antecedent and consequent are related temporally. (SMJ 333–36 substantially)

Ceratin (cer-A-tin) **188**—"the horned argument, [which] puts a matter in such terms that the propounder will win his point either way" (SMJ 201)—a *Captious Argument*

Characterismus (cha-rac-ter-IS-mus) **111**—"description of the body or mind" (SMJ 127), a species of Hypotyposis **108**

Charientismus (cha-ri-en-TIS-mus) **145**—"mollify[ing] threatening words by answering them with a smooth and appeasing mock" (SMJ 152)

Chiasmus—see Antimetabole **63**

Chria (CHRI-a) **78**—"a very short exposition of a deed or word, with the name of the author [or authority] recited" (SMJ 103)

Chronographia (chro-no-GRAPH-i-a) **116**—vivid reporting of events; in drama, events that occur off-stage (SMJ 129), a species of Hypotyposis **108**

Circumlocution—see Periergia **50**

Climax (CLI-max), also Gradation **65**—Anadiplosis **64** carried through three or more clauses (SMJ 83); a sorites involving "repetition of the last word of each sentence or clause at the beginning of the next, [marking] the degrees or steps in the argument" (SMJ 180), see under Grammar: Figures of Repetition and also under *Logos*: Logical Argumentation: Syllogistic Reasoning: Simple Syllogism: Sorites

Commoratio (com-mor-A-ti-o) **203**—insistent repetition of one's strongest point (SMJ 220), often joined to Epimone **204**—a figure of *Disputation*

Comparison—an argument based on the comparison of a subject to something greater, equal, or less (SMJ 147–55), see under *Logos*: Topics of Invention: Artificial Arguments: Division (A)

Compositio (com-po-SI-ti-o), or Composition **173**—attributing to a group what is applicable to individual members of the group (SMJ 193), joining of things that are to be severed (as asserting that five is both even and odd because it is made of two, which is even, and three, which is odd)—a *Material Fallacy* of ambiguity of language, the opposite of Division (B) **174**

Composition—see Compositio **173**

Compound Syllogism—a syllogism in one of three forms: *Hypothetical Syllogism, Disjunctive Syllogism*, and *Dilemma* (SMJ 185), see under *Logos*: Logical Argumentation: Syllogistic Reasoning: Valid Syllogistic Reasoning

Comprobatio (com-pro-BA-ti-o) **242**—commending "the good [the speaker] sees in the judges whose confidence he wishes to win" (SMJ 273)—a figure of *Ethos*

Concessio (con-CESS-i-o) **197**—granting a point that hurts the opponent to whom it is granted (SMJ 216)—a figure of *Disputation*

Conditional Proposition—see *Hypothetical Proposition*

Congeries—see Synathroesmus (B) **98**

Conjugates—"Words related to each other by derivation from the same root but differing in termination," as *just, justice, justly, justify*, etc. (SMJ 338), see under *Logos*: Topics of Invention: Artificial Arguments: Division (A): Notation and Conjugates, cf., *Notation*

Conjunction—"A conjunction of propositions is true only if all of its parts are true. It is false if any part is false," one of the three simple "arguable relations of propositions" (SMJ 174), the other two being contrariety and contradiction (which see under *Logos*: Topics of Invention: Artificial Arguments: Division (A): Contraries and Contradictories), see under *Logos*: Logical Argumentation

Consequent—follows upon an antecedent not causally (see *Cause*) but temporally and may be either necessary or contingent, see under *Logos*: Topics of Invention: Artificial Arguments: Division (A), cf., *Antecedent*

Consequent **180**—the fallacy of assuming "that a proposition is convertible simply when it is not," that is, that the subject and predicate may be reversed, as "All those at the court have good manners; therefore all who have good manners are at the court" (SMJ 197), or of assuming that the contrary of the antecedent must yield the contrary of the consequent, as "It is a man: *Ergo*, [i]t is a sensible body. It is no man: *Ergo*, it is no sensible body" (SMJ 371, quoting Thomas Blundeville, *Arte of Logick*, [1599], 1617)—a *Material Fallacy* of hidden assumption

Consonance **56**—repetition of internal consonant sounds (not included in SMJ)

Contradictories—contradictory propositions are such that if one is true the other must be false, and if one is false the other must be true; *white and not white* are contradictories (SMJ 130ff.), see under *Logos*: Topics of Invention: Artificial Arguments: Division (A), cf., *Contraries*

Contraries—opposites; contrary propositions cannot both be true, though they may both be false; *white and black* are contraries; "Shakespeare recognized the value of contraries as dramatic foils" (SMJ 130ff.), see under *Logos*: Topics of Invention: Artificial Arguments: Division (A), cf., *Contradictories*

Contrary Terms—terms that are "mutually repugnant" and therefore "serve to represent mental conflict and confusion" (SMJ 131), see under *Logos*: Topics of Invention: Artificial Arguments: Division (A): Contraries and Contradictories

Correctio (cor-REC-ti-o) **213**—advance warning of an unpleasant statement to come (RAL 28, not in SMJ)—a figure of *Pathos*

Crocodile's Argument—see Crocodilites **189**

Crocodilites (cro-co-DĬL-i-tēs? cro-co-DĬL-i-tēs? cro-co-dil-Ī-tēs?), also Crocodile's Argument, Crocodilite, Crocodility, Crocodillinae **189**—an argument that "harms the opponent either way" (SMJ 202), named for the "ancient illustration of the dilemma: A boy has been stolen by a crocodile, which promises to restore him if the boy's father [in some versions, mother] answers truly the crocodile's question 'Am I going to return this boy or not?' If he replies in the affirmative, the crocodile keeps the boy, and thus the father answers falsely; if in the negative, should the crocodile restore the boy the father will have answered falsely" (WNID)—a *Captious Argument*

Declamatio (de-cla-MA-ti-o)—see Periergia **50**

Deesis (de-Ē-sis), also Obtestatio (ob-tes-TA-ti-o) **226**—"vehement supplication" (SMJ 250)—a figure of *Pathos*

Definitio (de-fi-NI-ti-o), or Definition **86**—as defined by the logicians, the explanation of "the nature or essence of a subject in terms of its genus and difference" (SMJ 108), that is, the kind of thing it is and that which distinguishes it from others of its kind, in particular, its properties, see also Horismus **87** and Systrophe **88**

Definition—a species of *Artificial Argument*, see under *Logos*: Topics of Invention: Artificial Arguments

Definition—see Definitio **86**

Dehortatio (de-hor-TA-ti-o) **210**—dissuasion, which combines many figures to achieve its effect (SMJ 223)—a figure of *Disputation*

Diacope (di-A-co-pe) **69**—repetition of a word or short phrase with one or more other words between them, usually exclamatory (SMJ 88, 307), cf., Ploce (B) **68**

Diaeresis (di-AER-e-sis) **89**—"logical division of a genus into its species" (SMJ 111)

Dialectic—logical disputation, with the "capacity to generate arguments on both sides of a question" (SMJ 19), see *Logos*

Dialogismus (di-a-lo-JIS-mus) **114**—"the framing of speech suitable to the person speaking" (SMJ 128), a species of Hypotyposis **108**

Dialysis (di-AL-y-sis), or Dilemma (di-LEM-ma) **171**—"an abridged form [of Dilemma] with only the major premise stated and the rest implied" (SMJ 188)—see *Dilemma*

Diaphora (di-APH-or-a) **67**—"repetition of a common name so as to perform two logical functions: to designate an individual and to signify the qualities connoted by the common name" (SMJ 84)

Diastole (di-AS-to-lē), also Eciasis (ec-EYE-a-sis) **8**—lengthening (in English, altering the stress) of a syllable (SMJ 53)

Diasyrmus (di-a-SYR-mus) **200**—using a base similitude to disparage an opponent's argument or make it appear ridiculous (SMJ 218), (RAL 35)—a figure of *Disputation*

Diatyposis (di-a-typ-O-sis) **75**—"commending profitable rules and precepts to another" (SMJ 101), sometimes ironically

Diazeugma (di-a-ZEUG-ma) **24**—using one subject with many verbs (SMJ 59)

Dicaeologia (di-sē-o-LO-gi-a), or Anangeon (a-NAN-jun?, or a-nan-JĒ-on?) **207**—excusing one's word or action by pleading necessity (SMJ 221)—a figure of *Disputation*

Dilemma—a compound syllogism "having for its major premise a compound hypothetical proposition and for its minor premise a disjunctive proposition" (SMJ 188), "the most complex form of reasoning," see under *Logos*: Logical Argumentation: Syllogistic Reasoning: Valid Syllogistic Reasoning: Compound Syllogism, cf., *Compound Syllogism*

Dilemma—see Dialysis **171**

Dirimens Copulatio (DI-ri-mens cop-u-LA-ti-o) **148**—adding a point "to balance or outweigh what has already been said" (SMJ 153)

Disjunctive Proposition **100**—expressing "alternatives that divide the possibilities contemplated" (SMJ 118)

Disjunctive Syllogism—a compound syllogism that "has for its major premise a disjunctive [either/or] proposition, expressing alternatives, one of which the minor premise affirms or denies, while the conclusion in consequence affirms or denies the other" (SMJ 186), see under *Logos*: Logical Argumentation: Syllogistic Reasoning: Valid Syllogistic Reasoning: Compound Syllogism, cf., *Compound Syllogism*

Disputation—syllogistic reasoning exercised in "building up both sides of an argument," whether with oneself or with an opponent, using either valid syllogistic reasoning, fallacious reasoning, or both (SMJ 176, 203), see under *Logos*: Logical Argumentation: Syllogistic Reasoning

Dissimilarity—see *Similarity*

Distinctio (dis-TINC-ti-o), Distinction **162**—removing the ambiguity of words

Distinction—see Distinctio **162**

Division (A), or Divisio (di-VI-si-o)—an argument based on logical division of a subject into Genus and Species, Whole and Parts, Subject and Adjuncts, Cause and Effects, Antecedent and Consequents, Contraries and Contradictories, Similarity and Dissimilarity, Comparison (Greater, Equal, and Less), and Notation and Conjugates—see under *Logos*: Topics of Invention: Artificial Arguments

Division (B), or Divisio (di-VI-si-o) **174**—severing things that are to be joined, the reverse of Compositio, or Composition, **173** ("No instance of Shakespeare's use of [this figure] has been observed by the present writer" SMJ 194)—a material fallacy of ambiguity of language, see under *Logos*: Logical Argumentation: Syllogistic Reasoning: Fallacious Reasoning: Material Fallacy: Ambiguity of Language

Eciasis—see Diastole **8**

Eclipsis (e-CLIP-sis), or Ellipsis (e-LIP-sis) **20**—"omission of a word easily understood" (SMJ 58)

Ecphonesis (ec-pho-NĒ-sis) **218**—"exclamation, the most widely used figure of vehemence and one expressing every species of emotion" (SMJ 245)—a figure of *Pathos*

Effect—"that which is produced by the operation of all the causes" (SMJ 335), see *Cause*

Efficient Cause—see *Cause*

Elench—see Ignoratio Elenchi **179**

Ellipsis—see Eclipsis **20**

Emphasis (EM-pha-sis) **149**—giving "prominence to a quality or trait by conceiving it as constituting the very substance in which it inheres" (SMJ 153), in other words, treating a particular person (or thing) as identical with the universal abstraction of a quality to stress his (or its) exhibition of that quality

Enallage (en-AL-a-gē [MWCD], EN-al-lage [RAL]) **32**—"the deliberate use of one case, person, gender, number, tense, or mood for another" (SMJ 61), cf., Solecismus **37**

Enargia—see Hypotyposis **108**

Encomium (en-CO-mi-um) **102** "high praise and commendation of a person or thing by extolling the inherent qualities or adjuncts" (SMJ 123)

Enigma (e-NIG-ma) **163**—riddle, "the meaning of which is to be discovered or guessed" and which "hides its meaning under obscure or ambiguous allusions" (WNID) (SMJ 171)

Enthymeme—"an abridged syllogism" in which "only two of the three propositions...are expressed, while one is merely implicit" (SMJ 177), see under *Logos*: Logical Argumentation: Syllogistic Reasoning: Valid Syllogistic Reasoning: Simple Syllogism

Enumeratio (e-num-er-A-ti-o) **93**—division "of a subject into its adjuncts, a cause into its effects, an antecedent into its consequents" (SMJ 114)

Epanalepsis (ep-an-a-LEP-sis) **62**—"repetition at the end of a clause or sentence of the word with which it begins" (SMJ 80), cf., Antimetabole **63**

Epanodos (ep-A-no-dos) **97**—like Prolepsis **96**, but "repeating the terms of the general proposition in the amplification which particularizes it" (SMJ 116), see also Ploce **68**

Epanorthosis (e-pan-or-THO-sis) **147**—"correction, amend[ing] a first thought by altering it to make it stronger or more vehement" (SMJ 153)

Epenthesis (e-PEN-the-sis) **2**—"addition of a syllable or letter in the middle of a word" (SMJ 51)

Epergesis (ep-ER-ge-sis), also Appositio (a-po-SIT-i-o) **19**—"interrupts by interposing a word in apposition as an added interpretation" (SMJ 295), i.e., use of appositives or appositive phrases, sometimes including Metaphors **138** (SMJ 57), a species of Hyperbaton **13**

Epicrisis (e-PIC-ri-sis) **77**—adding the speaker's own opinion to a cited authority, agreeing, disagreeing, or making exceptions (SMJ 103)

Epilogus (e-pi-LO-gus) **168**—"Inferring what will follow from what has been spoken or done before" (RAL 43) (SMJ 185, 362)

Epimone (e-PI-mo-nē) **204**—repetition of the same point in the same words, somewhat in the manner of a refrain (SMJ 220), often joined to Commoratio **203**—a figure of *Disputation*

Epiphonema (ep-i-pho-NĒ-ma) **99**—"an epigrammatic summary, gather[ing] into a pithy, sententious utterance what has preceded" (SMJ 117)

Epiplexis (ep-i-PLEX-is), also Percontatio (per-con-TA-ti-o) **233**—asking questions in order to chide or reprehend (SMJ 256)—a figure of *Pathos*

Epistrophe (e-PIS-tro-phē), also Antistrophe (an-TIS-tro-phe) **60**—ending a series of clauses with the same word (SMJ 79–80)

Epitheton (e-PITH-e-ton) **104**—attributing a quality to a person or thing by addition of a modifying adjective (SMJ 124) (RAL 45)

Epitrope (e-PI-tro-pe) **130**—"ironical permission" (SMJ 139), see *Irony*

Epizeuxis (ep-i-ZEUX-is) **70**—repetition of a word or short phrase with no other words between them (SMJ 86)

Equivocation (e-qui-vo-CA-tion), also Antistasis (an-TI-sta-sis) **172**—use of the middle term in two different senses, involving the figures of Ambiguity (SMJ 191), especially Antanaclasis **159**, see under *Logos*: Logical Argumentation: Syllogistic Reasoning: Fallacious Reasoning: Material Fallacy—a *Material Fallacy* of ambiguity of language

Erotema (er-o-TĒ-ma), or Erotesis (er-o-TĒ-sis), or Interrogatio (in-ter-ro-GAT-i-o) **220**—"rhetorical question" (SMJ 246)—a figure of *Pathos*

Erotesis—see Erotema **220**

Ethopoeia (eth-o-PĒ-a) **112**—"description of natural propensities, manners and affections" (SMJ 127), a species of Hypotyposis **108**

Ethos—"the persuasion exerted upon the minds and hearts of the audience by the personal character of the speaker, causing them to believe in his sincerity, his truth, his ability, his good will toward them" (SMJ 272), one of the four major categories, along with Grammar, *Logos*, and *Pathos*, under which the figures of speech fall in the arrangement of Sister Miriam Joseph

Etymology (e-ty-MŎ-lo-gy) **158**—use of a word's etymology or derivation to illuminate meaning (SMJ 162)

Eucharistia (eu-char-IS-ti-a) **244**—giving thanks for benefits received (SMJ 274)—a figure of *Ethos*

Euche (EU-chē) **80**—a vow to keep a promise (SMJ 104)

Eulogia (eu-LO-gi-a) **240**—pronouncing a blessing (SMJ 261)—a figure of *Pathos*

Euphemismus (eu-phe-MIS-mus) **83**—prognostication of good (SMJ 106)

Eustathia (eu-stath-I-a) **81**—a pledge of constancy (SMJ 105)

Eutrepismus (eu-tre-PIS-mus) **92**—numbering and ordering parts of a whole (SMJ 113)

Exemplum—see Paradigma **134**

Exergasia (ex-er-GA-si-a), or Expolitio (ex-po-LI-ti-o) **151**—repeating the same thought in many figures (SMJ 154)

Expeditio—see Apophasis **169**

Expolitio—see Exergasia **151**

Exuscitatio (ex-us-ci-TA-ti-o, or ex-u-sci-TA-ti-o) **212**—showing deep emotion by which hearers are stirred to the like feeling (SMJ 244)—a figure of *Pathos*

Fable, also Apologue (AP-o-logue) **135**—"a short allegorical story that points a lesson or moral; the characters are frequently animals" (RAL 50) (SMJ 144), a species of Homoeosis **131**

Fallacies of Ambiguity of Language—six forms of *Material Fallacy*: Equivocation **172**, Amphibologia **41**, Compositio **173**, Division (B) **174**, Form of Speech **175**, and Accent **176** (SMJ 191), see under *Logos*: Logical Argumentation: Syllogistic Reasoning: Fallacious Reasoning: Material Fallacy

Fallacies of Hidden Assumption—seven forms of *Material Fallacy*: Accident **177**, Secundum Quid **178**, Ignoratio Elenchi **179**, Consequent **180**, False Cause **181**, Begging the Question **182**, and Many Questions **183** (SMJ 191), see under *Logos*: Logical Argumentation: Syllogistic Reasoning; Fallacious Reasoning: Material Fallacy

Fallacious Reasoning—"Fallacious reasoning, which has only the appearance of validity, may draw false conclusions even from true premises" (SMJ 176); "The sophist employs the outward forms of logic to hide the fallacy in his specious reasoning" (SMJ 190), see under *Logos*: Logical Argumentation: Syllogistic Reasoning

Fallacy—specious argument hidden in the outward forms of logic (SMJ 190)—see *Fallacious Reasoning, Formal Fallacy, Material Fallacy*

False Cause **181**—"putting for a cause that which is not a cause" (SMJ 198)—a *Material Fallacy* of hidden assumption

Feminine Rhyme **58** (B)—rhyming on the final stressed and following unstressed syllable (not in SMJ), see Rhyme **58**

Figures of Repetition—see under Grammar

Final Cause—see *Cause*

Form of Speech **175**—ambiguity in a verb phrase (SMJ 194)—a *Material Fallacy* of ambiguity of language

Formal Cause—see *Cause*

Formal Fallacy—"Formal fallacies are those which violate the rules of the syllogism and therefore yield no valid conclusion, even when the premises are true. The most common formal fallacy is that which ignores the necessity of using the middle term in its full extension in at least one of the premises" (SMJ 191)

Genus—in arguments of *Definition, genus* indicates the class of thing that a subject is, and *difference* indicates what distinguishes a subject from other members of its genus (SMJ 108), see under *Logos*: Topics of Invention: Artificial Arguments: Definition; in arguments of *Division* (A), a more comprehensive class of thing comprising the less comprehensive classes called *Species* (SMJ 111), see under *Logos*: Topics of Invention: Artificial Arguments: Division (A)

Gnome ([G]NOME or [G]NŌ-me)—see Proverb **74**

Gradation—see Climax **65**

Graecismus (gre-CIS-mus) **35**—use of a Greek idiom, usually by the confusion of two English constructions (SMJ 62)

Grammar—one of the four major categories, along with *Logos, Pathos,* and *Ethos,* under which the figures of speech fall in the arrangement of Sister Miriam Joseph; specifically, the category that includes stylistic modifications in the forms of words and the structure of sentences, including Schemes of Grammar (Schemes of Words and Schemes of Construction), Vices of Language, and Figures of Repetition

Heirmos—see Hirmus **30**

Hendiadys (hen-DĪ-a-dis) **33**—use of two nouns joined by "and" in place of a noun with its modifier (sometimes two coordinate adjectives joined by "and" in place of two cumulative adjectives) (SMJ 61)

"Hendiadys in Reverse" **34**—modifying a noun with a figurative adjective ("Here Shakespeare's creative art...outruns the precepts of the figurists, who...did not describe a turn of words like this.") (SMJ 62)

Heterogenium (het-er-o-GEN-i-um) **40**—"answering something utterly irrelevant to what is asked" (SMJ 66)

Hirmus (HIR-mus) **30** (also spelled Heirmos, Hyrmos, Irmus)—use of a periodic or suspended sentence (SMJ 60)

Homiologia (ho-mi-o-LO-gi-a) **49**—"tedious and inane repetition" (SMJ 69)

Homoeosis (hom-oe-O-sis) **131**—"the general figure of similitude" (SMJ 143), see also its species, Icon **132**, Parabola (also Parable) **133**, Paradigma (also Exemplum) **134**, and Fable (also Apologue) **135**

Homoioptoton—use of like case endings, see Homoioteleuton **29**

Homoioteleuton (hom-oi-o-te-LEU-ton) **29**—the use of like endings of words (SMJ 60), in English not distinguished from Homoioptoton (hom-oi-op-TO-ton), the use of like case endings

Horismus (ho-RIS-mus) **87**—the rhetoricians' imaginative form of Definitio **86** (the stricter and more precise form of the logicians) (SMJ 108)

Hypallage (hy-PAL-a-gē) **17**—exchange or application of words (A) in a perverted, absurd, or awkward way or (B) in a transferred epithet (SMJ 55–56), a species of Hyperbaton **13**

Hyperbaton (hy-PER-ba-ton) **13**—the general term for the alteration of normal word order (SMJ 54)

Hyperbole (hy-PER-bo-lē) **142**—amplification by exaggeration (SMJ 150), cf., Meiosis **143**

Hypothetical Proposition, also *Conditional Proposition*—An "if A...then B" statement. It may be either necessary (the two parts are connected by necessity—this yields knowledge) or contingent (the two parts are connected only by probability, or dubiously—this yields opinion) (SMJ 159–60, 336), see *Antecedent*

Hypothetical Proposition **156**—An "if A...then B" statement (SMJ 185), see *Hypothetical Proposition*

Hypothetical Syllogism—a compound syllogism "that has for its major premise a hypothetical proposition" (SMJ 185), see under *Logos*: Logical Argumentation: Syllogistic Reasoning: Valid Syllogistic Reasoning: Compound Syllogism, see *Compound Syllogism*

Hypotyposis (hy-po-ty-PO-sis), or Enargia (en-ar-GI-a) **108**—"the generic name given to figures of lively description or counterfeit representation," of which "the Elizabethans recognized many species, each with its own name signifying that it was a description of persons, manners, gestures, speech, events, places, or times, either real or imaginary" (SMJ 126), see figures **109**–**118**

Hypozeugma—see Zeugma **21**

Hypozeuxis (hy-po-ZEUX-is) **23**—(A) giving every clause in a series its own subject and verb (SMJ 58); (B) iteration (Puttenham, per SMJ 58)

Hyrmos—see Hirmus **30**

Hysteron Proteron (HYS-ter-on PRO-ter-on) **16**—putting first that which occurs later (SMJ 55), a species of Hyperbaton **13**

Icon (I-con) **132**—painting "the likeness of a person by imagery" (SMJ 143), "comparison of one person or thing with another, form with form, quality with quality" (SMJ 327), a species of Homoeosis **131**

Ignoratio Elenchi (ig-no-RA-ti-o e-LEN-chi) **179**—literally, ignorance of the nature of refutation: an unnoticed change in the argument (SMJ 197), specifically, "falsely assuming that the point at issue has been disproved when one merely resembling it has been disproved" (Triv 202)—a *Material Fallacy* of hidden assumption

Inartificial Argument—an argument offered from testimony as received, "either from men or from supernatural powers," both kinds of testimony having "the character of witnesses and the force of argument" and hence independent of artifice in the speaker or writer (SMJ 92), see under *Logos*: Topics of Invention, cf., *Artificial Argument, Invention, Topics*

Internal Rhyme **58** (D)—rhyming words in the middle of a line (not in SMJ), see Rhyme **58**

Interrogatio—see Erotema **220**

Inter Se Pugnantia (IN-ter SE pug-NAN-ti-a) **126**—pointing out hypocrisy or "discrepancy between theory and practice" (SMJ 138)

Invention—the general term for coming up with or figuring out what to say about the subject of a composition, how to develop or amplify the idea, from the Latin *invenire* (to come upon or discover, as distinct from the modern sense of original fabrication, which may or may not be involved in the process), the method being to draw the subject of a composition through a variety of established Topics or Places (SMJ 22, 92), see under *Logos*: Topics of Invention, cf., *Topics*

Irmus—see Hirmus **30**

Irony—the general category containing the specific figures Irony **127**, Antiphrasis **128**, Paralipsis **129**, and Epitrope **130** (SMJ 138), see under *Logos*: Topics of Invention: Artificial Arguments: Division (A): Contraries and Contradictories

Irony **127**—"naming one contrary [while intending] another, used in derision, mockery, jesting, dissembling" (SMJ 325); "perceived either by the contrariety of the matter or the manner of utterance, or both" (SMJ 325 quoting Dudley Fenner, *Artes of Logike and Rhetorike*, 1584), see *Irony*

Isocolon (i-so-COL-on), also Parison (PAR-i-son) **28**—using "phrases or clauses...of equal length and usually of corresponding structure" (SMJ 59)

Litotes (LI-to-tēs, li-TO-tēs) **119**—denying the contrary or contradictory of the predicate of a subject instead of affirming it (SMJ 135)

Locus, plural *Loci*—the Latin form of the Greek *topos*, *tupoi*—see *Topics*

Logical Argumentation—the second of the two divisions of *Logos*, the first being Topics of Invention (see *Topics*); Logical Argumentation is subdivided into Conjunction and Syllogistic Reasoning

Logos—the Greek word for reason or logic, one of the four major categories, along with Grammar, *Pathos*, and *Ethos*, under which the figures of speech fall in the arrangement of Sister Miriam Joseph; the category is subdivided into Topics of Invention (see *Topics*) and Logical Argumentation (see *Logical Argumentation*), cf., *Dialectic*

Macrologia—see Perissologia **46**

Malapropism—see Cacozelia **52** (B) and Acyrologia **53**

Many Questions **183**—"demanding a simple answer to a complex question" (SMJ 199)—a *Material Fallacy* of hidden assumption

Martyria (mar-TYR-i-a) **73**—argument based on one's own experience (SMJ 97)

Masculine Rhyme **58** (A)—rhyming on the final stressed syllable (not in SMJ), see Rhyme **58**

Material Cause—see *Cause*

Material Fallacy—"Material fallacies are those which have their root in the matter, that is, in the terms of a syllogism which appears to be formally correct. Logicians distinguish thirteen material fallacies, six occasioned by the ambiguity of language and seven by a false assumption hidden in the thought" (SMJ 191); in addition, Captious Arguments form seven more material fallacies, six of which may be illustrated by Shakespeare (SMJ 199), see under *Logos*: Logical Argumentation: Syllogistic Reasoning: Fallacious Rasoning, see *Fallacies of Ambiguity of Language*, *Fallacies of Hidden Assumption*, and *Captious Arguments*

Maxim—see Proverb **74**

Medela (me-DEL-a) **229**—seeking "to palliate by conciliatory words the offenses of a friend when they can [be neither] defended nor denied" (SMJ 253)—a figure of *Pathos*

Meiosis (mei-O-sis) **143**—belittling, opposite of Hyperbole **142**, including by reversing climactic order, opposite of Auxesis **141** (SMJ 151)

Mempsis (MEMP-sis) **227**—"a complaint against injuries and a craving for redress" (SMJ 251)—a figure of *Pathos*

Merismus (me-RIS-mus), also Partitio (par-TIT-i-o) or Partition **91**—dividing a whole into its parts (SMJ 112)

Mesozeugma—see Zeugma **21**

Metabasis (me-TAB-a-sis) **31**—"telling what has been said and what is to follow" (SMJ 60)

Metalepsis (me-ta-LEP-sis) **155**—attributing "a present effect to a remote cause" (SMJ 158)

Metaphor (MĚ-ta-phor) **138**—implicit comparison of one thing to another, using "a word or phrase literally denoting one kind of object or idea...in place of another to suggest a likeness or analogy between them" (MWCD) (SMJ 144)

Metastasis (me-TAS-ta-sis) **198**—turning back an objection against the one who made it (SMJ 217)—a figure of *Disputation*

Metathesis (me-TATH-e-sis) **10**—transposition or exchange of letters in a word, as Peacham's *brust* for *burst* (SMJ 53)

Metonymy (A) (me-TON-y-my) **107A**—"the substitution of subject for adjunct, or adjunct for subject" (SMJ 126), see under *Logos*: Topics of Invention: Artificial Arguments: Division (A): Subjects and Adjuncts

Metonymy (B) **107B**—the substitution of cause for effect or effect for cause (SMJ 158), see under *Logos*: Topics of Invention: Artificial Arguments: Division (A): Cause and Effect, Antecedent and Consequent

Mimesis (mī-ME-sis) **113**—"imitation of gesture, pronunciation, utterance" (SMJ 127), a species of Hypotyposis **108**

Mingle-mangle—see Soraismus **39**

Mycterismus (myc-ter-IS-mus) **231**—"a scornful mock, sometimes accompanied by a facial gesture, as drawing the lip awry" (SMJ 254)—a figure of *Pathos*

Negative Terms—"contradictories of the corresponding positive terms" (SMJ 133), see under *Logos*: Topics of Invention: Artificial Arguments: Division (A): Contraries and Contradictories

Noema (no-Ē-ma) **164**—"obscure and subtle speech" (SMJ 171)

Notation—regarding a word as a word, "that is, as a mark representing a sound," in relation to realities and to other words (SMJ 162, 338); "it may shed light on the thing it names through its etymology [see Etymology **158**], or it may occasion ambiguity or obscurity" (SMJ 339), see under *Logos*: Topics of Invention: Artificial Arguments: Division (A): Notation and Conjugates, cf., *Conjugates*

Obtestatio—see Deesis **226**

Occupatio—see Paralipsis **129**

Ominatio (o-min-A-ti-o) **85**—prognostication of evil (SMJ 106)

Onedismus (o ne-DIS-mus) **234**—"upbraiding another for ingratitude or impiety" (SMJ 256) —a figure of *Pathos*

Onomatopoeia (on-o-mat-o-PĒ-a) **136**—use of words or phrases that reproduce or imitate the sounds of what they signify (SMJ 144)

Optatio (op-TA-ti-o) **225**—"ardent wish or prayer" (SMJ 249)—a figure of *Pathos*

Orcos **79**—"an oath affirming that one speaks the truth" (SMJ 103)

Oxymoron (ox-y-MOR-on) **122**—self-contradiction in a single phrase (not in SMJ), see Paradox **121**

Paeanismus (pae-an-IS-mus) **241**—expressing exuberance of joy (SMJ 261)—a figure of *Pathos*

Parable—see Parabola **133**

Parabola (par-A-bo-la), also Parable **133**—parable, teaching a moral by means of "moral or mystical resemblance" (SMJ 143) or "by means of an extended metaphor" (RAL 70), a species of Homoeosis **131**

Paradiastole (pa-ra-di-AS-to-lē) **144**—"extenuat[ing] in order to flatter or soothe" (SMJ 152)

Paradiegesis (pa-ra-di-e-GE-sis) **152**—introductory narrative to open a speech (SMJ 155)

Paradigma (par-a-DIG-ma), also Exemplum (ex-EM-plum) **134**—"argument from example, judging the present from the past" (SMJ 144), a species of Homoeosis **131**

Paradox **121**—(A) self-contradiction, including Oxymoron **122**, which is a self-contradiction in a single phrase (not in SMJ); (B) an opinion contrary to that of most men (SMJ 136)

Paraenesis (pa-REE-ne-sis) **84**—warning of impending evil (SMJ 106)

Paragoge—see Proparalepsis **3**

Paralepsis—see Paralipsis **129**

Paralipsis (par-a-LIP-sis), also Paralepsis (par-a-LEP-sis) and Occupatio (oc-cu-PA-ti-o) **129**—"while pretending to pass over a matter, [telling] it most effectively" (SMJ 139), see *Irony*

Paramythia (pa-ra-MYTH-i-a) **228**—"seeking to console or diminish sorrow" (SMJ 252)—a figure of *Pathos*

Paraprosdokian (par-a-pros-DŌ-kē-an) **217**—the surprise or unexpected ending of a phrase, series, or sentence, a neologism not appearing in SMJ or other classical texts, see Aposiopesis **214**

Parecbasis (par-EC-ba-sis) **153**—digression (SMJ 155, 333)

Parechesis (par-e-CHE-sis) **57**—repetition of the same sound in words close together, in effect combining Alliteration **54**, Assonance **55**, and Consonance **56** in various ways (RAL 71–72, not included in SMJ)

Parelcon (par-EL-con) **47**—"the addition of a superfluous word" (SMJ 69)

Parenthesis (par-EN-the-sis) **18**—"interrupts a sentence by interposing words" (SMJ 295), "a word, phrase, or sentence inserted as an aside in a sentence complete in itself" (RAL), a species of Hyperbaton **13** (SMJ 57)

Pareuresis (par-EURE-e-sis) **208**—using an excuse of such might as to vanquish all objections (SMJ 222)—a figure of *Disputation*

Parison—see Isocolon **28**

Paroemia—see Proverb **74**

Paroemion—see Alliteration **54**

Paromoeion—see Alliteration **54**

Paromologia (par-o-mo-LO-gi-a) **196**—conceding a point unfavorable to one's own position and then bringing in a point that overthrows what was granted (SMJ 216)—a figure of *Disputation*

Paronomasia (par-on-o-MAS-i-a) **160**—using a word that sounds similar to but not exactly like a preceding word, differing from Antanaclasis **159** "in that the words repeated are nearly but not precisely alike in sound" (SMJ 166)

Parrhesia (par-RĒZ-i-a) **243**—showing humble respect "or, if necessity demands, [being] courageously outspoken in addressing those whom [one] ought to reverence or fear on a matter that concerns them or those near to them" (SMJ 273)—a figure of *Ethos*

Partitio—see Merismus **91**

Partition—see Merismus **91**

Pathos—the "form of persuasion by which one endeavors to put the auditor into whatever frame of mind is favorable to one's purpose" (SMJ 242), "the temper of mind induced in the hearers by the speaker" (SMJ 243), one of the four major categories, along with Grammar, *Logos*, and *Ethos*, under which the figures of speech fall in the arrangement of Sister Miriam Joseph

Percontatio—see Epiplexis **233**

Periergia (per-i-ER-gi-a) **50**—"overlabor to seem fine and eloquent, especially in a slight matter" (SMJ 70), related to Declamatio (de-cla-MA-ti-o), "elaborately ornamental or rehearsed speech" (RAL 29), and Circumlocution, talking all around the subject, neither included in SMJ

Periphrasis (pe-RIPH-ra-sis) **106**—"use of a descriptive phrase for a common name, often to give an air of solemnity or elevation or to avoid a harsh word" (SMJ 125)

Perissologia (per-iss-o-LO-gi-a), also Macrologia (ma-cro-LO-gi-a) **46**—"the addition of a superfluous clause which adds nothing to the meaning" (SMJ 69)

Peristasis (per-IST-a-sis) **101**—amplifying "by detailing the circumstances affecting a person or a thing" (SMJ 121)

Philophronesis (PHI-lo-phron-Ē-sis) **230**—"seeking to mitigate by gentle speech and humble submission the anger of an adversary whose might is too great to be overcome" (SMJ 253)—a figure of *Pathos*

Pleonasmus (ple-on-AS-mus) **48**—"the needless telling of what is already understood" (SMJ 69)

Places—see *Topics*

Ploce (PLO-cē) **68**, sometimes also Epanodos (ep-A-no-dos) **97**, Traductio (tra-DUC-ti-o), and Antistrophe (an-TIS-tro-phē)—(A) repetition of a proper name to designate a person and to signify his qualities (Peacham and Day, SMJ 84); or (B) the "speedy iteration of one word with some little intermission" (Puttenham, SMJ 85), especially "Emphatic repetition of a word with pregnant reference to its special significance" (WNID)—cf., Diacope **69**

Polyptoton (po-lyp-TO-ton) **66**—repetition of conjugates, words having the same derivation but different terminations (SMJ 162), see under Grammar: Figures of Repetition and also under *Logos*: Topics of Invention: Artificial Arguments: Division (A): Notation and Conjugates

Polysyndeton (pol-y-SYN-de-ton) **27**—using a conjunction between every two phrases or clauses (SMJ 59)

Pragmatographia (prag-ma-to-GRAPH-i-a) **115**—"the vivid description of an action or event" (SMJ 128), a species of Hypotyposis **108**

Privative Terms—expressing "the absence or the loss of a characteristic that ought to be present" (SMJ 134), see under *Logos*: Topics of Invention: Artificial Arguments: Division (A): Contraries and Contradictories

Procatalepsis (pro-ca-tal-EP-sis) **195**—confuting the objection that one's opponent is likely to make even before he has uttered it (SMJ 215)—a figure of *Disputation*

Proclees (PRO-clees) **236**—"provok[ing or goading] an adversary to the conflict by a vehement accusation or by a confident offer of justification" (SMJ 257)—a figure of *Pathos*

Proecthesis (pro-EC-the-sis) **206**—giving as excuse a defense of what one has said or done and a reason why he ought not to be blamed (SMJ 221)—a figure of *Disputation*

Prolepsis (pro-LEP-sis) **96**—"a general statement amplified by dividing it into parts" (SMJ 116)

Proparalepsis (pro-par-a-LEP-sis) **3**, also Paragoge (PAR-a-gō-gē, par-a-GŌ-gē)—"addition of a syllable at the end of a word" (SMJ 51)

Propositio (pro-pos-I-ti-o) **94**—"a brief summary of what is to follow" (SMJ 115)

Prosapodosis (pro-sa-PO-do-sis) **170**—arguing in support of each of several alternatives (SMJ 188), akin to the *Disjunctive Syllogism*

Prosopographia (pro-so-po-GRAPH-i-a) **109**—"lively description of a person" (SMJ 126), a species of Hypotyposis **108**

Prosopopoeia (pro-so-po-PĒ-a) **110**—"attribution of human qualities to dumb or inanimate creatures" (SMJ 126), a species of Hypotyposis **108**

Prosthesis (PROS-the-sis) **1**—"addition of a syllable at the beginning of a word" (SMJ 51)

Protozeugma—see Zeugma **21**

Protrope (PRO-tro-pē) **211**—persuasion "by joining promises, threats, and commands with mighty reasons to move the mind to the course desired" (SMJ 223)—a figure of *Disputation*

Proverb **74**, also Adage or Paroemia (pa-ROEM-i-a), Maxim, Apothegm (A-po-the[g]m), Sententia (sen-TEN-ti-a) or Sentence, Aphorismus (a-phor-IS-mus) (A) or Aphorism, and Gnome ([G]NOME or [G]NŌ-me)—The first two "represent the testimony of many men," the last five "the wisdom of one" (SMJ 98), "yet since the people sometimes seize upon and popularize the wise sayings of one man, a sharp line cannot be drawn between these two types of generalization" (SMJ 98); "The most difficult thing for the modern reader to remember is that the proverb...has been for most of formal rhetoric's history a means of *proof* rather than a substantiating ornament" (RAL 84); see under *Logos*: Topics of Invention: Inartificial Arguments: Testimony of Men

Prozeugma—see Zeugma **21**

Pseudomenos (pseu-DO-men-os) **186**—putting "another into such a position that whatever he says must needs be said amiss...as to ask whether a Cretan should be believed when he says, 'All Cretans are liars'" (SMJ 201)

Pysma (PYS-ma) **209**—asking "many questions requiring diverse answers, in order to gain attention, to provoke, to confirm, or to confute" (SMJ 222)—a figure of *Disputation*

Reditus ad Propositum (RED-i-tus ad pro-POS-i-tum) **154**—return from digression (SMJ 155, 333)

Restrictio (re-STRIC-ti-o) **95**—"excepting part of a statement already made" (SMJ 115) (RAL 86)

Rhyme **58**—Identical sounding terminations of words. (A) Masculine Rhyme is rhyming on the final stressed syllable; (B) Feminine Rhyme is rhyming on the final stressed and following unstressed syllable; (C) Triple Rhyme is rhyming on the three final syllables, usually with one stressed syllable followed by two unstressed syllables; (D) Internal Rhyme is rhyming with at least one word appearing in the middle of a verse line (not in SMJ)

Sarcasmus (sar-CAS-mus) **232**—"a more bitter taunt than mycterismus [**231**], a more open mock" (SMJ 255)—a figure of *Pathos*

Schematismus (sche-ma-TIS-mus) **165**—"circuitous speech" (SMJ 172)

Schemes—one of the two traditional divisions of figures of speech made by Renaissance rhetoricians (the other being *Tropes*) and categorized by them as either grammatical (see *Schemes of Grammar*) or rhetorical. The arrangement in Sister Miriam Joseph's *Shakespeare's Use of the Arts of Language*, on which the present work is based, largely dispenses with the distinction between schemes and tropes, about whose various definitions and subdivisions no two rhetoricians entirely agree, and arranges all the figures of speech in a clear way that reveals "the fundamental likeness" among all the sixteenth-century theorists.

Schemes of Construction—*Schemes of Grammar* in which stylistic modifications are made in the construction of sentences, see under Grammar: Schemes of Grammar

Schemes of Grammar—"patterns or fashionings of language" that "distinguish it from ordinary speech" (SMJ 48), that is, modifications of words and sentence structure that create variations from natural speech for stylistic purposes, including *Schemes of Words* and *Schemes of Construction*, see under Grammar

Schemes of Words—*Schemes of Grammar* in which "modifications of words [are] wrought by adding or subtracting a syllable or letter at the beginning, middle, or end, and by exchanging sounds," including selection of "less generally accepted" forms of words "current at the time" and coinage of "new forms" (SMJ 50), see under Grammar: Schemes of Grammar

Secundum Quid (se-CUN-dum QUID) **178**—assuming that what is true of a subject in a qualified sense is true of it absolutely or vice versa (SMJ 195)—a *Material Fallacy* of hidden assumption

Sentence—See Proverb **74**

Sententia (sen-TEN-ti-a)—see Proverb **74**

Similarity—along with *Dissimilarity*, a kind of argument based on similarities and differences between the subject and something else, see under *Logos*: Topics of Invention: Artificial Arguments: Division (A)

Simile (SI-mi-lē) **137**—explicit comparison of one thing to another by the use of like, as, etc. (SMJ 144)

Solecismus (so-le-CIS-mus) **37**—the ignorant misuse of cases, genders, and tenses (and presumably parts of speech) (SMJ 64), cf., Enallage **32**

Soraismus (sor-a-IS-mus), also spelled Soriasmus (sor-i-AS-mus) **39**—ignorant or pedantic mingling of different languages, also called Mingle-mangle (SMJ 65)

Soriasmus—see Soraismus **39**

Sorites (so-RI-tēs)—"a chain of reasoning, a series of abridged syllogisms or enthymemes" (SMJ 180), with or without Climax **65**, see under *Logos*: Logical Argumentation: Syllogistic Reasoning: Valid Syllogistic Reasoning: Simple Syllogism

Species—see *Genus*

Subject—in Grammar, that about which a sentence is predicated; in Logic, (A) that about which a proposition or statement is made, (B) that of which an adjunct is the property or attribute

Syllepsis (A) (syl-LEP-sis) **22A**—using one verb to govern a number of clauses with at least one of whose subjects it lacks grammatical congruence (SMJ 58), see under Grammar: Schemes of Grammar: Schemes of Construction: Omission, cf., Zeugma **21**

Syllepsis (B) **22B**—using "a word having simultaneously two different meanings, although it is not repeated" (SMJ 166), see under *Logos*: Topics of Invention: Artificial Arguments: Division (A): Notation and Conjugates: Ambiguity

Syllogism—a form of argument asserting a major premise, a minor premise, and a conclusion; it may be simple, even if in the form of a series of arguments (see *Sorites*), or compound (see *Compound Syllogism*), see under *Logos*: Logical Argumentation: Syllogistic Reasoning: Valid Syllogistic Reasoning

Syllogismus (syl-lo-GIS-mus) **167**—a "more abridged...form [of the *Enthymeme*], present[ing] a single vivid suggestion, from which the mind leaps to the desired inference without adverting to the process of reasoning which underlies it" (SMJ 179)

Syllogistic Reasoning—"a conjunction of propositions related not merely materially but formally as premises from which a conclusion spontaneously follows" (SMJ 176), subdivided into Valid Syllogistic Reasoning, Fallacious Reasoning, and Disputation, see under *Logos*: Logical Argumentation

Symploce (SYM-plo-cē) **61**—beginning and ending a series of clauses with the same words, a combination of Anaphora **59** and Epistrophe **60** (SMJ 79)

Synalepha—see Synaloepha **6**

Synaloepha (sin-a-LĒF-a) (also spelled Synalepha) **6**—elision of one of two vowels or of a single vowel, as *th' army for the army* (WNID) (SMJ 52)

Synathroesmus (syn-ath-RĒS-mus) **98**—(A) giving details and then gathering them up in recapitulation (SMJ 117); (B) Congeries, heaping together words of different meaning, without recapitulation (SMJ 117)

Synchoresis (syn-chor-E-sis) **194**—trusting so strongly in one's own cause that one freely gives one's questioner leave to judge him (SMJ 215)—a figure of *Disputation*

Syncope (SIN-co-pē) **5**—subtracting a letter or syllable from the middle of a word, as *foc's'le* for *forecastle* (MWCD) (SMJ 52)

Syncrisis (SYN-cri-sis) **124**—comparing "contrary things in contrasting clauses" (SMJ 137)

Synecdoche (sy-NEC-do-chē) **90**—"a trope [that] heightens meaning by substituting genus for species, species for genus, part for whole, whole for part" (SMJ 112)

Syngnome (SYN-gno-mē) **245**—forgiving injuries (SMJ 274)—a figure of *Ethos*

Synoeciosis (syn-oe-ci-O-sis) **120**—uniting contraries or seemingly incompatible terms (SMJ 135)

Synonymia (syn-o-NYM-i-a) **150**—iteration of "the same thing in many words of the same meaning to increase its force" (SMJ 54)

Systole (SIS-to-lē) **9**—shortening (in English, altering the stress) of a syllable (SMJ 53)

Systrophe (SYS-tro-phē) **88**—"the heaping together of many definitions of one thing" (SMJ 109), see Definitio **86**

Tapinosis (tap-in-O-sis) **42**—"the use of a base word to diminish the dignity of a person or thing" (SMJ 67)

Tasis (TA-sis) **12**—"not precisely a figure...a sweet and pleasant modulation or tunableness of the voice in pronunciation" (SMJ 53–54)

Tautologia (tau-to-LO-gi-a), also Tautology (tau-TO-lo-gy) **45**—"vain repetition of the same idea" in different words (SMJ 68)

Tautology—see Tautologia **45**

Taxis (TAX-is) **103**—"distribut[ing] to every subject its proper adjunct" (SMJ 123)

Testimony—see *Inartificial Argument*, see under *Logos*: Topics of Invention: Inartificial Arguments

Testimony of Men (**72–85**)—testimony from the authority of human witnesses and from "proverbs, apothegms, pledges, oaths" (SMJ 92), see under *Logos*: Topics of Invention: Inartificial Arguments

Testimony of Supernatural Powers **71**—testimony of scripture, of "oracles, soothsayers, augurs, prodigies, dreams, apparitions, ghosts, witches, prophecies," whether "for good or evil" (SMJ 92), and of curses, premonitions, trial by combat, and circumstantial evidence, which are located "On the borderline between the supernatural and the human forms of testimony" (SMJ 96–97), see under *Logos*: Topics of Invention: Inartificial Arguments

Thaumasmus (thau-MAS-mus) **219**—"exclamation of wonder" (SMJ 245)—a figure of *Pathos*

Threnos (THRE-nos) **223**—"a lament" (SMJ 248)—a figure of *Pathos*

Tmesis (TMĒ-sis or MĒ-sis) **15**—putting a word or words between the parts of a compound word (SMJ 55), a species of Hyperbaton **13**

Topics, also Places: from the Greek *topos* (= place), plural *topoi*—The topics or places of invention were the various established categories of logic and rhetoric through which a speaker might draw the subject of a composition in order to find things to say about it (see *Invention*). Aristotle enumerates twenty-eight topics; Cicero's *Topica*, the "standard text for beginning this study in the grammar schools of Tudor England" (SMJ 22), offers seventeen topics as an exhaustive list of the possible topics of invention: Definition, Division, the Name, Conjugates, Genus, Species, Similarity, Difference, Contraries, Adjuncts, Consequents, Antecedents, Incompatibles, Causes, Effects, Comparison with Lessers, Greaters, or Equals, and Testimony. See under *Logos*: Topics of Invention.

Topographia (top-o-GRAPH-i-a) **117**—"description of places" (SMJ 129), a species of Hypotyposis **108**

Topothesia (top-o-THES-i-a) **118**—"description of imaginary places" (SMJ 130), a species of Hypotyposis **108**

Traductio—see Ploce **68**

Triple Rhyme **58** (C)—three-syllable rhyme usually with one stressed syllable followed by two unstressed syllables (not in SMJ), see Rhyme **58**

Tropes—one of the two traditional divisions of figures of speech made by Renaissance rhetoricians (the other being *Schemes*): "A trope, such as a metaphor, turns the significance of a word or sentence from its proper meaning to another not proper, but yet near it in order to increase its force" (SMJ 33)—see *Schemes*

Utis (OO-tis) **190**—(A) An argument in which the proof is as uncertain as the thing to be proved: "No example has been noticed [in Shakespeare]" (SMJ 199)—a *Captious Argument*; (B) the same as Begging the Question **182** (SMJ 372)

Valid Syllogistic Reasoning—"If the premises are true, valid syllogistic reasoning yields true conclusions" (SMJ 176), see under *Logos*: Logical Argumentation: Syllogistic Reasoning

Vices of Language—the ignorant violation of grammatical rules, as opposed to figures of grammar, which are deliberate deviations from grammar for desired aesthetic effect, see under Grammar

Zeugma (ZEUG-ma) **21**—using one verb to govern a number of clauses with which it is grammatically congruent (SMJ 58), cf., Syllepsis (A) **22A**; in Prozeugma (or Protozeugma) the common verb or adjective is expressed in the first clause, in Mesozeugma in a middle clause, in Hypozeugma in the final clause